Matthias Horbach

Superposition-based Decision Procedures for Minimal Models

Matthias Horbach

Superposition-based Decision Procedures for Minimal Models

First-order Theorem Proving for Fixed Domain and Minimal Model Validity

Südwestdeutscher Verlag für Hochschulschriften

Impressum/Imprint (nur für Deutschland/only for Germany)
Bibliografische Information der Deutschen Nationalbibliothek: Die Deutsche Nationalbibliothek verzeichnet diese Publikation in der Deutschen Nationalbibliografie; detaillierte bibliografische Daten sind im Internet über http://dnb.d-nb.de abrufbar.
Alle in diesem Buch genannten Marken und Produktnamen unterliegen warenzeichen-, marken- oder patentrechtlichem Schutz bzw. sind Warenzeichen oder eingetragene Warenzeichen der jeweiligen Inhaber. Die Wiedergabe von Marken, Produktnamen, Gebrauchsnamen, Handelsnamen, Warenbezeichnungen u.s.w. in diesem Werk berechtigt auch ohne besondere Kennzeichnung nicht zu der Annahme, dass solche Namen im Sinne der Warenzeichen- und Markenschutzgesetzgebung als frei zu betrachten wären und daher von jedermann benutzt werden dürften.

Verlag: Südwestdeutscher Verlag für Hochschulschriften GmbH & Co. KG
Dudweiler Landstr. 99, 66123 Saarbrücken, Deutschland
Telefon +49 681 37 20 271-1, Telefax +49 681 37 20 271-0
Email: info@svh-verlag.de

Herstellung in Deutschland:
Schaltungsdienst Lange o.H.G., Berlin
Books on Demand GmbH, Norderstedt
Reha GmbH, Saarbrücken
Amazon Distribution GmbH, Leipzig
ISBN: 978-3-8381-2802-3

Imprint (only for USA, GB)
Bibliographic information published by the Deutsche Nationalbibliothek: The Deutsche Nationalbibliothek lists this publication in the Deutsche Nationalbibliografie; detailed bibliographic data are available in the Internet at http://dnb.d-nb.de.
Any brand names and product names mentioned in this book are subject to trademark, brand or patent protection and are trademarks or registered trademarks of their respective holders. The use of brand names, product names, common names, trade names, product descriptions etc. even without a particular marking in this works is in no way to be construed to mean that such names may be regarded as unrestricted in respect of trademark and brand protection legislation and could thus be used by anyone.

Publisher: Südwestdeutscher Verlag für Hochschulschriften GmbH & Co. KG
Dudweiler Landstr. 99, 66123 Saarbrücken, Germany
Phone +49 681 37 20 271-1, Fax +49 681 37 20 271-0
Email: info@svh-verlag.de

Printed in the U.S.A.
Printed in the U.K. by (see last page)
ISBN: 978-3-8381-2802-3

Copyright © 2011 by the author and Südwestdeutscher Verlag für Hochschulschriften GmbH & Co. KG and licensors
All rights reserved. Saarbrücken 2011

Abstract

Superposition is an established decision procedure for a variety of first-order logic theories represented by sets of clauses. A satisfiable theory, saturated by superposition, implicitly defines a minimal Herbrand model for the theory. This raises the question in how far superposition calculi can be employed for reasoning about such minimal models. This is indeed often possible when existential properties are considered. However, proving universal properties directly leads to a modification of the minimal model's term-generated domain, as new Skolem functions are introduced. For many applications, this is not desired because it changes the problem.

In this book, I will describe the first superposition calculus that can explicitly represent existentially quantified variables and can thus compute with respect to a given fixed domain. It does not eliminate existential variables by Skolemization, but handles them using additional constraints with which each clause is annotated. This calculus is sound and refutationally complete in the limit for a fixed domain semantics. For saturated Horn theories and classes of positive formulas, the calculus is even complete for proving properties of the minimal model itself, going beyond the scope of known superposition-based approaches.

The calculus is applicable to every set of clauses with equality and does not rely on any syntactic restrictions of the input. Extensions of the calculus lead to various new decision procedures for minimal model validity. A main feature of these decision procedures is that even the validity of queries containing one quantifier alternation can be decided. In particular, I prove that the validity of any formula with at most one quantifier alternation is decidable in models represented by a finite set of atoms and that the validity of several classes of such formulas is decidable in models represented by so-called disjunctions of implicit generalizations. Moreover, I show that the decision of minimal model validity can be reduced to the superposition-based decision of first-order validity for models of a class of predicative Horn clauses where all function symbols are at most unary.

Acknowledgements

This book is predominantly identical to my doctoral thesis (Horbach, 2010b), which I wrote at Max Planck Institute for Informatics under the supervision of Prof. Dr. Christoph Weidenbach. I am deeply grateful for the productive and enjoyable atmosphere that he and all my colleagues created during my time at the institute.

Contents

1 Introduction   **11**
- 1.1 Saturation-based First-Order Theorem Proving 11
- 1.2 First-order, Fixed Domain, and Minimal Model Semantics . . 14
- 1.3 Automated Theorem Proving in Minimal Models 18
  - 1.3.1 Proof by Consistency 18
  - 1.3.2 Implicit Induction 19
  - 1.3.3 The Saturation Approach 20
  - 1.3.4 The Completion Approach 24
  - 1.3.5 The Description-specific Approach 25
- 1.4 Contributions 26
  - 1.4.1 Superposition for Fixed Domain and Minimal Model Reasoning 27
  - 1.4.2 Disunification and Predicate Completion 28
  - 1.4.3 A Superposition-based Decision Procedure for DIG Interpretations 29
  - 1.4.4 Reducing the Decidability of Minimal Model Validity to Superposition-based First-order Decidability 30

2 Preliminaries   **33**
- 2.1 Mathematical Foundations 33
- 2.2 Syntax 35
  - 2.2.1 Terms and Formulas 35
  - 2.2.2 Constrained Clauses 38
  - 2.2.3 Substitutions 40
  - 2.2.4 Term and Clause Orderings 41
  - 2.2.5 Predicates 45
- 2.3 Semantics 45
  - 2.3.1 Interpretations and Entailment 45
  - 2.3.2 Semantics of Formulas and Constrained Clauses 46
- 2.4 Calculi 51
  - 2.4.1 Inferences, Redundancy and Derivations 51
  - 2.4.2 Soundness, Completeness and Termination 53

Contents

3 Disunification and Predicate Completion   **55**
- 3.1 Introduction 55
- 3.2 Disunification 57
  - 3.2.1 The Disunification Algorithm PDU 57
  - 3.2.2 Correctness and Termination of PDU 59
- 3.3 Predicate Completion 68
  - 3.3.1 The Predicate Completion Algorithm PC 68
  - 3.3.2 Disunification-based Quantifier Elimination 69
  - 3.3.3 Solved Form Computation 73
  - 3.3.4 Predicate Completion and Unique Herbrand Models . . 78
- 3.4 Decidability of the Satisfiability of Equational Formulas 79
- 3.5 Implementation 81
- 3.6 Conclusion 85

4 A Superposition Calculus for Fixed Domains   **87**
- 4.1 Introduction 87
- 4.2 First-Order Reasoning in Fixed Domains 87
  - 4.2.1 The Superposition Calculus for Fixed Domains SFD . . 89
  - 4.2.2 Model Construction and Refutational Completeness . . 95
  - 4.2.3 Other Herbrand Models of Constrained Clause Sets . . 106
- 4.3 Minimal Model Reasoning 111
  - 4.3.1 Relations between First-order, Fixed Domain and Minimal Model Validity 111
  - 4.3.2 The Inductive Superposition Calculus $\text{IS}(H)$ 117
- 4.4 Conclusion 123

5 A Superposition-Based Decision Procedure for Minimal Models   **127**
- 5.1 Introduction 127
- 5.2 The Constrained Ordered Resolution Calculus ORFD 129
- 5.3 Clausal Representations of Disjunctions of Implicit Generalizations 132
  - 5.3.1 Disjunctions of Implicit Generalizations 132
  - 5.3.2 Clausal Representations 134
  - 5.3.3 Completed Clausal Representations 135
- 5.4 Decidability Results 138
  - 5.4.1 Decidability of Ground Queries 138
  - 5.4.2 Decidability of DIG Equivalence 139
  - 5.4.3 Decidability of Formula Entailment 143
- 5.5 Implementation 145
- 5.6 Conclusion 150

Contents

6 Generic Superposition-based Decidability of Minimal Model Validity   **151**
    6.1   Introduction 151
    6.2   Preliminaries 154
          6.2.1   Substitution Expressions and Regular Constraint Clauses 154
          6.2.2   Semantics of Regular Constraint Clauses 156
          6.2.3   Inferences and Redundancy 159
    6.3   A Resolution Calculus for Regular Constraint Clauses 159
          6.3.1   Melting and the Calculus ORM 160
          6.3.2   Soundness and Completeness of ORM 165
          6.3.3   Termination of ORM 168
    6.4   Generalized Substitutions as Clause Sets 173
          6.4.1   Equivalence of Substitution Expressions and Clause Sets 176
          6.4.2   Predicate Completion for Substitution Expressions . . 182
    6.5   Decidability of Minimal Model Validity 186
    6.6   Conclusion 187

7 Conclusion   **189**
    7.1   Resumé 189
    7.2   Outlook 191

    Bibliography 193

    Index 203

List of Figures

1.1	The Elevator Example	14
1.2	The Elevator Example: Alternative Models	16
2.1	Negation Normal Form Transformation Rules	48
3.1	Normalization Rules of the Calculus PDU	59
3.2	Rules of the Calculus PDU for all Sorts	60
3.3	Rules of the Calculus PDU for Ultimately Periodic Sorts	61
3.4	Solved Form Conversion Rules	73
4.1	Rules of the Calculus SFD (1)	90
4.2	Rules of the Calculus SFD (2)	91
4.3	The Additional Rule of the Calculus SFD$^+$	107
4.4	The Induction Rule	119
5.1	Rules of the Calculus ORFD	130
5.2	Structure of the Implementation	146
6.1	The Ordered Query Resolution Rule	161
6.2	The Melting Rule	163

1 Introduction

In this book, I propose the first superposition calculus that can explicitly represent existentially quantified variables in computations with respect to a given fixed domain, giving rise to various new decision procedures for minimal model validity. The book is structured as follows: To give the reader an overview of the contents, I will in Chapter 1 present a historical background and an introduction to the problem of theorem proving with respect to a fixed domain or minimal model semantics as well as a synopsis of the contributions of this work. For this chapter, I assume that the reader is familiar with basic concepts of first-order logics, like the notions of first-order formulas and their (Herbrand) models. In Chapter 2, I will then thoroughly define all notions needed throughout the later chapters. This includes both a roundup of the syntax and semantics of first-order logics and an explanation of concepts that are newly introduced. The main contributions are presented in Chapters 3–6. Finally, I will in Chapter 7 give a resumé and an outlook on possible future developments.

1.1 Saturation-based First-Order Theorem Proving

Among the many ways to prove theorems in first-order logics, the one that has proven most useful for automation is *refutational theorem proving*, or *reductio ad absurdum*. In this style of reasoning, it is proved that a hypothesis ϕ is valid in all models of a finite set N of formulas, written $N \models \phi$, by showing that $N \cup \{\neg\phi\}$ is contradictory. For first-order reasoning, the formulas can without loss of generality be assumed to be in *clause normal form*, i.e. in the form $\forall x_1, \ldots, x_k . A_1 \wedge \ldots \wedge A_m \rightarrow B_1 \vee \ldots \vee B_n$, or $A_1, \ldots, A_m \rightarrow B_1, \ldots, B_n$ for short.

For *ground* (i.e. variable-free) clauses, unsatisfiability can be decided by *saturation*, i.e. by systematically adding implied ground clauses: Consider the following inference rules, where Γ stands for a conjunctively interpreted and Δ for a disjunctively interpreted list of atoms:

Chapter 1: Introduction

Ground Resolution:
$$\frac{\Gamma_1 \to \Delta_1, A \quad \Gamma_2, A \to \Delta_2}{\Gamma_1, \Gamma_2 \to \Delta_1, \Delta_2}$$

Ground Factoring:
$$\frac{\Gamma \to \Delta, A, A}{\Gamma \to \Delta, A}$$

This notation means that if the clauses above the line (the *premises*) are elements of the current clause set, then the one below the line (the *conclusion*) can be added. A set of equation-free ground clauses is unsatisfiable if, and only if, a contradiction, namely the empty clause, can be derived using these two inference rules.

For general clauses, the problem of deciding unsatisfiability can be reduced to the ground case: Herbrands theorem (Herbrand, 1930) states that a finite set of clauses is unsatisfiable if, and only if, there is a finite set of ground instances of these clauses that is unsatisfiable. Of course, blindly guessing the ground instances needed to derive a contradiction is infeasible, because there are usually infinitely many such ground instances. A first breakthrough to overcome this problem was the work by Robinson (1965). He showed how to interleave the instance-generation process with the derivation of a contradiction, namely by performing inferences directly on non-ground clauses that are only instantiated on a by-need basis along the way: A ground instance $\Gamma \to \Delta, A$ can only contribute to the refutation if there is another ground instance in which A appears on the left hand side of the implication. He showed that if a set of clauses is unsatisfiable, then the empty clause can be derived by saturating N with the following two inference rules:

Resolution:
$$\frac{\Gamma_1 \to \Delta_1, A_1 \quad \Gamma_2, A_2 \to \Delta_2}{(\Gamma_1, \Gamma_2 \to \Delta_1, \Delta_2)\sigma}$$

Factoring:
$$\frac{\Gamma \to \Delta, A_1, A_2}{(\Gamma \to \Delta, A_1)\sigma}$$

The unsatisfiability of full first-order clauses is not decidable, however it is semi-decidable and the rules Resolution and Factoring are *refutationally complete*: If a set N of clauses is inconsistent, then the empty clause can be derived using saturation with those two rules. But still, there is one important predicate which the resolution calculus cannot handle well: equality. The reason is that, if the axioms for equality (reflexivity, commutativity, transitivity and monotonicity) are explicitly added to the input, the search space explodes. A better way of treating equality is by integrating it directly into the calculus in the form of specialized rules like *Paramodulation* (Robinson and Wos, 1969; Brand, 1975):

Paramodulation:
$$\frac{\Gamma_1 \to \Delta_1, l{\simeq}r \quad \Gamma_2 \to \Delta_2, A_2[l']}{(\Gamma_1, \Gamma_2 \to \Delta_1, \Delta_2, A_2[r])\sigma}$$

(and similarly if A_2 is in the antecedent of the clause), where $\sigma = \mathrm{mgu}(l, l')$ unifies l and a non-variable subterm l' of A_2. The meaning of this rule is that an occurrence of $l'\sigma$ in A_2 can be replaced by $r\sigma$ if the side conditions of the equation $l{\simeq}r$ are fulfilled. This joins multiple applications of the monotonicity and possibly commutativity of equality in a single rule application and eliminates the need for the explicit application of the equality axioms. The combination of Paramodulation, Resolution, Factoring and Reflexivity is refutationally complete for clauses with equality, but although Paramodulation provides a serious improvement over just adding the axioms for equality, this rule is still too prolific to provide a decision procedure.

This problem still arises if only unit equations are considered, i.e. clauses of the form $\to s{\simeq}t$. Knuth and Bendix (1970) introduced the idea of driving the computation from more complicated to simpler equations: They used a term ordering $\succ$ to orient the equations and only enable Paramodulation inferences between the larger sides of equations. However, equations like $f(x,y){\simeq}f(x,z)$ cannot be oriented, so the algorithm fails for such equations. The solution in this context is *unfailing completion* (Hsiang and Rusinowitch, 1987; Bachmair, Dershowitz, and Plaisted, 1989), an extension of Knuth-Bendix completion the main element of which is that not the equations themselves but only the instances needed for an inference must be oriented. Then an inference between equations $\to l{\simeq}r$ and $\to s[l']{\simeq}t$ is possible if $l\sigma \succ r\sigma$ and $s\sigma \succ t\sigma$.

Combining this ordering-based idea with the treatment of full clauses by Paramodulation yields the most successful saturation-based calculus developed so far: *(Strict) Superposition* (Bachmair and Ganzinger, 1990, 1991, 1994; Nieuwenhuis and Rubio, 2001; Weidenbach, 2001), which restricts all inferences to maximal sides of maximal equations in each clause. Moreover, so-called *redundant* clauses that are implied by strictly smaller clauses need not be considered as premises to an inference. The success of Superposition is in particular demonstrated by Superposition-based calculi effectively deciding many known decidable classical subclasses of first-order logic, e.g. the monadic class with equality (Bachmair et al., 1993), the guarded fragment with equality (Ganzinger and Nivelle, 1999) and the Bernays-Schönfinkel class (Hillenbrand and Weidenbach, 2007), as well as a number of first-order classes

Chapter 1: Introduction

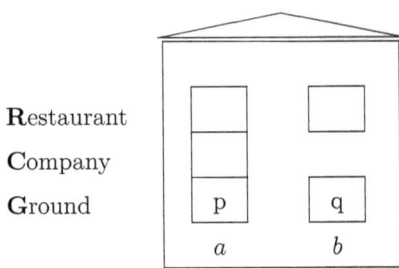

Figure 1.1: The Elevator Example

that have been proven decidable for the first time by means of the Superposition calculus (Nieuwenhuis, 1996; Jacquemard et al., 1998; Weidenbach, 1999; Jacquemard et al., 2006), for none of which there are decision procedures based on Resolution calculi in the style of Robinson or Paramodulation calculi in the style of Robinson and Wos.

1.2 First-order, Fixed Domain, and Minimal Model Semantics

The calculi presented so far derive conclusions ϕ that are provably valid in every model of a clause set N. This is, however, often too coarse an approach: For a number of applications, this semantics is not sufficient to determine an intended interpretation precisely and hence to prove all properties of interest. It is often essential to work more fine-grained, in the sense that the focus lies on statements that only hold in selected models of the premises.

Example 1.1 (Two Elevators)
Different semantics are of relevance, for example, in proving properties of computer systems. Consider the simple example of a building with three floors (Figure 1.1). The bottom ground floor and the top restaurant floor of the building are open to the public whereas the middle floor is occupied by a company and only open to its employees. In order to support this setting, there are two elevators a and b in the building. Elevator a is for the employees of the company and stops on all three floors whereas elevator b is for visitors of the restaurant, stopping solely on the ground and restaurant floors. Initially, there is a person p in elevator a and a person q in elevator b, both on the ground floor. Leaving out temporal aspects, the system can be modeled by three binary predicates G, C, R for the different floors, respectively, that take

1.2 First-order, Fixed Domain, and Minimal Model Semantics

as arguments an elevator and a person. For example, $G(a,p)$ means that person p stands in elevator a on the ground floor. The initial state of the system and the potential upward moves are modeled by the clause set N_E consisting of the following clauses:

Clause	Meaning
$\to G(a,p)$	Person p is on the ground floor in elevator a.
$\to G(b,q)$	Person q is on the ground floor in elevator b.
$G(a,x) \to C(a,x)$	Anyone on the ground floor in elevator a can reach the company floor with this elevator.
$C(a,x) \to R(a,x)$	Anyone on the company floor in elevator a can reach the restaurant floor with this elevator.
$G(b,x) \to R(b,x)$	Anyone on the ground floor in elevator b can reach the restaurant floor with this elevator.

Some structural properties of the system actually hold for all models of N_E, i.e. all buildings described by theses clauses. Some of these models are depicted in Figures 1.1 and 1.2. For example, whenever any person (not necessarily p or q) sits on the ground floor in elevator a, they can reach the restaurant floor, i.e. $N_E \models \forall x. G(a,x) \to R(a,x)$.

Other properties do not hold for every model: In the described system, every elevator can reach the restaurant floor. However, the given clauses allow for the existence of, say, a third elevator c for use by the company management that only connects the ground and company floors as in the right model in Figure 1.2. Of course, this third elevator was never mentioned in the system description. To exclude models containing such spurious elements, reasoning must be constrained to elements of the given domain, in this case to $\{a,b,p,q\}$. When models are considered in which only these two persons and two elevators exist, the restaurant floor is indeed reachable by all elevators, i.e. the formula $\forall x,y. G(y,x) \to R(y,x)$ holds in all these models.

But even if the domain is restricted to $\{a,b,p,q\}$, the description does not completely model the system: There are models of N_E in which elevator b also connects all three floors, e.g. the left model in Figure 1.2. The intended semantics of the elevator system, however, coincides with the so-called *minimal model* of N_E, where none but the specified elevator movements are possible. To prove that elevator b cannot reach the company floor, all non-minimal

Chapter 1: Introduction

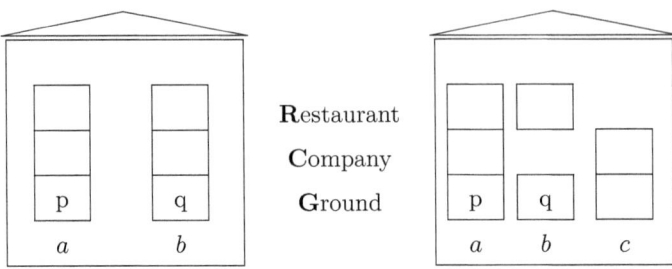

Figure 1.2: The Elevator Example: Alternative Models

models have to be excluded as well, such that only the one model remains for which the description was designed. In the remaining model, only the following ground atoms are true: $G(a,p), C(a,p), R(a,p), G(b,q), R(b,q)$.

Formally, models that are restricted to the given fixed domain Σ in this sense are the *Herbrand models* of N, i.e. models the universe of which consists of the terms built over Σ. The validity of ϕ in all such models of N is denoted by $N \models_\Sigma \phi$ and called *fixed domain validity*. The intended semantics for system descriptions is the one where only the minimal Herbrand model (minimal with respect to set inclusion) of N is considered, denoted by $\mathcal{I}_N$. In this model, intuitively every ground atom that is not explicitly made true by the clauses in N is false. If e.g. $N = \{P(a)\}$ and the signature contains two constants a and b, then $P(b)$ is false in $\mathcal{I}_N$. Validity of ϕ in this unique model is written $\mathcal{I}_N \models \phi$ or alternatively $N \models_{Ind} \phi$ and called *minimal model validity*. The notation $\models_{Ind}$ stems from the alternative widespread designation of minimal model validity as *inductive validity*. (If the clauses in N are not Horn, i.e. contain more than one positive literal, the minimal model is not necessarily unique. For example, the single clause $\{ \rightarrow P(a), P(b)\}$ has the two minimal models $\{P(a)\}$ and $\{P(b)\}$. The different minimal models can be distinguished by additionally fixing a term ordering that in turn induces an ordering on the models. For the sake of a more concise presentation, I ignore this complication for the moment.)

For the models that are considered in each of the three semantics *minimal model semantics, fixed domain semantics,* and *first-order semantics*, the following relations hold:

$$\mathcal{I}_N \in \{\mathcal{I} \mid \mathcal{I} \text{ is a Herbrand interpretation over } \Sigma \text{ and } \mathcal{I} \models N\}$$
$$\subseteq \{\mathcal{I} \mid \mathcal{I} \models N\}$$

Conversely, the following holds for the sets of formulas that are valid with

1.2 First-order, Fixed Domain, and Minimal Model Semantics

respect to the different semantics:

$$\{\phi \mid N \models_{Ind} \phi\} \supseteq \{\phi \mid N \models_{\Sigma} \phi\} \supseteq \{\phi \mid N \models \phi\}$$

In the simple elevator example, all appearing function symbols are constants and the Herbrand domain is finite. Hence the quantification over all elements of the domain, i.e. the restriction to $\models_{\{a,b,p,q\}}$, could be encoded explicitly by changing a query like $\forall y, x.G(y,x) \rightarrow R(y,x)$ to $\forall y, x.(y{\simeq}a \vee y{\simeq}b) \wedge (x{\simeq}p \vee x{\simeq}q) \wedge G(y,x) \rightarrow R(y,x)$. A property extended in this way is valid in all models of N_E if, and only if, it is valid in all Herbrand models of N_E, i.e. fixed domain reasoning can be reduced to first-order reasoning in this case. This reduction is, however, not possible when the domain is infinite.

This is exemplified by the following small example:

Example 1.2 (The "One Greater Than" Relation)
Consider the clause set

$$N_{GT} = \{\ \rightarrow GT(s(0), 0), \quad GT(x,y) \rightarrow GT(s(x), s(y))\ \}\ .$$

The minimal model $\mathcal{I}_{N_{GT}}$ in this example consists of all atoms $GT(t_1, t_2)$ where t_2 is a ground term over the signature $\Sigma_{\text{nat}} = \{s, 0\}$ and $t_1 = s(t_2)$. So the domain of $\mathcal{I}_{N_{GT}}$ is isomorphic to the naturals and the interpretation of GT in $\mathcal{I}_{N_{GT}}$ is the "one greater than" relation.

Consider some formulas that are valid with respect to the different semantics:

- The formula $GT(s(s(0)), s(0))$ can be derived by resolution from the clauses in N_{GT}, so it is valid in every model of N_{GT}.

- The formula $\forall x.GT(s(x), x)$ is valid in every Herbrand model of N_{GT} over the domain Σ_{nat}. However, it is not valid in every model of N_{GT}, for example not in a model containing an additional copy $a, s(a), s(s(a)), \ldots$ of the natural numbers such that $GT(t_1, t_2)$ never holds if t_1, t_2 are elements of this copy.

- The formula $\forall x.\neg GT(x,x)$ holds in the minimal model of N_{GT}, because no natural number is one greater than itself. It does not hold in the model over the natural numbers in which GT is interpreted as the "one greater than or equal to" relation.

So the following validity relations hold for the different formulas and semantics:

$N_{GT} \models GT(s(s(0)), s(0))$ $\quad N_{GT} \models_{\Sigma_{\text{nat}}} GT(s(s(0)), s(0))$ $\quad N_{GT} \models_{Ind} GT(s(s(0)), s(0))$
$N_{GT} \not\models \forall x.GT(s(x), x)$ $\quad N_{GT} \models_{\Sigma_{\text{nat}}} \forall x.GT(s(x), x)$ $\quad N_{GT} \models_{Ind} \forall x.GT(s(x), x)$
$N_{GT} \not\models \forall x.\neg GT(x,x)$ $\quad N_{GT} \not\models_{\Sigma_{\text{nat}}} \forall x.\neg GT(x,x)$ $\quad N_{GT} \models_{Ind} \forall x.\neg GT(x,x)$

Chapter 1: Introduction

1.3 Automated Theorem Proving in Minimal Models

Minimal model ($\models_{Ind}$) and fixed-domain ($\models_\Sigma$) theorem proving are more difficult problems than first-order ($\models$) theorem proving: It follows from Gödel's incompleteness theorem (Gödel, 1931) that minimal model validity is neither decidable nor semi-decidable, and the same holds for fixed domain validity. In fact, the standard model of Peano arithmetic can be encoded in a fixed domain setting as follows: Given the signature $\Sigma_{PA} = \{s, 0, +, \cdot\}$, let N_{PA} consist of the clauses $x+0 \simeq x$ and $x+s(y) \simeq s(x+y)$ defining addition, $x \cdot 0 \simeq 0$ and $x \cdot s(y) \simeq (x \cdot y) + x$ defining multiplication, and $s(x) \not\simeq 0$ and $s(x) \simeq s(y) \rightarrow x \simeq y$ stating that all numbers are different. Then N_{PA} has exactly one Herbrand model over Σ_{PA}, and this model is isomorphic to the natural numbers. So an arithmetic formula ϕ is valid over the natural numbers if, and only if, $N_{PA} \models_{Ind} \phi$ if, and only if, $N_{PA} \models_{\Sigma_{PA}} \phi$.

In spite of this complication, there are several approaches to automated theorem proving with respect to the minimal model of a set of clauses. They are either targeted at a decidable fragment of the problem or they sacrifice completeness or termination guarantees to be as widely applicable as possible. In what follows, I will give a short overview of some of the most important such approaches.

1.3.1 Proof by Consistency

Classically, the first extensively studied interpretations given as minimal models of clause sets were data type specifications. To manually prove properties of such specifications, structural induction is usually the method of choice. However, induction always requires non-trivial steps like choosing the induction variables, a suitable problem instance to apply the induction hypothesis to, and intermediate lemmas required for the induction to work. Hence explicit induction usually requires user interaction.

To automatize proofs that would normally use induction, several authors like Musser (1980), Goguen (1980), Lankford (1981) and Huet and Hullot (1980) proposed the alternative approach of *proof by consistency*. In the terminology of Musser (1980), proofs are performed as follows: Specifications of data types can be expressed by a finite set of orientable equations, i.e. by a rewrite system. If equality can be *completely defined*, i.e. if an equality predicate eq and constants c_{true} and c_{false} can be added to the minimal model

1.3 Automated Theorem Proving in Minimal Models

$\mathcal{I}$ of the specification such that

$$\mathcal{I} \models t_1 \simeq t_2 \iff \mathcal{I} \models \text{eq}(t_1, t_2) \simeq c_{\text{true}} \quad \text{and}$$
$$\mathcal{I} \models t_1 \not\simeq t_2 \iff \mathcal{I} \models \text{eq}(t_1, t_2) \simeq c_{\text{false}},$$

(where t_1, t_2 are not true, false or $\text{eq}(u_1, u_2)$) then a set E of equations holds in the minimal model of the specification if, and only if, adding E to the original equations and completing the equations by using the Knuth-Bendix procedure does not lead to an inconsistency (i.e. an equality true$\simeq$false).

Example 1.3
For the data type of integers with constructors 0 and s, the following equations form a complete definition of equality:

$$\text{eq}(x, x) \simeq c_{\text{true}}$$
$$\text{eq}(s(x), 0) \simeq c_{\text{false}}$$
$$\text{eq}(0, s(x)) \simeq c_{\text{false}}$$
$$\text{eq}(s(x), s(y)) \simeq \text{eq}(x, y)$$

The equation $s(s(0)) \simeq s(0)$ can be disproved by adding it to the above clauses and completing the set: Overlapping the new equation with the fourth equation defining equality, $\text{eq}(s(x), s(y)) \simeq \text{eq}(x, y)$, leads to the equation

$$\text{eq}(s(0), s(y)) \simeq \text{eq}(s(0), y).$$

A further overlap of this equation with the first equation, $\text{eq}(x, x) \simeq c_{\text{true}}$, leads to $\text{eq}(s(0), 0) \simeq c_{\text{true}}$, which reduces to $c_{\text{false}} \simeq c_{\text{true}}$ using the second equation.

The requirement of complete definitions of equality is quite strong: Even simple sets of equations like $\{s(p(x)) \simeq x, p(s(x)) \simeq x\}$ cannot be completely defined in a finite way. Nevertheless, replacing induction by a completion procedure has become the base of a variety of approaches to minimal model theorem proving. In fact, all approaches presented in the following sections have their roots in these ideas.

1.3.2 Implicit Induction

Explicit induction cannot be automatized, but a related concept called *implicit induction* can: In implicit induction, the induction schema is not predefined, but an individual schema (which, in essence, is a finite representation of the minimal model) is computed for each problem that then serves as the basis of a proof by consistency.

Chapter 1: Introduction

Well-known methods in the area of implicit induction are the test set (Bouhoula and Rusinowitch, 1995; Bouhoula and Jouannaud, 1997; Bouhoula and Jacquemard, 2008; Kapur, Narendran, and Zhang, 1991), as well as cover set (Zhang, Kapur, and Krishnamoorthy, 1988) and rewriting methods (Reddy, 1990). Implicit induction led to the development of several dedicated tools for minimal model theorem proving, among them the test set-based RLL (Kapur and Zhang, 1988) and the cover set-based SPIKE (Bouhoula, Kounalis, and Rusinowitch, 1992), and to combinations of implicit induction methods with existing decision procedures (Kapur and Subramaniam, 2000; Giesl and Kapur, 2003; Falke and Kapur, 2006). In this short overview, I will concentrate on the test set method.

Roughly, implicit induction using test sets works as follows: To prove that a conjecture equation $t_1 \simeq t_2$ holds in the minimal model of a set of equations given as a rewrite system R, a test set for R is computed. A test set consists of a finite set of terms that describe the ground terms that are irreducible with respect to the R. Then the induction variables of the conjecture are instantiated with these terms. Finally, it is proved that the instantiated conjectures follow from the specification and smaller instances of the conjecture by showing the consistency of the overall set.

Example 1.4 (Bouhoula et al., 1995)
Consider the positive natural numbers with a subtraction operator (with cut-off) specified by the following rewrite system:

$$x - 0 \to x$$
$$0 - x \to 0$$
$$s(x) - s(y) \to x - y$$

A test set for this specification is the set $\{0, s(x)\}$. To prove that the equation $x - x \simeq 0$ holds in the minimal model of this specification, the variable x in this equation is instantiated with the elements of the test set, and these instances are then checked by simplification.

The instance $0 - 0 \simeq 0$ is directly reduced to the trivial identity $0 \simeq 0$. The instance $s(x) - s(x) \simeq 0$ is reduced to the same trivial identity using the rule $s(x) - s(y) \to x - y$ and the induction hypothesis $x - x \to 0$. Hence the equation is valid.

1.3.3 The Saturation Approach

For the analysis of more general representations of interpretations, it is useful to notice that there is a strong connection between saturation with Superposition and the minimal model semantics: The model $\mathcal{I}_N$ can explicitly be

1.3 Automated Theorem Proving in Minimal Models

constructed from a saturated and consistent clause set N. For Horn clauses, this construction roughly takes the form of iteratively including an atom A in the model when there is a ground instance $B_1, \ldots, B_n \to A$ of an element of N for which all antecedent atoms $B_1, \ldots, B_n$ are already known to be valid in the model. If $B_1, \ldots, B_n \to A$ is the smallest clause from which a new atom can be derived, it is said to *produce* A. The technical details of the model construction will be explained in Section 2.3.2.

Its success in the first-order world raises the question whether Superposition can also be employed for reasoning with respect to the minimal model semantics without the use of induction. Based on initial work by Stuber (1991), Ganzinger and Stuber (1992) addressed exactly this question. In a first-order world, the consistency of $N \cup \{C\}$ is decided by computing a saturation N^* of $N \cup \{C\}$ and checking whether this saturation contains the empty clause. If it does and if N itself is not contradictory, then $N \models \exists \vec{x}. \neg C$ and hence also $N \models_{Ind} \exists \vec{x}. \neg C$. On the other hand, if N^* does not contain the empty clause, this does not necessarily mean that $\mathcal{I}_N$ is a model of N^*:

Example 1.5
Consider a unary function symbol s, a constant 0 and a binary relation GE, intended to describe the "greater than or equal to" relation on natural numbers. Let N_{GE} contain the following two clauses:

(1) $\qquad\qquad\qquad\qquad \to GE(x, 0)$
(2) $\qquad\qquad\qquad GE(x, y) \to GE(s(x), s(y))$

This clause set is saturated (for every partial ordering $\succ$ for which it holds that $G(s(x), s(y)) \succ G(x, y)$) and the model $\mathcal{I}_{N_{GE}}$ is indeed isomorphic to the natural numbers with the less-or-equal relation. If one of the clauses

$C_1 \qquad\qquad\qquad GE(0, s(0)) \to$
$C_2 \qquad\qquad\qquad\qquad \to GE(0, s(0))$
$C_3 \qquad\qquad\qquad\qquad \to GE(s(0), s(0))$

is added, then $N \cup \{C_i\}$ is still saturated. However, adding one of these clauses affects the minimal model of the overall clause set in different ways:

The clause C_1 is purely negative, so it does not contribute to the minimal model and $\mathcal{I}_{N_{GE} \cup \{C_1\}} = \mathcal{I}_{N_{GE}}$, which implies $N_{GE} \models_{Ind} C_1$.

The clause C_2 adds the ground atom $GE(0, s(0))$ to the minimal model, i.e. $\mathcal{I}_{N_{GE} \cup \{C_2\}} \supsetneq \mathcal{I}_{N_{GE}}$, which implies $N_{GE} \not\models_{Ind} C_2$.

The clause C_3 does not fit nicely into this picture: It does contribute the atom $GE(s(0), s(0))$ to the minimal model, but this atom would otherwise have been produced by clause (2) anyway. So although C_3 is productive, $\mathcal{I}_{N_{GE} \cup \{C_3\}} = \mathcal{I}_{N_{GE}}$ and $N_{GE} \models_{Ind} C_3$.

The idea of Ganzinger and Stuber was to try and exclude the possibility that $N^* \setminus N$ contains any clauses for which they cannot decide productivity. They made use of two ingredients:

(i) They assumed that the validity of ground clauses in $\mathcal{I}_N$ was decidable by external means. They claim that this is a reasonable assumption, since otherwise theorem proving for the minimal model of N would be hopeless anyway. (I will later discard that prerequisite.) Decidability of ground clauses can be achieved by restricting N to *universally reductive* clauses, i.e. clauses that are either purely negative or that have a unique maximal positive literal (with respect to the term ordering used for Superposition) containing all variables of the clause.

(ii) They used *negative literal selection* (Bachmair and Ganzinger, 1994). This is a well-known technique in first-order saturation, where negative literals of each clause can be selected, and inferences using such a clause must work on one of the selected literals. This does not affect refutational completeness, and if a clause in a saturated set contains a selected literal, then it cannot be productive.

So the key was to make all derived non-ground clauses contain a selected literal. Since positive clauses like $\to P(x)$ do not contain any selectable literals, Ganzinger and Stuber artificially added negative literals:

(i) They introduced a new unary predicate *Gnd* supposed to hold for all ground terms. The set N over signature Σ was then enriched by the clause set

$$N_{Gnd} = \{Gnd(x_1), \ldots, Gnd(x_n) \to Gnd(f(x_1, \ldots, x_n)) \mid f \in \Sigma\} \ .$$

(ii) Finally, the conjecture $C = \Gamma \to \Delta$ was changed to

$$Gnd(C) = Gnd(y_1), \ldots, Gnd(y_m), \Gamma \to \Delta \ ,$$

where the y_i are the variables of C.

This procedure is sound in the sense that $N \models_{Ind} \exists \vec{x}. \neg C$ if, and only if, $N \cup N_{Gnd} \models_{Ind} \exists \vec{x}. \neg Gnd(C)$. By selecting one of the *Gnd* literals in the antecedent of $Gnd(C)$ and every derived clause, it can be avoided that any derived non-ground clause is productive.

Example 1.6
Consider a unary function symbol s, a constant 0 and a binary relation GE, intended to describe the "greater than or equal to" relation on natural numbers. Let N_{GE} contain the following two clauses:

1.3 Automated Theorem Proving in Minimal Models

(1) $\rightarrow GE(x,0)$
(2) $GE(x,y) \rightarrow GE(s(x),s(y))$

The model $\mathcal{I}_{N_{GE}}$ is indeed isomorphic to the natural numbers with the less-or-equal relation. The set of ground terms is defined by

(3) $\rightarrow Gnd(0)$
(4) $Gnd(x) \rightarrow Gnd(s(x))$

To prove that the relation is total, i.e. for all x,y it holds that $GE(x,y)$ or $GE(y,x)$, the clause

(5) $\underline{Gnd(x)}, Gnd(y) \rightarrow GE(x,y), GE(y,x)$

is added. The underlining indicates that the atom $Gnd(x)$ is selected in this clause. Each of the two clauses (3) and (4) can be resolved with the selected atom in clause (5), which results in the following two clauses:

(6) $\underline{Gnd(y)} \rightarrow GE(0,y), GE(y,0)$
(7) $Gnd(x), \underline{Gnd(y)} \rightarrow GE(s(x),y), GE(y,s(x))$

The first clause is redundant because of clause (1) and does not have to be considered for further inferences. The clauses (3) and (4) can be resolved with the selected atom in clause (7), which results in:

(7) $Gnd(x), \rightarrow GE(s(x),0), GE(0,s(x))$
(8) $Gnd(x), \underline{Gnd(y)} \rightarrow GE(s(x),s(y)), GE(s(y),s(x))$

The first clause is redundant because of clause (1) and the second clause is redundant because of clauses (2) and (5). There are no additional inferences between non-redundant clauses, i.e. the clause set $\{(1),\ldots,(8)\}$ is saturated. Since all derived clauses in this set contain a selected atom, they are not productive, which means that the relation LE is indeed total in $\mathcal{I}_{N_{LE}}$, i.e. $N_{LE} \models_{Ind} GE(x,y) \vee GE(y,x)$

The greatest drawback of this approach is the requirement to select a negative Gnd literal, because this selection effectively makes the algorithm often not terminate. The reason for this is that the selection basically initiates an enumeration of all ground instances of a clause. For example for the conjecture $\rightarrow P(x)$ and empty N, all the ground clauses $\rightarrow P(s(\ldots s(0)\ldots))$ are successively derived. In Example 1.6, this enumeration could be avoided by a carefully chosen selection strategy, it is not known how to derive this strategy automatically. In particular, no decidability results based on approach by Ganzinger and Stuber have been known so far.

1.3.4 The Completion Approach

The main problem with the approach by Ganzinger and Stuber is the that an enumeration of all ground terms is used to decide whether the derivation always talks about $\mathcal{I}_N$. Comon and Nieuwenhuis (2000) started from a different angle: If the initial clause set is consistent, then every model of the final saturated set is also a model of the (also saturated) input set N. If N has at most a single Herbrand model, then this property is clearly maintained throughout the derivation. Hence Comon and Nieuwenhuis propose to *complete* N, i.e. to add a new set N' of clauses such that $\mathcal{I}_N$ is the only Herbrand model of $N \cup N'$. Then a fair saturation of $N \cup N' \cup \{C\}$ produces (in the limit) an empty clause if, and only if, $N \not\models_{Ind} C$.

Example 1.7

Consider again the "greater than or equal to" relation on natural numbers from Example 1.6 described by the clause set N_{GE} containing the following two clauses:

(1) $\quad\quad\quad\quad\quad\quad\quad\quad\quad \to GE(x, 0)$
(2) $\quad\quad\quad\quad\quad GE(x, y) \to GE(s(x), s(y))$

Note that the literal $GE(s(x), s(y))$ is maximal in the second clause, so every inference with clause (2) has to use this literal. A completion of this clause set is given by the following clauses:

(3) $\quad\quad\quad\quad\quad\quad GE(0, s(y)) \to$
(4) $\quad\quad\quad\quad\quad GE(s(x), s(y)) \to GE(x, y)$

This completion is computed using a predicate completion procedure that will be the central theme of Chapter 3. Note that there are no non-trivial inferences between the clauses (1)–(4). To prove again that the relation is total, i.e. for all x, y it holds that $GE(x, y)$ or $GE(y, x)$, the clause

(5) $\quad\quad\quad\quad\quad\quad\quad\quad\quad \to GE(x, y), GE(y, x)$

is added. There are two possible inferences using (without loss of generality) the left literal of clause (5), namely either with clause (3) or (4), leading to:

(6) $\quad\quad\quad\quad\quad\quad\quad\quad\quad \to GE(s(y), 0)$
(7) $\quad\quad\quad\quad\quad\quad\quad\quad\quad \to GE(x, y), GE(s(y), s(x))$

Clause (6) is an instance of (1) and can be ignored, and the only remaining inference, between clauses (7) and (4), leads back to clause (5). So the set $\{(1), \ldots, (7)\}$ is saturated and, since it does not contain the empty clause, consistent. This means that $\{(1), \ldots, (7)\}$ has a Herbrand model over $\{s, 0\}$,

1.3 Automated Theorem Proving in Minimal Models

and since $\{(1),\ldots,(4)\}$ has only one such model, namely $\mathcal{I}_{N_{GE}}$, in particular clause (5) must be valid in $\mathcal{I}_{N_{GE}}$. This means that $N_{GE} \models_{Ind} \forall x,y.\, GE(x,y) \vee GE(y,x)$ is proved.

While this approach is more likely than the one of Ganzinger and Stuber to result in a terminating procedure once the completion has been computed, it still suffers from several shortcomings:

(i) Completion as presented by Comon and Nieuwenhuis only works if all clauses in N are universally reductive and Horn.

(ii) Completion is also restricted to clause sets in which no positive equations occur.

(iii) Even if the completion N' of N is computable, it does not inherit nice properties from N: Even if N is Horn and non-equational, the same does not hold for $\mathcal{I}_N$. For example, the clause set $\{P \to Q(x,y), \to Q(x,x)\}$ is completed by the clause $Q(x,y) \to P, x \simeq y$, which is not Horn and contains an equation. So termination arguments for $N \cup \{C\}$ do not carry over to $N \cup N' \cup \{C\}$.

Due to these problems, the approach by Comon and Nieuwenhuis also did not give rise to new decidability results. However, I will use the idea of completion in settings where suitable extensions of conditions (i) and (ii) are met and refine the idea of completing the input N in such a way that the problem (iii) vanishes.

1.3.5 The Description-specific Approach

The previously mentioned approaches all try to tackle model descriptions of a maximal variety. When the range of descriptions is reduced, decision procedures become more easily available. I will concentrate here on two types of descriptions:

A Herbrand interpretation can be regarded as a (usually infinite) set of ground atoms. The most natural finite representations of Herbrand models are finite sets of possibly non-ground atoms, so-called *Atomic Representations of Term Models (ARMs)*, representing the interpretation where all ground instances of these atoms hold. For example, the ARM $\{P(0), P(s(s(x))\}$ denotes the interpretation containing all atoms of the form $P(0)$ or $P(s(s(t)))$, where t is a ground term over s and 0.

To examine more expressive interpretations, Lassez and Marriott (1987) studied so-called *Disjunctions of Implicit Generalizations*, which are sets of non-ground atoms each of which is equipped with a set of restriction atoms. For example, a single implicit generalization might take the form

$$P(x)/\{P(0), P(s(s(x)))\},$$

which denotes the interpretation where all instances of the left hand side $P(x)$ of this expression hold, except those that are instances of an atom on the right hand side, i.e. of $P(0)$ or $P(s(s(x)))$. In this example, this leaves only the ground atom $P(s(0))$.

For both kinds of representations, several decidability results are known: Gottlob and Pichler (2001) showed that the validity of a clause in an interpretation represented by an ARM is decidable, as is the equivalence of two ARMs. Fermüller and Pichler (2005; 2007) proved the same results for DIGs.

The methods used to derive these decidability results are specialized for the given problems, and I will not detail them here. However, I will later revisit both types of representations: Taking a different approach, namely a specialization of an algorithm in the spirit of Comon and Nieuwenhuis to DIGs, I will extend the mentioned decidability results and show the decidability of the validity of more expressive formula classes.

1.4 Contributions

In this book, I will show how to extend Superposition to a sound and refutationally complete calculus for the fixed domain semantics. The algorithm can handle equality and is not restricted to clauses of any special syntactic form. Based on an additional induction rule, I further extend the calculus to reason over minimal models. I also show how the calculus can be used as a decision procedure for validity in interpretations that are represented by ARMs and DIGs, extending the fragment for which validity in such interpretations is known to be decidable. Finally, I present a generic method to derive minimal model decidability results for Horn clauses over signatures of at most unary function symbols from saturation-based first-order decidability results. All these calculi use variants of disunification and predicate completion. I extend disunification and predicate completion accordingly and justify the initial use of disunification in predicate completion that was proposed by Comon and Nieuwenhuis. The main contributions are detailed in the following sections.

1.4.1 Superposition for Fixed Domain and Minimal Model Reasoning

Conceptual problems in using Superposition for fixed domain and minimal model reasoning arise when a conjecture contains both universally and existentially quantified variables. In this case, Superposition cannot be used for fixed domain and minimal model reasoning any more: Universally quantified conjectures that become existentially quantified after negation cannot be handled by standard Superposition because Superposition works only on universally quantified clauses. The usual remedy for this problem in first-order reasoning is to *Skolemize* the existential variables. But as soon as this happens, the computation no longer works over the initial signature Σ, but over $\Sigma \cup \{f_1, \ldots, f_n\}$, where $f_1, \ldots, f_n$ are the introduced Skolem functions. This approach is in general not faithful to the problem: In the Elevator Example 1.1, $N_E \models_{\{a,b,p,q\}} \forall y.\exists x.G(y,x)$, i.e. there is a person in every elevator on the ground floor (namely p in elevator a and q in elevator b), but the negation $\exists y.\forall x.\neg G(y,x)$ becomes $\forall x.\neg G(c,x)$ after Skolemization, where c is the fresh Skolem constant introduced for y. This formula corresponds to the query $\exists x.G(c,x)$ which does not hold in the minimal model $\mathcal{I}_{N_E}$ because there is no elevator c in this model. In particular, the approach is not refutationally complete: Even if $N \models_\Sigma \phi$, the empty clause cannot always be derived.

This inability to Skolemize leads to another problem: If existential quantification is somehow incorporated into the notion of clauses, the scope of existential quantifiers must not be restricted to single clauses but they must range over the whole clause set. Otherwise a calculus for clauses with existential variables cannot be complete: Consider for example the unsatisfiable set $\{P(x)\rightarrow Q(x),\ P(x),Q(x)\rightarrow,\ \exists y.\rightarrow P(y)\}$. Resolution of the first and third clauses yields $\exists z.\rightarrow Q(z)$, and resolution of this clause with the second one yields $\exists w.P(w)\rightarrow$. But a contradiction can only be derived by keeping track of the fact that w can be instantiated by the same value as y.

In Chapter 4, I show how to address these complications by explicitly integrating existential variables (the scope of which ranges over a whole clause set) directly into the calculus. To this end, Skolemization is avoided; instead, clauses are enriched by constraints that keep track of instantiations of the existential variables. For example, the negated conjecture in the example above results in the constrained clause $v \simeq y \parallel G(y,x) \rightarrow$ with existential variable v. This constrained clause represents the formula $\exists v.\forall x, y.\ v \simeq x \rightarrow G(y,x)$. The extended notion of constrained clauses gives rise to the Superposition calculus SFD for fixed domains. In addition to standard first-order equational reasoning, the inference and reduction rules of this calculus also take care of the constraint. SFD is sound and refutationally complete for the fixed domain se-

Chapter 1: Introduction

mantics and queries of the form $\forall^*\exists^*\phi$, where ϕ is quantifier-free (Section 4.2). On a set of unconstrained clauses, SFD behaves just like first-order Superposition.

A fixed domain unsatisfiability proof of a constrained clause set with SFD in general requires the computation of infinitely many empty clauses, which means that compactness is lost. This does not come as a surprise because it must be proved that an existentially quantified clause cannot be satisfied in a term-generated infinite domain. For Example 1.2, proving the unsatisfiability of the set $N_{GT} \cup \{v \simeq x \parallel GT(s(x), x) \to\}$ over the signature $\{0, s\}$ amounts to the successive derivation of the clauses $v \simeq 0 \parallel \Box$, $v \simeq s(0) \parallel \Box$, $v \simeq s(s(0)) \parallel \Box$, and so on. In order to represent such an infinite set of empty clauses finitely, an induction rule, based on the minimal model semantics, can be employed (Section 4.3).

In contrast to previous calculi, SFD is extremely flexible: It is neither restricted to special model descriptions like DIGs nor to clauses that satisfy a given syntactic property like universal reductiveness, and it can handle a quantifier alternation, which has not been possible before.

Most of the results in this chapter have been published as (Horbach and Weidenbach, 2008, 2009e, 2010).

1.4.2 Disunification and Predicate Completion

A set of constrained clauses that is saturated by SFD is Herbrand-unsatisfiable if, and only if, the constraints of the empty clauses are *covering*. For example, the constrained clause set $\{v \simeq 0 \parallel \Box, v \simeq s(x) \parallel \Box\}$ is covering for the signature $\{s, 0\}$ because whatever value is chosen for the shared existential variable v, an instance of one of the clauses is a contradiction; for $v \mapsto s(s(0))$, for example, instantiating x by $s(0)$ leads to the instance $s(s(0)) \simeq s(s(0)) \parallel \Box$, which provides a contradiction. Hence the clause set does not have a Herbrand model over $\{s, 0\}$.

The decision of coverage is a so-called *disunification problem*. While *unification* is the task of finding for an equation $s \simeq t$ substitutions σ of the variables in s and t such that $s\sigma$ and $t\sigma$ are syntactically equal, i.e. such that $s\sigma \simeq t\sigma$ holds in the free term algebra $\mathcal{T}(\Sigma)$, *disunification* is the more general task of finding the instantiations of the free variables of a given equational formula under which this formula holds in $\mathcal{T}(\Sigma)$. In the example, the the formula $v \not\simeq 0 \wedge \forall x. v \not\simeq s(x)$ must be considered, which does not have any solutions in $\mathcal{T}(\Sigma_{\text{nat}})$. In a more general framework, instances making the formula valid in a specific interpretation are computed, for example interpretations in which some function symbols are interpreted as associative or commutative.

Disunification is also the basic ingredient of *predicate completion*, the procedure that Comon and Nieuwenhuis use to guarantee that a given predicative Horn clause set has a unique Herbrand model. Predicate completion plays an important role in further developing SFD into a decision procedure for various classes of interpretations in Chapters 5 and 6 (cf. the overview in Sections 1.4.3 and 1.4.4). The clause classes arising in the development of the decision procedures of Chapter 5 are partially non-Horn and I extend predicate completion in Section 3.3 to predicative non-Horn clauses sets and to clause sets containing a simple form of equations (see below). As a side product, I also give the first correctness proof of the original predicate completion proposed by Comon and Nieuwenhuis.

The first part of Chapter 3 is devoted to reviewing a disunification algorithm by Comon and Delor (1994) and extending it to *ultimately periodic interpretations*. Ultimately periodic interpretations are Herbrand interpretations in which equations of the form $s^l(x) \simeq s^k(x)$ hold, and they occur for example as models of formulas of propositional linear time temporal logic. As a first application of the extended disunification algorithm, I prove in Section 3.4 that the satisfiability of equational formulas in ultimately periodic interpretations is decidable. Considering these interpretations is not essential for the remainder of this book. However, they provide candidates for interpretations in which also validity of predicative clauses is decidable using a suitable version of SFD. The presented algorithms have been implemented on top of the automated theorem prover SPASS (Weidenbach et al., 2009). The implementation is described in Section 3.5 and in (Horbach, 2011b). To my knowledge, it provides the first publicly available program for disunification and predicate completion.

The main results of this chapter have been published as (Horbach, 2010a, 2011a).

1.4.3 A Superposition-based Decision Procedure for DIG Interpretations

For special representations of interpretations like DIGs, decision procedures for (minimal model) validity of clauses do already exist (cf. Section 1.3.5). As a first evidence to the practical usefulness of SFD, I show in Chapter 5 that a fragment of SFD, the resolution calculus ORFD, provides a decision procedure on the basis of which all known decidability results for DIGs can be derived. Moreover, ORFD allows me to extend these results considerably.

To do so, I first show how to translate DIGs into sets of constrained clauses (Section 5.3). Left and right hand sides of a DIG are described separately, for example the very simple DIG $\{P(x,y)/\{P(a,y), P(x,b)\}\}$ over the two-element domain $\{a, b\}$, that describes the interpretation containing only $P(b, a)$, is translated into the clauses

- $\rightarrow \dot{P}(x,y)$ describing the left hand side,
- $\rightarrow \check{P}(a,y)$ and $\rightarrow \check{P}(x,b)$ describing the restrictions, and
- $\dot{P}(x,y) \rightarrow \check{P}(x,y), P(x,y)$ linking the two descriptions.

Then the predicates in this non-Horn clause set are completed using the extended predicate completion algorithm from Chapter 3, which results in a clause set N. The only Herbrand model of N over the given signature is just the original DIG-represented interpretation. Because this obviously implies that the minimal model and fixed domain semantics agree for N, ORFD is complete with respect to the minimal model semantics for N. I show in Section 5.4 how this allows me to recover the known results that the equivalence of interpretations and the validity of clauses are decidable (cf. Fermüller and Pichler, 2005, 2007), and how decidability extends to several more expressive classes of queries, for example queries of the form $\forall \vec{x}.\exists \vec{y}.C$ where C is a clause or queries $\forall \vec{x}.\exists \vec{y}.\phi$ and $\exists \vec{x}.\forall \vec{y}.\phi$ where ϕ is a purely positive or purely negative quantifier-free formula. For ARMs, i.e. minimal models of finitely many non-ground atoms, I even prove that the validity of any formula with at most one quantifier alternation is decidable. The calculus ORFD has also been implemented on top of SPASS and the implementation is described in Section 5.5.

These decidability results have been published as (Horbach and Weidenbach, 2009a,d).

1.4.4 Reducing the Decidability of Minimal Model Validity to Superposition-based First-order Decidability

Superposition terminates on many fragments of first-order logic, thus providing a decision procedure for these fragments. The similarities between standard Superposition and SFD raises the question whether similar results can be achieved for minimal model reasoning. In particular: Is it possible to reduce the (higher-order) problem of minimal model decidability in a generic way to first-order decidability?

In Chapter 6, I pursue this question. In the presence of clauses with equality, it is easy to see that termination of Superposition on unconstrained clauses does not carry over to constrained clauses even for very simple problems. For example, unconstrained Superposition terminates on ground unit clauses, but SFD does not terminate on $\rightarrow s(0) \simeq 0$ and $v \simeq 0 \,\|\, \Box$, because it enables the successive derivation of all clauses of the form $v \simeq s(\ldots(s(0))\ldots) \parallel \square$. The situation improves considerably when only predicative clauses are considered. I show in Section 6.3 that, if the description N consists of unconstrained predicative Horn clauses and a query of the form $\forall x. \exists y_1, \ldots, y_m. \bigvee_i \bigwedge_j A_{ij}$ (corresponding after negation to the constrained clauses $\vec{v} \simeq \vec{x} \parallel A_{i1}, \ldots, A_{in_i} \rightarrow$) is considered, termination of Superposition on

$$N \cup \{A_{11}, \ldots, A_{1m_1} \rightarrow, \ldots, A_{n1}, \ldots, A_{nm_n} \rightarrow\}$$

already almost implies termination of the calculus SFD on the constrained clause set

$$N \cup \{\vec{v} \simeq \vec{x} \parallel A_{11}, \ldots, A_{1m_1} \rightarrow, \ldots, \vec{v} \simeq \vec{x} \parallel A_{n1}, \ldots, A_{nm_n} \rightarrow\}.$$

Almost because the only reason for non-termination is a regular increase in the constraints. This increase can be captured by an extension of the notion of a constraint to regular expressions like $v \simeq s^*(0)$ and by an additional Melting inference rule. In the example above, Melting would derive the constrained clause $v \simeq s^*(0) \parallel \square$ from $v \simeq 0 \parallel \square$ and $v \simeq s(0) \parallel \square$. This constrained clause comprises all the constrained clauses $v \simeq s(\ldots(s(0))\ldots) \parallel \square$ and effectively prevents non-termination.

I show that Melting is sound for the considered fragment and use this rule as the basis of an inference calculus that terminates on every constrained clause set of the form

$$N \cup \{\vec{v} \simeq \vec{x} \parallel A_{11}, \ldots, A_{1m_1} \rightarrow, \ldots, \vec{v} \simeq \vec{x} \parallel A_{n1}, \ldots, A_{nm_n} \rightarrow\}.$$

Deciding Herbrand-unsatisfiability is more complex for clauses with these more expressive constraints than for the original constrained clauses used in the context of SFD and ORFD. The reason is that coverage of such constrained clauses cannot directly be translated into a disunification problem. In Section 6.4, I show how the decision of coverage can instead again be regarded as a problem of minimal model validity. This problem is decidable if all function symbols in the signature are constant or unary and the positive literal in every clause on N is linear. In Section 6.5, I combine these results to prove that it is decidable whether $N \models_{Ind} \forall x. \exists y_1, \ldots, y_m. \bigvee_i \bigwedge_j A_{ij}$ holds whenever

(i) all function symbols in Σ are at most unary,

(ii) N is a set of Horn clauses and all positive literals in N are linear, and

(iii) $N \cup \{A_{11}, \ldots, A_{1m_1} \rightarrow, \ldots, A_{n1}, \ldots, A_{nm_n} \rightarrow\}$ belongs to a class that can be finitely saturated by Ordered Resolution.

These results have been published as (Horbach and Weidenbach, 2009b,c).

2 Preliminaries

2.1 Mathematical Foundations

In this section, I will shortly recall the basic definitions of multisets, orderings and equivalence relations. In the context of superposition calculi, equations and clauses are traditionally defined as multisets of terms or literals, respectively. While a definition using sets instead of multisets is equally possible, multisets have the advantage of being more explicit and closer to actual implementations (cf. Definitions 2.9 and 2.10).

The extensive use of orderings on the literals in a clause and of the terms in an equation is, as noted in the introduction, one of the major advantages of superposition compared to previous calculi and throughout this book, I will make use of several such orderings (see e.g. Definitions 2.21 and 2.27). Finally, there is a strong correspondence between equivalence relations on terms that are compatible with the term structure and Herbrand interpretations (cf. Definition 2.29).

Definition 2.1 (Natural Numbers)
The set $\mathbb{N}$ of natural numbers contains all non-negative integers, i.e. $\mathbb{N} = \{0, 1, 2, \ldots\}$.

Definition 2.2 (Multisets)
A *multiset* M over a set T is a function $M : T \to \mathbb{N}$. The *union* M_1, M_2 of two multisets M_1 and M_2 over T is the function mapping $t \in T$ to $M_1(t) + M_2(t)$. The *element-of* relation for multisets is defined by $t \in M$ if, and only if, $M(t) \neq 0$. A multiset M over T is *empty* if $M(t) = 0$ for all $t \in T$. Like the empty set, the empty multiset is denoted by $\emptyset$.

If M is a multiset over T and $S \subseteq T$ is a subset of T, $M \subseteq S$ means that $M(t) \neq 0$ implies $t \in S$ for all $t \in T$ and $M \cap S = \emptyset$ means that $t \in S$ implies $M(t) = 0$ for all $t \in T$.

Multisets are written in a set-like notation, e.g. $\{t, t, t\}$ denotes the multiset M where $M(t) = 3$ and $M(t') = 0$ for all $t' \neq t$ in T. If M is a multiset over T and $t \in T$, then M, t denotes the multiset union $M \cup \{t\}$.

Definition 2.3 (Orderings)
A *partial ordering* $\succeq$ on a set T is a binary relation on T that is

(i) *reflexive*, i.e. $t \succeq t$ for all $t \in T$,

(ii) *antisymmetric*, i.e. $t_1 \succeq t_2$ and $t_2 \succeq t_1$ implies $t_1 = t_2$ for all $t_1, t_2 \in T$, and

(iii) *transitive*, i.e. $t_1 \succeq t_2$ and $t_2 \succeq t_3$ implies $t_1 \succeq t_3$ for all $t_1, t_2, t_3 \in T$.

A *strict partial ordering* $\succ$ on a set T is a binary relation on T that is

(i) *asymmetric*, i.e. $t_1 \succ t_2$ implies $t_2 \not\succ t_1$ for all $t_1, t_2 \in T$, and

(ii) *transitive*, i.e. $t_1 \succ t_2$ and $t_2 \succ t_3$ implies $t_1 \succ t_3$ for all $t_1, t_2, t_3 \in T$.

If $=$ is the identity relation on T and $\succeq$ is a partial ordering on T, then the relation $\succ$ defined as $\succ = (\succeq \setminus =)$ is a strict partial ordering. Conversely, if $\succ$ is a strict partial ordering on T, then the relation $\succeq$ defined as $\succeq = (\succ \cup =)$ is a partial ordering.

A partial ordering $\succeq$ is *total* or an *ordering* on $T' \subseteq T$ if $t_1 \succeq t_2$ or $t_2 \succeq t_1$ for all $t_1, t_2 \in T'$. A strict partial ordering $\succ$ is *total* or a *strict ordering* on $T' \subseteq T$ if $t_1 \succ t_2$ or $t_2 \succ t_1$ or $t_1 = t_2$ for all $t_1, t_2 \in T'$.

Definition 2.4 (Lexicographic and Multiset Orderings)

A strict partial ordering $\succ$ on a set T can be extended to a strict partial ordering $\succ^{mul}$ on multisets over T as follows: $M \succ^{mul} N$ if

(i) $M \neq N$ and

(ii) whenever there is a $t \in T$ such that $N(t) \succ M(t)$, then $M(t') \succ N(t')$ for some $t' \succ t$.

It can be extended to a strict partial ordering $\succ^{lex}$ on n-tuples over T as follows: $(t_1, \ldots, t_n) \succ^{lex} (t'_1, \ldots, t'_n)$ if there is an index $1 \leq i \leq n$ such that

(i) $t_j = t'_j$ for all $1 \leq j < i$ and

(ii) $t_i \succ t'_i$.

Analogously, a partial ordering $\succeq$ on a set T can be extended to a partial ordering $\succeq^{mul}$ on multisets over T and a partial ordering $\succeq^{lex}$ on n-tuples over T.

Definition 2.5 (Minimal and Maximal Elements)

Let $\succ$ be a strict partial ordering on a set T and let S be a subset of T or a multiset over T. With respect to $\succ$ and S, an element $t \in S$ is called

- *maximal* if there is no element $s \in S$ with $s \succ t$,

- *minimal* if there is no element $s \in S$ with $t \succ s$,

- *strictly maximal* if t is maximal and, if S is a multiset, $S(t) = 1$,
- *strictly minimal* if t is minimal and, if S is a multiset, $S(t) = 1$.

Definition 2.6 (Reflexive, Symmetric and Transitive Closure)
Let R be a binary relation on a set T. The relation $R \cup \{(t,t) \mid t \in T\}$ is the *reflexive closure* of R, and $R \cup \{(t_1, t_2) \mid R(t_2, t_1)\}$ is the *symmetric closure* of R.

Let relations R^n be inductively defined by
(i) $R^0 = \{(t,t) \mid t \in T\}$ and
(ii) $R^{n+1} = \{(t_1, t_2) \mid R(t_1, t')$ and $R^n(t', t_2)$ for some $t' \in T\}$.

The union $\bigcup_{n \in \mathbb{N}} R^n$ is the *transitive closure* of R.

Definition 2.7 (Equivalence Relations and Quotients)
An *equivalence relation* $\cong$ on a set T is a binary relation on T that is
(i) *reflexive*, i.e. $t \cong t$ for all $t \in T$,
(ii) *symmetric*, i.e. $t_1 \cong t_2$ implies $t_2 \cong t_1$ for all $t_1, t_2 \in T$, and
(iii) *transitive*, i.e. $t_1 \cong t_2$ and $t_2 \cong t_3$ implies $t_1 \cong t_3$ for all $t_1, t_2, t_3 \in T$.

For every element $t \in T$, the subset $[t]_\cong = \{t' \in T \mid t \cong t'\}$ of T is called the *equivalence class* of t. Note that $t \cong t'$ if, and only if, $[t]_\cong = [t']_\cong$. The set $T/_\cong = \{[t]_\cong \mid t \in T\}$ is the *quotient of T by* $\cong$. If the considered equivalence relation is unambiguous, $[t]_\cong$ is also written simply as $[t]$.

2.2 Syntax

I will now introduce the syntax of terms, clauses and formulas as well as of term rewrite systems, partially relying on definitions from Baader and Snyder (2001), Bachmair and Ganzinger (2001) and Comon (2001). The only non-standard concepts are those of substitutions and their domains, which are defined in an unusual way, and of the constrained clauses that I introduce to include existential variables into the notion of clauses.

2.2.1 Terms and Formulas

Definition 2.8 (Signatures)
A *(many-sorted) signature* is a tuple $\Sigma = (\mathcal{S}, \mathcal{F}, \mathcal{X}, \tau_\mathcal{S})$, where
(i) $\mathcal{S}$ is a finite and non-empty set of *sort symbols*,
(ii) $\mathcal{F}$ is a finite and non-empty set of *function symbols*,
(iii) $\mathcal{X}$ is an infinite set of *variables*

Chapter 2: Preliminaries

(iv) $\mathcal{F}$ and $\mathcal{X}$ are disjoint, and

(v) $\tau_\mathcal{S}$ is a *sort assignment*, i.e. a mapping that assigns

    a) to every symbol in $\mathcal{F}$ a non-empty tuple of sorts and

    b) to every variable in $\mathcal{X}$ a sort, such that infinitely variables are mapped to each sort,

such that for every sort $S \in \mathcal{S}$ there is at least one symbol $f \in \mathcal{F}$ with $\tau_\mathcal{S}(f) = S$.

A sort assignment $\tau_\mathcal{S}(x) = S$ for $x \in \mathcal{X}$ or $\tau_\mathcal{S}(f) = (S_1, \ldots, S_n, S)$ for $f \in \mathcal{F}$ and $n \geq 0$ is usually written as $x : S$ or $f : S_1, \ldots, S_n \to S$, respectively. The number n is called the *arity* of f. A function symbol of arity 0 is called a *constant*, a function symbol of arity 1 is called *unary* and a function symbol of arity 2 is called a *binary*.

The letter S is usually used as a sort symbol, f, g are used as as function symbols, and u, v, x, y, z as variables.

Σ will often only contain a single sort and the current set of variables and the sort assignment for all function symbols will be clear from the context. In this case, it is sometimes given (ambiguously) as $\Sigma = \mathcal{F}$.

The restriction to a *finite* set of function symbols is necessary because disunification, one of the basic algorithms used throughout this book, is restricted to finitely many function symbols.

Definition 2.9 (Terms)
Let $\Sigma = (\mathcal{S}, \mathcal{F}, \mathcal{X}, \tau_\mathcal{S})$ be a signature. The set $\mathcal{T}_S(\Sigma, \mathcal{X})$ of *terms (over Σ) of sort S* is defined as the smallest set such that

(i) $x \in \mathcal{T}_S(\Sigma, \mathcal{X})$ for all $x : S$ in $\mathcal{X}$

(ii) $f(t_1, \ldots, t_n) \in \mathcal{T}_S(\Sigma, \mathcal{X})$ whenever $f : S_1, \ldots, S_n \to S$ and $t_i \in \mathcal{T}_{S_i}(\Sigma, \mathcal{X})$

For a subset $\mathcal{X}' \subseteq \mathcal{X}$, the subset of $\mathcal{T}_S(\Sigma, \mathcal{X})$ of terms of sort S the construction of which uses only variables from $\mathcal{X}'$ in step (i) is denoted by $\mathcal{T}_S(\Sigma, \mathcal{X}')$; the subset of terms of sort S that are constructed without the use of step (i) is also denoted by $\mathcal{T}_S(\Sigma)$.

The relation $t \in \mathcal{T}_S(\Sigma, \mathcal{X})$ is also written as $t : S$. The set $\mathcal{T}(\Sigma, \mathcal{X})$ of *terms (over Σ)* is defined as $\mathcal{T}(\Sigma, \mathcal{X}) = \bigcup_{S \in \mathcal{S}} \mathcal{T}_S(\Sigma, \mathcal{X})$, and analogously $\mathcal{T}(\Sigma, \mathcal{X}') = \bigcup_{S \in \mathcal{S}} \mathcal{T}_S(\Sigma, \mathcal{X}')$ and $\mathcal{T}(\Sigma) = \bigcup_{S \in \mathcal{S}} \mathcal{T}_S(\Sigma)$.

To improve readability, a list $t_1, \ldots, t_n$ of terms is often written as $\vec{t}$, and the n-fold application $f(\ldots (f(t))\ldots)$ of a unary function symbol f to a term t is written as $f^n(t)$.

2.2 Syntax

Definition 2.10 (Equations)
Let Σ be a signature. An *equation over* Σ is a multiset of two terms t_1, t_2 of the same sort, written as $t_1 \simeq t_2$.

Definition 2.11 (Atoms, Literals, and Formulas)
Let Σ be a signature. An *atom over* Σ is an equation over Σ.
The set of *formulas over* Σ is the smallest set such that

(i) every atom is a formula,

(ii) the two logical constants $\top$ and $\bot$ (true and false) are formulas,

(iii) if ϕ_1, ϕ_2 are formulas, then so are the *negation* $\neg \phi_1$, the *conjunction* $\phi_1 \wedge \phi_2$ and the *disjunction* $\phi_1 \vee \phi_2$, and

(iv) if $x \in \mathcal{X}$ and ϕ is a formula, then $\exists x.\phi$ and $\forall x.\phi$ are formulas.

A *literal* is a formula of the form A or of the form $\neg A$, where A is an atom. A literal $\neg(t_1 \simeq t_2)$, called *disequation*, is also written as $t_1 \not\simeq t_2$. A literal is called *positive* if it is an atom, and *negative* otherwise. A general formula that does not use the constructor symbol $\neg$ is also called *positive*.

Definition 2.12 (Abbreviations for Formulas)
Formulas are often written in a more intuitive or compressed form. Let $\phi, \phi_1, \ldots, \phi_n$ be formulas and let $\vec{x} = x_1, \ldots, x_m$ be a list of variables:

- A multiset $s_1 \simeq t_1, \ldots, s_n \simeq t_n$ of equations is often written as $\vec{s} \simeq \vec{t}$.
- The notation $\phi_1 \to \phi_2$ denotes the formula $\neg \phi_1 \vee \phi_2$.
- The notations $\bigvee_{i \in I} \phi_i$ and $\bigwedge_{i \in I} \phi_i$, where I is a set, are inductively defined as follows:

  (i) $\bigvee_{i \in \emptyset} \phi_i = \bot$ and $\bigwedge_{i \in \emptyset} \phi_i = \top$

  (ii) $\bigvee_{i \in \{i_0\}} \phi_i = \phi_{i_0}$ and $\bigwedge_{i \in \{i_0\}} \phi_i = \phi_{i_0}$

  (iii) $\bigvee_{i \in I \cup \{i_0\}} \phi_i = (\bigvee_{i \in I} \phi_i) \vee \phi_{i_0}$ and
  $\bigwedge_{i \in I \cup \{i_0\}} \phi_i = (\bigwedge_{i \in I} \phi_i) \wedge \phi_{i_0}$ for $I \not\ni \emptyset$.

  This notation is ambiguous because the order of the indices (and hence of the formulas) is not fixed.
- The notation $\forall \vec{x}.\phi$ denotes the formula $\forall x_1 \ldots \forall x_m.\phi$, and $\exists \vec{x}.\phi$ denotes the formula $\exists x_1 \ldots \exists x_m.\phi$. In the case where $\vec{x}$ is empty, $\forall \emptyset.\phi$ and $\exists \emptyset.\phi$ both denote ϕ.

Definition 2.13 (Subterms and Subformulas)
Let Σ be a signature. An *expression over* Σ is a term or a formula over Σ. A *path* is a finite sequence of natural numbers, and concatenation of two paths p, q is denoted by $p.q$. For an expression e and a path p, the *subexpression* $e|_p$ *of e at position p* is defined recursively as

- $e|_p = e$ if p is empty, and
- $e|_p = e_i$ if $p = i.q$ and either
  - $e = f(e_1, \ldots, e_n)$ and $i \leq n$, or
  - $e = e_1 \vee e_2$ or $e = e_1 \wedge e_2$ and $i \leq 2$, or
  - $e = \neg e_1$ or $e = \exists x.e_1$ or $e = \forall x.e_1$ and $i = 1$.

The expression e is said to *contain* e' and e' *occurs* in e if e' is a subexpression of e. If e' is a subexpression of e and $e' \neq e$, then e' is a *strict subexpression* of e. A *subformula* is a subexpression that is a formula and a *subterm* is a subexpression that is a term. The number of paths p for which $e|_p$ is defined is called the *size* of e and denoted by $|e|$. A formula is *quantifier-free* if it does not contain a subformula $\exists x.\phi$ or $\forall x.\phi$.

If e_1, e_2 are two expressions and p is a position in e_1 such that $e_1|_p$ and e_2 are two formulas or two terms of the same sort, then $e_1[e_2]_p$ is the result of replacing $e_1|_p$ by e_2 in e_1: Formally, $e = e_1[e_2]_p$ is the unique expression such that

- $e|_q = e_2|_{p'}$ if q is a path of the form $q = p.p'$ and $e_2|_{p'}$ is defined, and
- $e|_q = e_1|_q$ if q is not of this form and $e_1|_q$ is defined.

Definition 2.14 (Variables and Universal and Existential Closure)
Let Σ be a signature and let e be a formula or a term over Σ. The set $\text{var}(e)$ of *variables of* e is defined as the set of all variables that are subterms of e. If e does not contain any variables, it is *ground*. In particular, $\mathcal{T}(\Sigma)$ is the set of all ground terms over Σ.

A variable x *occurs freely* in a formula ϕ if $\phi|_{i_1\ldots i_n} = x$ and none of the subexpressions $\phi|_{i_1\ldots i_m}$, $m \leq n$, is of the form $\phi|_{i_1\ldots i_m} = \exists x.\phi_1$ or $\phi|_{i_1\ldots i_m} = \forall x.\phi_1$. A formula that does not contain any free variable occurrences is *closed*. If $x_1, \ldots, x_n$ are the free variables in ϕ, then $\forall x_1.\cdots \forall x_n.\phi$ and $\exists x_1.\cdots \exists x_n.\phi$ are the *universal closure* and *existential closure* of ϕ, respectively.

2.2.2 Constrained Clauses

To model problems that encompass both universal and existential variables, I will employ *constrained clauses*. They consist of two parts: A clause $\Gamma \to \Delta$ that, as usual, captures the universal fragment of the problem, and a constraint α consisting of equations and disequations that keep track of instantiations of the existential variables.

Definition 2.15 (Clauses)
Let $\Sigma = (\mathcal{S}, \mathcal{F}, \mathcal{X}, \tau_\mathcal{S})$ be a signature. A *clause over* Σ is a pair (Γ, Δ) of multisets of atoms over Σ, written $\Gamma \to \Delta$. The multiset Γ is called *antecedent*

2.2 Syntax

and the multiset Δ is called the *succedent* of the clause. A clause $\Gamma \to \Delta$ is a *(syntactical) tautology* if Δ contains an equation $t \simeq t$ or $\Gamma \cap \Delta$ is non-empty. The clause is *Horn* if Δ contains at most one atom. The *empty clause*, where $\Gamma = \Delta = \emptyset$, is denoted by $\square$.

The set var(C) of *variables occurring in C* contains exactly the variables occurring in a literal of Γ or Δ.

Definition 2.16 (Universal and Existential Variables)
Let $\Sigma = (\mathcal{S}, \mathcal{F}, \mathcal{X}, \tau_\mathcal{S})$ be a signature. Let $\mathcal{V} = \{v_1, \ldots, v_n\} \subseteq \mathcal{X}$ be a finite set of variables. The elements of $\mathcal{V}$ are called *existential variables* and those in $\mathcal{X} \setminus \mathcal{V}$ *universal variables*.

Existential variables are usually denoted by u or v.

Definition 2.17 (Constraints)
Let $\Sigma = (\mathcal{S}, \mathcal{F}, \mathcal{X}, \tau_\mathcal{S})$ be a signature and let $\mathcal{V} = \{v_1, \ldots, v_n\} \subseteq \mathcal{X}$ be a finite set of existential variables, where the v_i are pairwise distinct. A *constraint* α *over* Σ *and* $\mathcal{V}$ is a multiset of equations $s \simeq t$ and disequations $t \not\simeq t'$ where $s \in \mathcal{T}(\Sigma, \mathcal{X})$ and $t, t' \in \mathcal{T}(\Sigma, \mathcal{X} \setminus \mathcal{V})$ and every existential variable occurs at most once in α.

The multiset of equations in α is denoted by $\alpha^\simeq$ and the multiset of disequations by $\alpha^{\not\simeq}$. The constraint $\alpha^\simeq$ is the *positive part* of α and α is *positive* if $\alpha = \alpha^\simeq$.

The notion of *subterms* naturally lifts to positive constraints containing each existential variable by the definition $\alpha|_{i.p} = t_i|_p$, where $v_i \simeq t_i$ is the unique equation in α containing v_i.

The set var(α) of *variables of α* is defined as the set of all variables that occur in one of the equations or disequations of α. If α does not contain any *universal* variables, it is *ground*.

Definition 2.18 (Constrained Clauses)
A *constrained clause* $\alpha \,\|\, C$ *over* Σ *and* $\mathcal{V}$ consists of a constraint α over Σ and $\mathcal{V}$ and a clause C over Σ, such that

(i) the positive part $\alpha^\simeq$ of α contains exactly one equation for each element of $\mathcal{V}$, i.e. $\alpha^\simeq = v_1 \simeq t_1, \ldots, v_n \simeq t_n$, and

(ii) C does not contain any existential variables, i.e. var(C) $\cap \mathcal{V} = \emptyset$.

If α is a positive constraint, then $\alpha \,\|\, C$ is called a *positively constrained clause*.

The set var(α) $\cup$ var(C) of variables occurring in α or C is denoted by var($\alpha \,\|\, C$). A constrained clause $\alpha \,\|\, C$ is called *ground* if it does not contain any universal variables, i.e. if var($\alpha \,\|\, C$) $\subseteq \mathcal{V}$ (and hence var($\alpha \,\|\, C$) = $\mathcal{V}$). I regularly omit constraint equations between variables that do not occur elsewhere in the constrained clause, i.e. I abbreviate $(\alpha^\simeq, \beta) \,\|\, C$ as $\beta \,\|\, C$ if

(i) all equations in $\alpha^\simeq$ are of the form $v_i{\simeq}x_i$ for a variable x_i,
(ii) $\mathrm{var}(\alpha^\simeq) \cap (\mathrm{var}(\beta) \cup \mathrm{var}(C)) = \emptyset$, and
(iii) no variable appears twice in $\alpha^\simeq$.

Such a constrained clause is called *unconstrained* if β is empty. Clauses are regarded as a special case of constrained clauses by identifying a clause C with $\parallel C$.

For example for $\mathcal{V} = \{u, v\}$, I write $u{\simeq}x \parallel P(x)$ for $u{\simeq}x, v{\simeq}y \parallel P(x)$. These abbreviations are justified because all constrained clauses $(\alpha^\simeq, \beta) \parallel C$ that are abbreviated as $\beta \parallel C$ have the same semantics (cf. Lemma 2.42).

2.2.3 Substitutions

Definition 2.19 (Substitutions)
Let $\Sigma = (\mathcal{S}, \mathcal{F}, \mathcal{X}, \tau_\mathcal{S})$ be a signature. A Σ-*substitution* (or simply *substitution*) σ is a map from a finite set $\mathcal{X}' \subseteq \mathcal{X}$ of variables to $\mathcal{T}(\Sigma, \mathcal{X})$ such that if x is mapped to t, then x and t are of the same sort. The set $\mathrm{dom}(\sigma) = \mathcal{X}'$ is called the *domain* of σ. The application of a substitution σ to a variable x is denoted by $x\sigma$, and the *image* of σ is the term set $\mathrm{im}(\sigma) = \{x\sigma \mid x \in \mathrm{dom}(\sigma)\}$.

If $\mathcal{X}'' \subseteq \mathcal{X}$, then the *restriction* $\sigma|_{\mathcal{X}''}$ of σ to $\mathcal{X}''$ denotes the substitution with domain $\mathcal{X}''$ that agrees with σ on $\mathcal{X}'' \cap \mathcal{X}'$ and maps every variable in $\mathcal{X}'' \setminus \mathcal{X}'$ to itself.

A substitution σ is *linear* if no variable occurs twice in $\mathrm{im}(\sigma)$. A bijective substitution $\sigma : \mathcal{X}' \to \mathcal{X}''$ is a *variable renaming*. If $\sigma : \mathcal{X}' \to \mathcal{X}''$ is a variable renaming, then the unique renaming $\sigma^{-1} : \mathcal{X}'' \to \mathcal{X}'$ satisfying $x\sigma\sigma^{-1}$ is the *inverse renaming* of σ.

A substitution σ is identified with its homomorphic extension to terms, quantifer-free formulas, clauses and constrained clauses, where it is applied to both constraint and clausal part. A substitution σ is *grounding* for a term (or quantifier-free formula or clause or constrained clause) t if $t\sigma$ is ground.

The notion of substitution is extended to all formulas by defining the application of a substitution to a quantified term as $(\forall x.\phi)\sigma = \forall y.(\phi\sigma')$, where

(i) y is a fresh variable of the same sort as x and
(ii) $\sigma' : \mathcal{X}' \cup \{x\} \to \mathcal{T}(\Sigma, \mathcal{X})$ is defined by $x\sigma' = y$ and $x'\sigma' = x'\sigma$ for $x' \in \mathcal{X}' \setminus \{x\}$.

The way substitutions and their domains and images are defined here is non-standard: Usually, a substitution is considered as a map $\mathcal{X} \to \mathcal{T}(\Sigma, \mathcal{X})$ defined on all variables while its domain is the set of all variables on which the substitution operates non-trivially. However, I want to be able to distinguish between substitutions like $\{x \mapsto f(x)\}$ and $\{x \mapsto f(x), y \mapsto y\}$. This

2.2 Syntax

has several reasons. One is that it simplifies several proofs, notably in Section 4.3. But more importantly, it is essential for the definition of *substitution expressions*, a generalization of substitutions that is introduced in Chapter 6: In this chapter, I will use predicative atoms (those are formally defined in Section 2.2.5 below) to describe substitutions, and clauses for substitution expressions. The arity of these predicates corresponds to the size of the substitution's domain. The substitutions $\sigma = \{x \mapsto x\}$ and $\tau = \{x \mapsto a\}$, for example, are described by the atoms $P_\sigma(x)$ and $P_\tau(a)$, and the composition $\sigma \circ \tau$ of the two substitutions by the clause set $\{\to P_\tau(a),\ P_\tau(x) \to P_\sigma(x)\}$. An important feature of this clause set is that the succedent in each clause contains all variables of the clause. Were σ considered as a substitution with empty domain, as one would classically do, and described by the propositional atom P'_σ, the clause set for $\sigma \circ \tau$ would be $\{\to P_\tau(a),\ P_\tau(x) \to P'_\sigma\}$ and the succedent in the second clause would not contain the variable x.

The price to pay for this increased expressivity is that the definition of most general unifiers is slightly more awkward than usual:

Definition 2.20 (Unifiers and Most General Unifiers)
Let Σ be a signature. Two terms s, t over Σ are *unifiable* if they are of the same sort and there is a substitution σ such that $s\sigma = t\sigma$. Two atoms A, B are *unifiable* if there is a substitution σ such that $A\sigma = B\sigma$. The substitution σ is called a *unifier*.

Let $\mathcal{X}'$ be the variables in s and t (or of A and B, respectively). If the restriction $\tau|_{\mathcal{X}'}$ of every unifier τ of s and t (or of A and B) is of the form $(\sigma\tau')|_{\mathcal{X}'}$, then σ is called a *most general unifier* of s and t (or of A and B). The most general unifier is unique up to a variable renaming and up the addition to or retraction from its domain of variables that are mapped to themselves. It is (ambiguously) denoted by $\operatorname{mgu}(s, t)$ (or $\operatorname{mgu}(A, B)$).

If $s_1, \ldots, s_n$ and $t_1, \ldots, t_n$ are terms over Σ such that, for every index $i \in \{1, \ldots, n\}$, s_i and t_i are of the same sort, then a substitution σ is a *simultaneous unifier* of $(s_1, t_1), \ldots, (s_n, t_n)$ if $s_i\sigma = t_i\sigma$ for all i. Most general simultaneous unifiers are defined accordingly, and they are again unique up to a variable renaming and domain elements that are mapped to themselves. If α_1 and α_2 are positive constraints of the form $\alpha_1 = v_1 \simeq s_1, \ldots, v_n \simeq s_n$ and $\alpha_2 = v_1 \simeq t_1, \ldots, v_n \simeq t_n$, then $\operatorname{mgu}(\alpha_1, \alpha_2)$ denotes a most general simultaneous unifier of $(s_1, t_1), \ldots, (s_n, t_n)$.

2.2.4 Term and Clause Orderings

One of the strengths of superposition is that only inferences involving maximal literals in a clause have to be considered, and that the conclusion of an inference is always smaller than the maximal premise. To state such ordering conditions, a given ordering on terms must be extended to literal occurrences inside a clause, to clauses and to constrained clauses.

Definition 2.21 (Clause Orderings)
Let $\Sigma = (\mathcal{S}, \mathcal{F}, \mathcal{X}, \tau_\mathcal{S})$ be a signature. A partial ordering $\succeq$ on $\mathcal{T}(\Sigma)$ induces a partial ordering $\succeq$ on $\mathcal{T}(\Sigma, \mathcal{X})$ by $t_1 \succeq t_2$ if, and only if, $t_1\sigma \succeq t_2\sigma$ for all grounding substitutions σ. This partial ordering can in turn be extended to atoms over $\mathcal{T}(\Sigma, \mathcal{X})$ (which are multisets of terms) as its multiset-extension.

Clauses are considered as multisets of occurrences of atoms. The occurrence of an atom A in the antecedent is identified with the multiset $\{A, A\}$; the occurrence of an atom A in the succedent is identified with the multiset $\{A\}$. Now a partial ordering on atoms lifts to atom occurrences as its multiset extension, and to clauses as the multiset extension of this partial ordering on atom occurrences. By abuse of notation, all these partial orderings are denoted by $\succeq$.

If, for example, $u \succ t \succ s$, then the atom occurrences in the clause $s \simeq t, t \simeq t \rightarrow s \simeq u$ are ordered as $s \simeq u \succ t \simeq t \succ s \simeq t$, because $\{s \simeq u\} \succ \{t \simeq t, t \simeq t\} \succ \{s \simeq t, s \simeq t\}$. Note that an occurrence of an atom A in the antecedent is strictly larger than an occurrence of the same equation in the succedent because $\{A, A\} \succ \{A\}$.

The partial ordering $\succeq$ extends to positive constraints by

$$v_1 \simeq s_1, \ldots, v_n \simeq s_n \succeq v_1 \simeq t_1, \ldots, v_n \simeq t_n \text{ if, and only if, } s_1 \succeq t_1 \wedge \ldots \wedge s_n \succeq t_n.$$

and to negative parts of constraints as the multiset extension $\succeq^{mul}$ of $\succeq$. General constraints are ordered with priority on their positive parts, i.e. $\alpha \succeq \beta$ if, and only if,

(i) $\alpha^\simeq \succeq \beta^\simeq$ and
(ii) $\alpha^\simeq = \beta^\simeq$ implies $\alpha^{\not\simeq} \succeq \beta^{\not\simeq}$.

Constrained clauses are ordered lexicographically with priority on the constraint, i.e. $\alpha \parallel C \succeq \beta \parallel D$ if, and only if,

(i) $\alpha \succeq \beta$ and
(ii) $\alpha = \beta$ implies $C \succeq D$.

It is also possible to consider positive constraints as multisets when ordering them, or to extend the partial ordering lexicographically. While all results of this book remain valid in both cases, the latter approach is less natural because it relies on an ordering on the existential variables.

When a superposition calculus is defined on clauses, an ordering that is total on all ground clauses is usually required. The partial ordering on ground

2.2 Syntax

constrained clauses defined here is not total, e.g. the constrained clauses $u \simeq a, v \simeq b \,\|\, \Box$ and $u \simeq b, v \simeq a \,\|\, \Box$ are incomparable, but the ordering is strong enough to support an extension of the usual notion of redundancy to constrained clauses an the completeness results that are based on this notion.

Definition 2.22 (Universal Reductiveness)
Let $\succeq$ be a partial term ordering that is total on ground terms. A clause $\Gamma \rightarrow \Delta$ is *universally reductive* if either $\Delta = \emptyset$ or if $\Delta = \Delta', s \simeq t$ such that

(i) all variables of $\Gamma \rightarrow \Delta$ occur in s and

(ii) for every grounding substitution σ, it holds that $s\sigma \succ t\sigma$ and $(s \simeq t)\sigma$ is strictly maximal in $(\Gamma \rightarrow \Delta)\sigma$.

Example 2.23
The clauses $x \simeq 0 \rightarrow s(x) \simeq 0$ and $P(x), Q(y) \rightarrow S(z), T(x, y, z)$ are universally reductive. The clause $P(x), Q(y) \rightarrow S(z), T(x, y, y)$ is not universally reductive because no succedent atom contains all three variables, and $x \simeq 0 \rightarrow s(x) \simeq s(0)$ is not universally reductive because both sides of the equation $s(0) \simeq s(0)$ in the ground instance $0 \simeq 0 \rightarrow s(0) \simeq s(0)$ are equal.

Definition 2.24 (Properties of Relations on Terms)
Let $\Sigma = (\mathcal{S}, \mathcal{F}, \mathcal{X}, \tau_\mathcal{S})$ be a signature. Let R be a binary relation on $\mathcal{T}(\Sigma, \mathcal{X})$.

Then R is *well-founded* if there is no infinite chain $t_1, t_2, \ldots$ such that $R(t_i, t_{i+1})$ for all i. It has the *subterm property* if $R(t[t']_p, t')$ for all t, t' where $t[t']_p \neq t'$. It is *stable under substitutions* if $R(t, t')$ implies $R(t\sigma, t'\sigma)$ for all t, t' and all substitutions σ. It is *monotonic* if $R(t, t')$ implies $R(u[t]_p, u[t']_p)$ for all terms u and positions p in u.

Let f be a binary function symbol and let $\cong_{AC(f)}$ be the smallest congruence such that $f(x, y) \cong_{AC(f)} f(y, x)$ and $f(f(t_1, t_2), t_3) \cong_{AC(f)} f(t_1, f(t_2, t_3))$ for all $t_1, t_2, t_3 \in \mathcal{T}(\Sigma, \mathcal{X})$. The relation R is *compatible with associativity and commutativity of* f if $R(t_1, t_2)$ and $t_1 \cong_{AC(f)} t'_1$ and $t_2 \cong_{AC(f)} t'_2$ implies $R(t'_1, t'_2)$.

A *congruence relation* is a monotonic equivalence relation on terms.

A *reduction ordering* is a well-founded partial ordering on terms that has the subterm property and is stable under substitutions.

Definition 2.25 (Rewrite Systems)
Let $\Sigma = (\mathcal{S}, \mathcal{F}, \mathcal{X}, \tau_\mathcal{S})$ be a signature. A binary relation $\rightarrow$ on $\mathcal{T}(\Sigma, \mathcal{X})$ is a *rewrite relation* if it is

(i) stable under substitutions and

(ii) monotonic.

Chapter 2: Preliminaries

The symbol $\leftrightarrow$ denotes the symmetric closure of $\rightarrow$, and $\stackrel{*}{\rightarrow}$ (and $\stackrel{*}{\leftrightarrow}$, respectively) denotes the reflexive and transitive closure of $\rightarrow$ (and $\leftrightarrow$).

A set R of equations is called a *rewrite system* with respect to a strict partial term ordering $\succ$ if $s \succ t$ or $t \succ s$ for each equation $s \simeq t \in R$. Elements of R are called *rewrite rules*. A position p in a term u is a *redex* for a rewrite rule $s \rightarrow t$ if $u|_p = s$. If $s \succ t$, then $s \simeq t \in R$ is also written $s \rightarrow t \in R$. The relation $\rightarrow_R$ is defined as the smallest rewrite relation for which $s \rightarrow_R t$ whenever $s \rightarrow t \in R$. A term s is *reducible* by R if there is a term t such that $s \rightarrow_R t$, and *irreducible* or *in normal form* (with respect to R) otherwise. The same notions also apply to formulas and to positive constraints instead of terms.

The rewrite system R is *ground* if all equations in R are ground. It is *terminating* if $\rightarrow$ is well-founded, and it is *confluent* if for all terms t, t_1, t_2 satisfying $t \stackrel{*}{\rightarrow}_R t_1$ and $t \stackrel{*}{\rightarrow}_R t_2$ there is a term t_3 such that $t_1 \stackrel{*}{\rightarrow}_R t_3$ and $t_2 \stackrel{*}{\rightarrow}_R t_3$.

If R is a rewrite system, then $\stackrel{*}{\rightarrow}_R$ is a partial ordering. If furthermore R is terminating, i.e. $\stackrel{*}{\rightarrow}_R \setminus = $ is a well-founded partial ordering, it can be used for Noetherian induction.

There are several ways to extend partial orderings on the set $\mathcal{F}$ of function symbols to the set $\mathcal{T}(\Sigma)$ of terms over Σ. The ones presented here are the recursive path ordering (Dershowitz, 1982) and the associative path ordering (Bachmair and Plaisted, 1985). Let $\mathcal{F}$ be a set of function symbols equipped with a partial ordering $\succ$ and let $stat : \mathcal{F} \rightarrow \{lex, mul\}$ be a function assigning to every function symbol either lexicographic or multiset status.

Definition 2.26 (Recursive Path Ordering)
The *recursive path ordering* $\succ_{\text{rpo}}$ on $\mathcal{T}(\Sigma)$ is given as follows: For terms $t = f(t_1, \ldots, t_m)$ and $t' = g(t'_1, \ldots, t'_n)$ over Σ, $t \succ_{\text{rpo}} t'$ holds if either

(i) $t_i = t'$ or $t_i \succ_{\text{rpo}} t'$ for some i or

(ii) $t \succ_{\text{rpo}} t'_i$ for all $1 \leq i \leq n$ and either

   a) $f \succ g$ or
   b) $f = g$ and $(t_1, \ldots, t_m) \succ_{\text{rpo}}^{stat(f)} (t'_1, \ldots, t'_n)$.

Definition 2.27 (Associative Path Ordering)
Let $\mathcal{F}$ contain the symbols $\wedge$ and $\vee$. For a term $t \in \mathcal{T}(\Sigma)$, let $t\downarrow$ be the normal form of t with respect to the distributivity rule $t_0 \wedge (t_1 \vee t_2) \rightarrow (t_0 \wedge t_1) \vee (t_0 \wedge t_2)$. Define the *associative path ordering* $\succ_{\text{apo}}$ on $\mathcal{T}(\Sigma)$ as follows: $t \succ_{\text{apo}} t'$ if

(i) $t\downarrow \succ_{\text{rpo}} t'\downarrow$ or

(ii) $t\!\downarrow = t'\!\downarrow$ and $|t'| > |t|$.

The ordering $\succ_{\text{apo}}$ is monotonic, has the subterm property, is compatible with the associativity and commutativity of $\wedge$ and $\vee$, and is well-founded.

2.2.5 Predicates

This notion of formulas and clauses does not natively support predicates. However, predicates can as usual be included as follows: First the signature is extended by

(i) a new sort S_{bool},

(ii) a new constant $c_{\text{true}} : S_{bool}$ of the new sort, and

(iii) for each predicate symbol P taking arguments of sorts $S_1, \ldots, S_n$ a new function symbol f_P of sort $S_1, \ldots, S_n \to S_{bool}$.

Then an expression $P(t_1, \ldots, t_n)$ is regarded as an abbreviation for the equation $f_P(t_1, \ldots, t_n) \simeq c_{\text{true}}$. A given partial term ordering $\succ$ is extended to the new symbols such that c_{true} is minimal.

Atoms, formulas or clauses that only contain equations between terms of the form $t \simeq c_{\text{true}}$ and no variables of sort S_{bool}, are called *predicative*. On the other hand, an atom, formula or clause that does not contain equations of sort S_{bool} (and, in the case of a formula, no quantifier binding a variable of sort S_{bool}) is called *equational*. The exclusion of variables of the predicative sort S_{bool} is made to avoid that substitutions introduce symbols of this sort.

Signatures with predicates will often be given as $\Sigma = (\mathcal{S}, \mathcal{P}, \mathcal{F}, \mathcal{X}, \tau_\mathcal{S})$, denoting the signature $\Sigma = (\mathcal{S} \cup \{S_{bool}\}, \mathcal{F} \cup \{c_{\text{true}}\} \cup \{f_P \mid P \in \mathcal{P}\}, \mathcal{X}, \tau_\mathcal{S})$. Again, an abbreviation is used if $\mathcal{S}$ contains only a single sort and the set of variables and the sort assignments are clear from the context: $\Sigma = (\mathcal{P}, \mathcal{F})$.

2.3 Semantics

2.3.1 Interpretations and Entailment

Definition 2.28 (Interpretations)
Let $\Sigma = (\mathcal{S}, \mathcal{F}, \mathcal{X}, \tau_\mathcal{S})$ be a signature. A *first-order interpretation* over Σ, or *interpretation* for short, is a pair $\mathcal{I} = (U, I)$ consisting of a non-empty set U, the *domain* or *universe*, and a function I that assigns

(i) to every sort S in $\mathcal{S}$ a subset $I(S)$ of U such that the sets assigned to different sorts are disjoint, and

(ii) to every function symbol $f : S_1, \ldots, S_n \to S$ in the set $\mathcal{F}$ a function $I(f)$ of type $I(S_1) \times \ldots \times I(S_n) \to S$.

An *assignment* for $\mathcal{I}$ is a function $\mu : \mathcal{X}' \to U$ such that $\mathcal{X}' \subseteq \mathcal{X}$ and $\mu(x) \in I(\tau_\mathcal{S}(x))$ for all variables $x \in \mathcal{X}'$. The homomorphic extension of μ to terms in $\mathcal{T}(\Sigma, \mathcal{X}')$ is denoted by I_μ, i.e. I_μ is the unique map $\mathcal{T}(\Sigma, \mathcal{X}') \to U$ such that

(i) $I_\mu(x) = \mu(x)$ for $x \in \mathcal{X}'$ and
(ii) $I_\mu(f(t_1, \ldots, t_n)) = I(f)(I_\mu(t_1), \ldots, I_\mu(t_n))$ for $f \in \mathcal{F}$.

Definition 2.29 (Herbrand Interpretations)
An interpretation $\mathcal{I} = (U, I)$ over $\Sigma = (\mathcal{S}, \mathcal{F}, \mathcal{X}, \tau_\mathcal{S})$ is a *Herbrand interpretation* if

(i) there is a congruence relation $\cong$ on $\mathcal{T}(\Sigma)$ such that $U = \mathcal{T}(\Sigma)/{\cong}$ is a quotient of $\mathcal{T}(\Sigma)$ and

(ii) every ground term over Σ is interpreted by its equivalence class, i.e. it holds that $I(f)([t_1]_\cong, \ldots, [t_n]_\cong) = [f(t_1, \ldots, t_n)]_\cong$ for every function symbol f and all terms $t_i \in \mathcal{T}(\Sigma)$, where $[t]_\cong$ is the $\cong$ equivalence class of t.

As a Herbrand interpretation is uniquely defined by its universe U, it will often be denoted by U alone. For example, $\mathcal{T}(\Sigma)$ or $\mathcal{T}(\Sigma)/{\cong}$ denote Herbrand interpretations over Σ. If E is a set of equations over Σ, then $\mathcal{T}(\Sigma)/E$ stands for the Herbrand interpretation $\mathcal{T}(\Sigma)/{\cong_E}$, where $\cong_E$ is the smallest congruence relation on $\mathcal{T}(\Sigma)$ containing E.

A Herbrand interpretation $\mathcal{T}(\Sigma)/{\cong}$ is sometimes identified with $\cong$. This can be a more natural point of view, especially when describing the semantics of formulas and clauses (see below).

Definition 2.30
Let Σ be a signature, let $\mathcal{I} = \mathcal{T}(\Sigma)/{\cong}$ be a Herbrand interpretation over Σ, and let Γ, Δ be multisets of equations over Σ. Write

- $\Gamma \subseteq \mathcal{I}$ if $t_1 \cong t_2$ for every equation $t_1 {\simeq} t_2 \in \Gamma$, and
- $\Delta \cap \mathcal{I} = \emptyset$ if $t_1 \not\cong t_2$ for every equation $t_1 {\simeq} t_2 \in \Delta$.

2.3.2 Semantics of Formulas and Constrained Clauses

Definition 2.31 (Semantics of Formulas)
Let $\Sigma = (\mathcal{S}, \mathcal{P}, \mathcal{F}, \tau_\mathcal{S})$ be a signature and let $\mathcal{I} = (U, I)$ be an interpretation over a Σ. An assignment $\mu : \mathcal{X}' \to U$ for $\mathcal{I}$ *satisfies* a formula ϕ over Σ containing only free variables from $\mathcal{X}'$, written $\mathcal{I}, \mu \models \phi$ if

- $\phi = \top$, or

- $\phi = t_1 {\simeq} t_2$ and $I_\mu(t_1) = I_\mu(t_2)$, or
- $\phi = \neg \phi_1$ and $\mathcal{I}, \mu \not\models \phi_1$, pr
- $\phi = \phi_1 \vee \phi_2$ and $\mathcal{I}, \mu \models \phi_1$ or $\mathcal{I}, \mu \models \phi_2$, or
- $\phi = \phi_1 \wedge \phi_2$ and $\mathcal{I}, \mu \models \phi_1$ and $\mathcal{I}, \mu \models \phi_2$, or
- $\phi = \exists x. \phi_1$ and there is an element $u \in U$ of the universe such that $\mathcal{I}, \mu' \models \phi_1$, where $\mu' : \mathcal{X}' \cup \{x\} \to U$ maps x to u and is identical to μ on all other variables of its domain, or
- $\phi = \forall x. \phi_1$ and for every element $u \in U$ of the universe it holds that $\mathcal{I}, \mu' \models \phi_1$, where $\mu' : \mathcal{X}' \cup \{x\} \to U$ maps x to u and is identical to μ on all other variables of its domain.

A formula ϕ is *satisfiable in $\mathcal{I}$* if $\mathcal{I}, \mu \models \phi$ for some assignment μ of the free variables of ϕ. It is called *satisfiable* if there is an interpretation $\mathcal{I}$ such that ϕ is satisfiable in $\mathcal{I}$. An interpretation $\mathcal{I}$ *entails* ϕ, written $\mathcal{I} \models \phi$, if $\mathcal{I}, \mu \models \phi$ for every assignment μ of the free variables of ϕ for $\mathcal{I}$. The same statement is expressed by saying that ϕ is *valid* in $\mathcal{I}$ or that $\mathcal{I}$ is a *model* of ϕ.

It is often not only of interest whether a formula is satisfiable in an interpretation, but also which assignments are witnesses of this satisfiability:

Definition 2.32 (Solutions)
Let $\mathcal{I} = (I, U)$ be an interpretation and ϕ a formula over $\Sigma = (\mathcal{S}, \mathcal{F}, \mathcal{X}, \tau)$ and let $\mathcal{X}' \subseteq \mathcal{X}$. The set $\mathrm{Sol}(\phi, \mathcal{X}', \mathcal{I})$ of *solutions of ϕ in $\mathcal{I}$ with respect to $\mathcal{X}'$* is defined as

$$\mathrm{Sol}(\phi, \mathcal{X}', \mathcal{I}) = \{\mu : \mathcal{X}' \to U \mid \mathcal{I}, \mu \models \phi\} \,.$$

Two formulas ϕ, ϕ' are *equivalent with respect to $\mathcal{I}$* if they have identical solutions in $\mathcal{I}$, i.e. if $\mathrm{Sol}(\phi, \mathcal{X}', \mathcal{I}) = \mathrm{Sol}(\phi', \mathcal{X}', \mathcal{I})$, where $\mathcal{X}'$ consists of the free variables of ϕ and ϕ'. Two formulas are *equivalent* if they are equivalent with respect to every interpretation.

If $\mathcal{I}$ is a Herbrand interpretation over the signature Σ, then $\mathrm{Sol}(\phi, \mathcal{X}', \mathcal{I})$ is the substitution set $\mathrm{Sol}(\phi, \mathcal{X}', \mathcal{I}) = \{\sigma : \mathcal{X}' \to \mathcal{T}(\Sigma) \mid \mathcal{I} \models \phi\sigma\}$.

Definition 2.33 (Negation Normal Form)
A formula ϕ is in *negation normal form* if

(i) every subformula of ϕ of the form $\neg \phi_1$ is a literal and

(ii) no strict subformula of ϕ equals $\top$ or $\bot$.

The formula ϕ is in *conjunctive normal form* if it is in negation normal form and

Chapter 2: Preliminaries

Propagation of Negation:

$\neg \top \twoheadrightarrow \bot$ $\qquad$ $\neg(\phi \vee \phi') \twoheadrightarrow \neg\phi \wedge \neg\phi'$ $\qquad$ $\neg(\exists x.\phi) \twoheadrightarrow \forall x.\neg\phi$

$\neg \bot \twoheadrightarrow \top$ $\qquad$ $\neg(\phi \wedge \phi') \twoheadrightarrow \neg\phi \vee \neg\phi'$ $\qquad$ $\neg(\forall x.\phi) \twoheadrightarrow \exists x.\neg\phi$

$\neg\neg\phi \twoheadrightarrow \phi$

Propagation of Truth and Falsity:

$\top \wedge \phi \twoheadrightarrow \phi$ $\qquad$ $\top \vee \phi \twoheadrightarrow \top$ $\qquad$ $\exists x.\top \twoheadrightarrow \top$

$\bot \wedge \phi \twoheadrightarrow \bot$ $\qquad$ $\bot \vee \phi \twoheadrightarrow \phi$ $\qquad$ $\exists x.\bot \twoheadrightarrow \bot$

$\phi \wedge \top \twoheadrightarrow \phi$ $\qquad$ $\phi \vee \top \twoheadrightarrow \top$ $\qquad$ $\forall x.\top \twoheadrightarrow \top$

$\phi \wedge \bot \twoheadrightarrow \bot$ $\qquad$ $\phi \vee \bot \twoheadrightarrow \bot$ $\qquad$ $\forall x.\bot \twoheadrightarrow \bot$

Figure 2.1: Negation Normal Form Transformation Rules

(iii^c) no subformula of ϕ of the form $\phi_1 \vee \phi_2$ contains a subformula of the form $\psi_1 \wedge \psi_2$.

The formula ϕ is in *disjunctive normal form* if it is in negation normal form and

(iii^d) no subformula of ϕ of the form $\phi_1 \wedge \phi_2$ contains a subformula of the form $\psi_1 \vee \psi_2$.

It is well-known that the rewrite system from Figure 2.1 is confluent and terminating and transforms every formula into a unique equivalent formula in negation normal form.

Definition 2.34 (Semantics of Clauses)
Clauses are interpreted as the conjunction of the antecedent atoms implying the disjunction of the succedent atoms, i.e. an interpretation $\mathcal{I}$ over Σ *entails* a clause $C = A_1, \ldots, A_m \to B_1, \ldots, B_n$, written $\mathcal{I} \models C$, if it entails the formula $\forall \vec{x}.\phi_C$, where $\phi_C = A_1 \wedge \ldots \wedge A_m \to B_1 \vee \ldots \vee B_n$ and $\vec{x}$ are the variables occurring in C. Clause sets are interpreted conjunctively, i.e. $\mathcal{I}$ *entails* a clause set N, written $\mathcal{I} \models N$, if it entails every clause in N. In this case, $\mathcal{I}$ is a *model* of N.

If $\mathcal{I}$ is a Herbrand model, then $\mathcal{I}$ entails a ground clause $C = \Gamma \to \Delta$ if, and only if, $\Gamma \not\subseteq \mathcal{I}$ or $\Delta \cap \mathcal{I} \neq \emptyset$ (cf. Definition 2.30).

Bachmair and Ganzinger (1994) introduced the construction of a special Herbrand interpretation $\mathcal{I}_N^{\succ}$ derived from a clause set N and an ordering $\succ$:

Definition 2.35 ($\mathcal{I}_N^{\succ}$)
Let $\succ$ be a well-founded strict reduction ordering that is total on ground

2.3 Semantics

terms. Proceed by induction on the clause ordering $\succ$ to define ground rewrite systems Prod_C and R_C and Herbrand interpretations I_C for ground clauses C over Σ.

If $C = \Gamma \to \Delta, s \simeq t$ is a ground instance of a clause from N such that

(i) $s \simeq t$ is a strictly maximal occurrence of an atom in C and $s \succ t$,

(ii) s is irreducible by R_C,

(iii) $\Gamma \subseteq I_C$, and

(iv) $\Delta \cap I_C = \emptyset$,

then let $\text{Prod}_C = \{s \to t\}$. In this case, C is *productive* and C produces $s \to t$, respectively. Otherwise $\text{Prod}_C = \emptyset$. In both cases, define $R_C = \bigcup_{C \succ C'} \text{Prod}_{C'}$ and $I_C = \{s \simeq t \mid s \to t \in R_C^*\}$. Finally, define a ground rewrite system $R_N = \bigcup_C \text{Prod}(C)$ as the set of all produced rewrite rules and the Herbrand interpretation $\mathcal{I}_N^{\succ}$ over $\mathcal{T}(\Sigma)$ as the quotient $\mathcal{I}_N^{\succ} = \mathcal{T}(\Sigma)/R_N$. If the ordering is clear from the context, $\mathcal{I}_N^{\succ}$ is usually abbreviated as $\mathcal{I}_N$.

In Section 4.2.2, I will extend this construction of $\mathcal{I}_N$ to constrained clauses (Definition 4.5). At several points in later chapters, I will use the following properties of $\mathcal{I}_N^{\succ}$ that have been proved by Bachmair and Ganzinger:

Lemma 2.36 (Properties of $\mathcal{I}_N^{\succ}$)
The rewrite system R_N is confluent and terminating. If N is consistent and saturated with respect to a refutationally complete inference system (see below), then $\mathcal{I}_N$ is a minimal model of N with respect to set inclusion.

Definition 2.37 (Semantics of Constraints)
Constraints are interpreted as conjunctions and $\simeq$ and $\not\simeq$ as syntactic equality and disequality, respectively:

For a constraint α over Σ and $\mathcal{V}$, let $\phi_\alpha = \bigwedge_{L \in \alpha} L$ be a conjunction of all equations and disequations in α. The constraint α is *satisfiable* if there is a substitution $\sigma : \mathcal{V} \to \mathcal{T}(\Sigma)$ such that $\mathcal{T}(\Sigma) \models \forall \vec{x}.\phi_\alpha \sigma$, where $\vec{x}$ are the universal variables in α.

The negative part $\alpha^{\not\simeq}$ of α is *syntactically valid* if $\mathcal{T}(\Sigma) \models \forall \vec{x}.\phi_{\alpha^{\not\simeq}}$.

Definition 2.38 (Clauses and Constraints as Formulas)
Let α be a constraint and let C be a clause. By a slight abuse of notation, α and ϕ_α as well as C and ϕ_C are occasionally identified. For example, $\mathcal{I} \models \forall \vec{x}.C$ is a shorthand notation of $\mathcal{I} \models \forall \vec{x}.\phi_C$.

Definition 2.39 (Coverage)
A set A of constraints over a signature Σ is *covering (for Σ)* if for every positive ground constraint β over Σ there is a satisfiable ground instance $\alpha \tau$ of a constraint $\alpha \in A$ such that $\beta = \alpha^{\simeq} \tau$.

Example 2.40
For the signature $\Sigma_{\text{nat}} = \{s, 0\}$ with a unary function symbol s and a constant function symbol 0, each of the constraint sets

(i) $\{v{\simeq}0,\ \ v{\simeq}s(0),\ \ v{\simeq}s(s(0)),\ \ \ldots\}$,
(ii) $\{v{\simeq}0,\ \ v{\simeq}s(x)\}$, and
(iii) $\{v{\simeq}x\}$

is covering. However, the singleton constraint set $\{v{\simeq}x, s(x){\not\simeq}s(s(0))\}$ is not covering because the ground constraint $v{\simeq}s(0)$ does not appear as the positive part of a satisfiable ground instance: It appears in the ground instance $v{\simeq}s(0), s(s(0)){\not\simeq}s(s(0))$, but this instance is not satisfiable.

When considering constrained clauses, the usual definition of the semantics of a constrained clause $\alpha \parallel C$ (where all variables are universally quantified) in the literature is simply the set of all ground instances $C\sigma$ such that σ is a solution of α (cf. Bachmair and Ganzinger, 2001; Nieuwenhuis and Rubio, 2001). This definition does not meet the current needs because the constraints here contain existentially quantified variables, and as explained in the introduction (Section 1.4.1), these are supposed to interconnect all clauses in a given constrained clause set.

Definition 2.41 (Semantics of Constrained Clause Sets)
Let N be a constrained clause set over Σ and $\mathcal{V}$, A Herbrand interpretation $\mathcal{I} = (U, I)$ over Σ entails N, written $\mathcal{I} \models N$, if there is a substitution $\sigma : \mathcal{V} \to \mathcal{T}(\Sigma)$ such that for every constrained clause $\alpha \parallel C \in N$ and every substitution $\tau : \text{var}(\alpha \parallel C) \setminus \mathcal{V} \to \mathcal{T}(\Sigma)$, it holds that $\mathcal{I} \models \alpha\sigma\tau \to C\tau$. In this case, $\mathcal{I}$ is a *model* of N.

A constrained clause set N is *Herbrand-satisfiable (over Σ)* if it has a Herbrand model over Σ, and *Herbrand-unsatisfiable (over Σ)* otherwise.

Let M and N be two (constrained or unconstrained) clause sets. The expression $N \models_\Sigma M$ means that each Herbrand model of N over Σ is also a model of M, and $N \models_{\text{Ind}} M$ means that $\mathcal{I}_N \models N$ and $\mathcal{I}_N \models M$.

Constrained clauses are considered equal up to renaming of non-existential variables. For example, the two constrained clauses $u{\simeq}x, v{\simeq}y \parallel \to P(x)$ and $u{\simeq}y, v{\simeq}x \parallel \to P(y)$ are considered equal (x and y have been exchanged), but they are both different from the constrained clause $u{\simeq}y, v{\simeq}x \parallel \to P(x)$, where u and v have been exchanged:

Lemma 2.42 (Renaming of Universal Variables)
Let $N \cup \{\alpha \parallel C\}$ be a set of constrained clauses over $\Sigma = (\mathcal{S}, \mathcal{F}, \mathcal{X}, \tau_\mathcal{S})$ and $\mathcal{V}$ and let $\rho : \text{var}(\alpha \parallel C) \setminus \mathcal{V} \to \mathcal{X} \setminus \mathcal{V}$ be a variable renaming. Then $N \cup \{\alpha \parallel C\} \models_\Sigma N \cup \{(\alpha \parallel C)\rho\}$.

Proof. Let $\mathcal{I}$ be a Herbrand model of $N \cup \{\alpha \,\|\, C\}$ over Σ. By definition, there is a substitution $\sigma : \mathcal{V} \to \mathcal{T}(\Sigma)$ such that for every constrained clause $\alpha_0 \,\|\, C_0 \in N \cup \{\alpha \,\|\, C\}$ and every substitution $\tau : \mathrm{var}(\alpha_0 \,\|\, C_0) \setminus \mathcal{V} \to \mathcal{T}(\Sigma)$, it holds that $\mathcal{I} \models \alpha_0 \sigma \tau \to C_0 \tau$. It suffices to show that this implication also holds for $\alpha \,\|\, C$.

Let $\tau : \mathrm{var}(\alpha \,\|\, C) \setminus \mathcal{V} \to \mathcal{T}(\Sigma)$. Then $\mathcal{I} \models \alpha \rho \sigma \tau$ if, and only if, $\mathcal{I} \models \alpha \sigma \rho \tau$, because the domains and codomains of σ and ρ are disjoint. Because $\mathcal{I}$ is a Herbrand model of $N \cup \{\alpha \,\|\, C\}$, this implies $\mathcal{I} \models C\rho\tau$. ◇

Lemma 2.43 (Coverage of Empty Clause Constraints and Herbrand-Unsatisfiability)
Let N be a set of constrained empty clauses over Σ and $\mathcal{V}$. If the constrained clause set $\{\alpha \mid (\alpha \,\|\, \Box) \in N\}$ is covering for Σ, then N does not have a Herbrand model over Σ.

Proof. Let $\mathcal{I}$ be a Herbrand model of N over Σ. Then there is a substitution $\sigma : \mathcal{V} \to \mathcal{T}(\Sigma)$ such that for every constrained clause $\alpha \,\|\, C \in N$ and every substitution $\tau : \mathrm{var}(\alpha \,\|\, C) \setminus \mathcal{V} \to \mathcal{T}(\Sigma)$, it holds that $\mathcal{I} \models \alpha \sigma \tau \to C\tau$. I show that the constraint $\alpha_\sigma = v_1 \simeq v_1\sigma, \ldots, v_n \simeq v_n\sigma$ is not covered by A_N.

It clearly holds that $\mathcal{I} \models \alpha_\sigma \sigma$ because $\alpha_\sigma \sigma$ only consists of equations of the form $t \simeq t$. If the constraint α_σ were of the form $\alpha_\sigma = \alpha\tau$ for a constrained clause $\alpha \,\|\, \Box \in N$ and some substitution τ, it would thus follow that $\mathcal{I} \not\models \alpha \,\|\, \Box$, which contradicts the fact that $\mathcal{I}$ is a model of N. ◇

This shows that coverage is a generalization of the first-order concept of a contradiction (the empty clause): While a set of unconstrained clauses is unsatisfiable if it contains the empty clause, a set of constrained clauses is Herbrand-unsatisfiable if it contains a set of constrained empty clauses with covering constraints.

2.4 Calculi

2.4.1 Inferences, Redundancy and Derivations

Calculi that reason about sets of constrained clauses will be described by inference rules that characterize how a new constrained clause can be derived from the given constrained clauses.

Definition 2.44 (Inference Calculi)
An *inference rule* is a relation on constrained clauses. Its elements are called *inferences* and written as

$$\frac{\alpha_1 \,\|\, C_1 \quad \ldots \quad \alpha_k \,\|\, C_k}{\alpha \,\|\, C} \ .$$

Chapter 2: Preliminaries

The constrained clauses $\alpha_1 \| C_1, \ldots, \alpha_k \| C_k$ are called the *premises* and $\alpha \| C$ the *conclusion* of the inference. An *inference calculus*, or simply *calculus*, is a set of inference rules.

Given a calculus C, there are two ways how to alter a given constrained clause set N: The obvious way is to use inferences with premises in N to derive new constrained clauses. Additionally, the set can be condensed by eliminating so-called *redundant* constrained clauses, that are already implied by smaller constrained clauses in N. The notion of redundancy is also a means to reduce the number of inferences that need to be considered, which is one of the reasons why superposition calculi have become so successful; for example, an inference involving a redundant premise will only lead to information that could equally well be deduced using only smaller clauses, so it need not be performed.

Definition 2.45 (Redundancy and Saturation)
A ground constrained clause $\alpha \| C$ is called *redundant* with respect to a set N of constrained clauses if α is unsatisfiable or if there are ground instances $\alpha_1 \| C_1, \ldots, \alpha_k \| C_k$ of constrained clauses in N with satisfiable constraints and the common positive constraint part $\alpha_1^{\approx} = \ldots = \alpha_k^{\approx} = \alpha^{\approx}$ such that $\alpha_i \| C_i \prec \alpha \| C$ for all i and $C_1, \ldots, C_k \models C$ (or $C_1, \ldots, C_k \models_\Sigma C$, which is equivalent because $\models$ and $\models_\Sigma$ agree on ground clauses). A non-ground constrained clause is redundant if all its ground instances are redundant.

A ground inference with conclusion $\alpha \| C$ is *redundant* with respect to N if

(i) some premise is redundant, or

(ii) there are ground instances $\alpha_1 \| C_1, \ldots, \alpha_k \| C_k$ of constrained clauses in N with satisfiable constraints and the common positive constraint part $\alpha_1^{\approx} = \ldots = \alpha_k^{\approx} = \alpha^{\approx}$ such that

  a) all $\alpha_i \| C_i$ are smaller than the maximal premise of the inference and

  b) $C_1, \ldots, C_k \models C$.

A non-ground inference is *redundant* if all its ground instances are redundant.

A constrained clause set N is *saturated* with respect to a calculus C if every inference in C with premises in N is redundant with respect to N.

Definition 2.46 (Derivations and Fairness)
Let C be a calculus. A pair (N, N') of constrained clause sets is called a *C-derivation step* if either

(i) there is an inference in C with premises in N and conclusion $\alpha \| C$ such that $N' = N \cup \{\alpha \| C\}$, or

(ii) there is a clause $\alpha \parallel C \in N$ that is redundant with respect to N and $N' = N \setminus \{\alpha \parallel C\}$.

A *C-derivation* is a finite or infinite sequence $N_0, N_1, \ldots$ of constrained clause sets such that for each i, (N_i, N_{i+1}) is a C-derivation step.

A C-derivation $N_0, N_1, \ldots$ is *fair* if every inference in C with premises in the constrained clause set $N_\infty = \bigcup_j \bigcap_{k \geq j} N_k$ is redundant with respect to $\bigcup_j N_j$.

2.4.2 Soundness, Completeness and Termination

The most important property of every calculus is its *soundness*, i.e. that only inferences can be made that do not change the semantics of the problem.

Definition 2.47 (Soundness)
A calculus C is *sound* with respect to a set S of constrained clauses and an entailment relation $\vdash$ (typically $\vdash$ is one of $\models, \models_\Sigma$ or $\models_{Ind}$) if $N \vdash N'$ for every C-derivation step (N, N') with $N \subseteq S$.

If a calculus is supposed to result in a (semi) decision procedure, it must also derive an obvious contradiction whenever the input is contradictory. In the introduction, I have already presented several calculi like Robinson's Resolution calculus that are refutationally complete for unconstrained clauses. In the unconstrained setting, a contradiction is reached when an empty clause has been derived. For constrained clauses, coverage of the derived constrained empty clauses is the right generalization of this concept (cf. Lemma 2.43):

Definition 2.48 (Refutational Completeness)
A calculus C is *refutationally complete* with respect to a set S of constrained clauses and an entailment relation $\vdash$ (typically $\vdash$ is one of $\models, \models_\Sigma$ or $\models_{Ind}$) if for every set $N \subseteq S$ of constrained clauses over a signature Σ that is saturated with respect to C and that satisfies $N \vdash \bot$, the set $A_N = \{\alpha \mid (\alpha \parallel \Box) \in N\}$ of constraints of empty constrained clauses in N is covering.

Usually, the set S is clear from the context and not explicitly given. For example, first-order Resolution is sound and refutationally complete with respect to the set of unconstrained clauses.

The final ingredient for a decision procedure is its termination. Usually, many different inferences can be applied to a given constrained clause set, and the choice in which order they are performed will naturally have an impact on a calculus' termination behavior.

Definition 2.49 (Strategies)
A *derivation strategy* for a calculus C is a mapping S from sets of constrained

clauses to sets of constrained clauses such that $(N, N \cup \{\alpha \,\|\, C\})$ is a C-derivation step for every $\alpha \,\|\, C \in S(N)$.

A C-derivation $N_0, N_1, \ldots$ *follows* a strategy S if $N_{i+1} \subseteq N_i \cup S(N_i)$ for each index i.

Definition 2.50 (Termination)
A calculus C with a derivation strategy S is *terminating* if every C-derivation $N_0, N_1, \ldots$ that follows the strategy S is finite.

Note that while I follow Ganzinger and Stuber (1992) in regarding refutational completeness as a a property that talks about static objects (namely saturated sets), it is sometimes considered as talking about dynamic objects (fair derivations). In this case, termination of the calculus is usually included in the completeness notion. Then the notion defined above might be called *refutational completeness in the limit*, meaning that a contradiction would be derived in the limit of each fair derivation (independently of termination).

3 Disunification and Predicate Completion

3.1 Introduction

Originally, *unification* (Robinson, 1965) was the task of finding solutions to an equation $t \simeq t'$ of terms with respect to the free term algebra $\mathcal{T}(\Sigma)$, i.e. substitutions σ that instantiate the free variables of t and t' in such a way that $t\sigma$ and $t'\sigma$ are syntactically equal. The notion was then generalized to solving systems (i.e. conjunctions) of equations, and unification was recognized as a procedure that can be expressed using transformations of such systems (Jouannaud and Kirchner, 1991; Baader and Snyder, 2001).

From there on, the idea of unification was extended in at least two directions that are relevant for this work: On the one hand, Lassez et al. (1986) examined systems of disequations, and later on a unified framework for the analysis of both equations and disequations was finally found in *disunification* (Mal'cev, 1971; Maher, 1988; Comon and Lescanne, 1989). Algorithmically, disunification procedures are algorithms rewriting first-order formulas over syntactic equality atoms into an equivalent normal form. On the theoretical side, they provide a decision procedure for the satisfiability in $\mathcal{T}(\Sigma)$ of (possibly quantified) formulas containing equality $\simeq$ as the only predicate symbol. Disunification has various applications, in particular in areas such as logic programming (Colmerauer, 1984), automated model building (Caferra and Zabel, 1992; Fermüller and Leitsch, 1996) and minimal model theorem proving (Comon, 1991; Comon and Nieuwenhuis, 2000, and Chapters 5 and 6).

On the other hand, Plotkin (1972) integrated sets E of equational axioms into the transformation rules used for unification, effectively unifying with respect not to $\mathcal{T}(\Sigma)$ but to quotients $\mathcal{T}(\Sigma)/E$ (see also Jouannaud and Kirchner, 1986). Similar extensions were also made to disunification: Comon (1988) developed disunification algorithms with respect to quotients $\mathcal{T}(\Sigma)/E$ where E is a so-called quasi-free or compact axiomatization. Examples of such axiomatizations include sets of associativity and commutativity axioms. Fernández (1992) used a narrowing-based approach to show that if E is a ground convergent rewrite system, then the existential fragment of disunifi-

Chapter 3: Disunification and Predicate Completion

cation is semi-decidable but in general not decidable even if E-unification is decidable and finitary (i.e. there are always only finitely many different most general E-unifiers).

In this chapter, I extend disunification to more general interpretations: Instead of considering only quotients of $\mathcal{T}(\Sigma)$, I allow minimal many-sorted Herbrand models of predicative clauses and equations of the form $s^l(x){\simeq}s^k(x)$ for some sorts. I will call such interpretations *ultimately periodic*. They occur naturally as quotients of the natural numbers or when models of formulas from propositional linear time temporal logics are described by clause sets (Ludwig and Hustadt, 2009). The extended algorithm gives rise to a decision procedure for the satisfiability of equational formulas in ultimately periodic interpretations.

My algorithm is based on the disunification algorithm by Comon and Delor (1994). While there are other disunification algorithms available, this one has the advantage of being flexible in the sense that the control on its rules is kept as weak as possible. Earlier algorithms like the ones of Comon and Lescanne (1989) and Comon (1991) required an often inefficient normal form (e.g. conjunctive normal form) computation after every step. The weak control used by Comon and Delor leaves wide space for the development of efficient instances in concrete implementations, which is important because disunification over an infinite domain is NP-complete (NP-hardness can easily be shown by encoding SAT by $x \mapsto x{\simeq}$true and $\neg x \mapsto x{\simeq}$false; for completeness see Pichler, 2003). On the downside, the weak control makes the termination argument considerably more complicated than when formulas are kept strongly normalized.

In addition to flexibility, the emphasis in Comon and Delor's algorithm lies in a very rich constraint-based sort structure. This sort structure and the consideration of quotient algebras are orthogonal problems. To restrict the presentation of the current results to its essential kernel, I will mostly ignore the sort constraints here.

Predicative atoms are often integrated into a multi-sorted equational framework not explicitly but by adding a new sort `bool`, replacing each atom $P(t_1, \ldots, t_n)$ by an equation $f_P(t_1, \ldots, t_n){\simeq}$true between terms of this sort (cf. Section 2.2.5), and then using algorithms designed for the purely equational setting. This is not so trivial for disunification because it does not prevent the need to extend disunification to a quotient $\mathcal{T}(\Sigma)/_E$, where E encodes the set of valid predicative atoms.

The addition of predicative atoms often makes disunification applicable for the completion of predicates, i.e. for the computation of those instances of a predicate that do not hold in a given interpretation. Comon and Nieuwenhuis (2000) gave an algorithm how to complete predicates in minimal Herbrand models of universally reductive Horn clause sets but did not formally prove its correctness. I will generalize their approach to ultimately periodic models and prove the correctness of this generalization, which also implies the correctness of the original algorithm.

This chapter is structured as follows: In Section 3.2, I will present a disunification algorithm for ultimately periodic interpretations and prove it correct and terminating. As a first application, I will show in Section 3.3 how to use disunification to compute the completion of predicates in ultimately periodic interpretations and in minimal models of saturated non-Horn clause sets. In Section 3.4, I combine results from the previous sections to prove that the satisfiability of equational formulas in ultimately periodic interpretations is decidable. Finally, I will shortly present an implementation of the various presented algorithms in Section 3.5.

The main results of this chapter have been published as (Horbach, 2010a, 2011a,b).

3.2 Disunification

3.2.1 The Disunification Algorithm PDU

Disunification provides a means to transform an equational formula ϕ into a simpler equational formula ϕ' for which satisfiability with respect to the considered interpretation is easily decidable.

Example 3.1
Consider the most elementary case of reasoning with respect to the Herbrand interpretation $\mathcal{T}(\Sigma)$. In the formula $\phi_f = \exists y. f(x,y) \not\simeq f(s(s(x)), 0) \land f(x,y) \not\simeq f(s(s(x)), s(0))$ over a signature containing two sorts S, T and the function symbols $0 : S$, $s : S \rightarrow S$ and $f : S, S \rightarrow T$, the disequations can be decomposed as $x \not\simeq (s(s(x))) \lor y \not\simeq 0$ and $x \not\simeq (s(s(x))) \lor y \not\simeq s(0)$, respectively. Because for every instantiation σ the two terms $x\sigma$ and $s(s(x))\sigma$ are syntactically different, the subformula $x \not\simeq (s(s(x)))$ is equivalent to the constant $\top$, which means that the whole formula is equivalent to $\top$. Since $\top$ is trivially satisfiable with respect to $\mathcal{T}(\{0,s,f\})$, so is the initial formula ϕ_f.

Disunification algorithms usually have the aim to simplify a formula while preserving its solution set with respect to an interpretation. The base algorithm can in general not compute the solutions with respect to a general equational theory $\mathcal{T}(\Sigma)/E$, where E is a set of equations: For $E = \{s(s(x)) \simeq x\}$, the formula ϕ from Example 3.1 is unsatisfiable in $\mathcal{T}(\{0, s, f\})/E$. One of the problems is that $x \not\simeq (s(s(x)))$ is *not* equivalent to $\top$ in this interpretation.

Chapter 3: Disunification and Predicate Completion

Because a terminating disunification procedure with respect to an equational theory $\mathcal{T}(\Sigma)/E$ directly results in a decision procedure for satisfiability in $\mathcal{T}(\Sigma)/E$, disunification with respect to equational theories is in general not possible. I will now show that disunification can nevertheless be extended to interpretations as in the previous example, where the equalities in E are restricted to the form $s^l(x){\simeq}s^k(x)$.

Definition 3.2 (Ultimately Periodic Interpretation)
Let $\Sigma = (\mathcal{S}, \mathcal{P}, \mathcal{F}, \mathcal{X}, \tau)$ be a signature. Let $S_1, \ldots, S_n$ be n different sorts such that all ground terms of sort S_i are of the form $s_i^m(0_i)$ for two function symbols $s_i, 0_i$. A finite set $E = \{s_1^{l_1}(x){\simeq}s_1^{k_1}(x), \ldots, s_n^{l_n}(x){\simeq}s_n^{k_n}(x)\}$ of equations between terms in $S_1, \ldots, S_n$, with $l_i > k_i$ for all i is called a *set of ultimate periodicity equations*. Each sort S_i, $1 \leq i \leq n$, is called *ultimately periodic of type* (k_i, l_i). All other sorts are called *free*.

Let $\succ$ be a well-founded strict reduction ordering that is total on ground terms and let N be a finite set of predicative and universally reductive clauses that is saturated with respect to a refutationally complete calculus such that $N \cup E$ is satisfiable. The Herbrand interpretation $\mathcal{I}_{N \cup E}$ of $N \cup E$ with respect to $\succ$ (cf. Definition 2.35) is called an *ultimately periodic interpretation*.

The disunification procedure for ultimately periodic interpretations is based on a disunification algorithm by Comon and Delor (1994), which I will call DU. They treat the sorting discipline explicitly by enriching formulas (over an unsorted signature) with sorting constraints of the form $t \in S$, where t is a term and S is a so-called sort expression, e.g. Nat $\vee$ f(Nat, Nat). On the one hand, this allows very rich sort structures. On the other hand, it constitutes an additional considerable technical complication of the algorithm. Since multi-sorting can nicely be expressed by formulas over a sorted signature and the addition of sort constraints is a rather orthogonal problem, the variation of the algorithm used below does not rely on explicit sort constraints but on implicit well-sortedness.

Since most rules occur in two dual versions, it will be useful to be able to talk about equations and disequations at the same time.

Definition 3.3 ($t_1 \dot\simeq t_2$)
Let t_1, t_2 be two terms of the same sort. The expression $t_1 \dot\simeq t_2$ stands for either $t_1 \simeq t_2$ or $t_1 \not\simeq t_2$.

Definition 3.4 (PDU)
Let E be a set of ultimate periodicity equations. The *Periodic Disunification Calculus PDU for E* consists of the rules in Figures 3.1, 3.2 and 3.3. All

3.2 Disunification

Normalization:
The Normalization rules comprise the negation normal form transformation rules from Figure 2.1 and the two rules

P1: $\forall \vec{x}.\phi[\forall \vec{y}.\phi']_p \twoheadrightarrow \forall \vec{x}, \vec{y}.\phi[\phi']_p$
P2: $\exists \vec{x}.\phi[\exists \vec{y}.\phi']_p \twoheadrightarrow \exists \vec{x}, \vec{y}.\phi[\phi']_p$

if $\vec{x}$ and $\vec{y}$ are not empty and there is none of the symbols $\neg, \forall, \exists$ between the two joined quantifiers; if a variable of $\vec{y}$ occurs in $\phi[\top]_p$, it is renamed to avoid capturing.

Formulas are always kept normalized with respect to these rules.

Figure 3.1: Normalization Rules of the Calculus PDU

rules can be applied at any position in a formula and they are applied modulo associativity and commutativity of $\vee$ and $\wedge$ and modulo the identities $\exists \vec{x}, \vec{y}.\phi = \exists \vec{y}, \vec{x}.\phi$ and $\forall \vec{x}, \vec{y}.\phi = \forall \vec{y}, \vec{x}.\phi$.

The rules of Figures 3.1 and 3.2 are essentially identical to the rules of DU. The only exceptions are Q7/8, Finite Sort Reduction, and Explosion, which differ from the original formulation in that they are a straightforward combination of originally unsorted rules with rules that manipulate explicit sorting constraints. The original rule Ex1 also always required $\vec{x}$ to be non-empty. This is too weak for the completion algorithm of Section 3.3, which is why PDU uses a version of Ex1 by Comon and Lescanne (1989).

Example 3.5
For Example 3.1 and $E_2 = \{s(s(x)) \simeq x\}$, the normalization with respect to PDU runs as follows:

$\phi \twoheadrightarrow^*_{D2} \exists y.(x \not\simeq s(s(x)) \vee y \not\simeq 0) \wedge (x \not\simeq s(s(x)) \vee y \not\simeq s(0))$
$\twoheadrightarrow^*_{PR} \exists y.(x \not\simeq x \vee y \not\simeq 0) \wedge (x \not\simeq x \vee y \not\simeq s(0)) \twoheadrightarrow^*_{\text{normalize}} \exists y.y \not\simeq 0 \wedge y \not\simeq s(0)$
$\twoheadrightarrow^*_{PS2} (0 \not\simeq 0 \wedge 0 \not\simeq s(0)) \vee (s(0) \not\simeq 0 \wedge s(0) \not\simeq s(0)) \twoheadrightarrow^*_{\text{normalize}} \bot$

3.2.2 Correctness and Termination of PDU

I will first show that $\twoheadrightarrow_{\text{PDU}}$ rewrite steps do not change the solutions of a formula.

Theorem 3.6 (Correctness)
Let $\mathcal{I} = \mathcal{I}_{N \cup E}$ be an ultimately periodic interpretation and let ϕ, ϕ' be two formulas such that $\phi \twoheadrightarrow_{\text{PDU}} \phi'$. Let $\mathcal{X}'$ be a set of variables containing the free variables of ϕ. Then $\text{Sol}(\phi, \mathcal{X}', \mathcal{I}) = \text{Sol}(\phi', \mathcal{X}', \mathcal{I})$.

Chapter 3: Disunification and Predicate Completion

Decomposition, Clash, and Occurrence Check:
D1: $f(u_1, \ldots, u_n) \simeq f(u'_1, \ldots, u'_n) \rightarrowtail u_1 \simeq u'_1 \wedge \ldots \wedge u_n \simeq u'_n$
D2: $f(u_1, \ldots, u_n) \not\simeq f(u'_1, \ldots, u'_n) \rightarrowtail u_1 \not\simeq u'_1 \vee \ldots \vee u_n \not\simeq u'_n$
C1: $f(u_1, \ldots, u_m) \simeq g(u'_1, \ldots, u'_n) \rightarrowtail \bot$ if $f \neq g$
C2: $f(u_1, \ldots, u_m) \not\simeq g(u'_1, \ldots, u'_n) \rightarrowtail \top$ if $f \neq g$
O1: $t \simeq u[t] \rightarrowtail \bot$ if $u[t] \neq t$
O2: $t \not\simeq u[t] \rightarrowtail \top$ if $u[t] \neq t$
if $f(u_1, \ldots, u_n)$, t and $u[t]$ belong to a free sort

Quantifier Elimination:
Q1: $\exists \vec{x}.\phi_1 \vee \phi_2 \rightarrowtail (\exists \vec{x}.\phi_1) \vee (\exists \vec{x}.\phi_2)$ if $\vec{x} \cap \text{var}(\phi_1, \phi_2) \neq \emptyset$
Q2: $\forall \vec{x}.\phi_1 \wedge \phi_2 \rightarrowtail (\forall \vec{x}.\phi_1) \wedge (\forall \vec{x}.\phi_2)$ if $\vec{x} \cap \text{var}(\phi_1, \phi_2) \neq \emptyset$
Q3: $\exists \vec{x}, x.\phi \rightarrowtail \exists \vec{x}.\phi$ if $x \notin \text{var}(\phi)$
Q4: $\forall \vec{x}, x.\phi \rightarrowtail \forall \vec{x}.\phi$ if $x \notin \text{var}(\phi)$
Q5: $\forall \vec{x}, x.x \not\simeq t \vee \phi \rightarrowtail \forall \vec{x}.\phi\{x \mapsto t\}$ if $x \notin \text{var}(t)$
Q6: $\exists \vec{x}, x.x \simeq t \wedge \phi \rightarrowtail \exists \vec{x}.\phi\{x \mapsto t\}$ if $x \notin \text{var}(t)$
Q7: $\forall \vec{z}, \vec{x}.y_1 \simeq t_1 \vee \ldots \vee y_n \simeq t_n \vee \phi \rightarrowtail \forall \vec{z}.\phi$
Q8: $\exists \vec{z}, \vec{x}.y_1 \not\simeq t_1 \wedge \ldots \wedge y_n \not\simeq t_n \wedge \phi \rightarrowtail \exists \vec{z}.\phi$
if in Q7 and Q8 $y_i \neq t_i$ and $\text{var}(y_i \simeq t_i) \cap \vec{x} \neq \emptyset$ for all i and $\text{var}(\phi) \cap \vec{x} = \emptyset$
and the sorts of all variables in $\vec{x}$ contain infinitely many semantically distinct
ground terms (in particular, all t_i are of a free sort).
Q1 and Q2 also require that no redex for P1 or P2 is created.

Finite Sort Reduction:
S1: $\forall \vec{x}, x.\phi \rightarrowtail \forall \vec{x}.\phi\{x \mapsto t_1\} \wedge \ldots \wedge \phi\{x \mapsto t_n\}$
S2: $\exists \vec{x}, x.\phi \rightarrowtail \exists \vec{x}.\phi\{x \mapsto t_1\} \vee \ldots \vee \phi\{x \mapsto t_n\}$
if the sort S of x is free and finite and $t_1, \ldots, t_n$ are the ground terms in S.

Distribution:
N1: $\forall \vec{x}.\phi[\phi_0 \vee (\phi_1 \wedge \phi_2)]_p \rightarrowtail \forall \vec{x}.\phi[(\phi_0 \vee \phi_1) \wedge (\phi_0 \vee \phi_2)]_p$
N2: $\exists \vec{x}.\phi[\phi_0 \wedge (\phi_1 \vee \phi_2)]_p \rightarrowtail \exists \vec{x}.\phi[(\phi_0 \wedge \phi_1) \vee (\phi_0 \wedge \phi_2)]_p$
if ϕ_0, ϕ_1, ϕ_2 are quantifier-free, $\text{var}(\phi_1) \cap \vec{x} \neq \emptyset$, ϕ_1 is not a conjunction in N1
and not a disjunction in N2 and does not contain a redex for N1 or N2, and
there is no negation and no quantifier in ϕ along the path p.

Explosion:
Ex1: $\exists \vec{x}.\phi \rightarrowtail \bigvee_{f \in \mathcal{F}'} \exists \vec{x}, \vec{x}_f.y \simeq f(\vec{x}_f) \wedge \phi\{y \mapsto f(\vec{x}_f)\}$
if y is free in ϕ, no other rule except Ex2 can be applied, there is in ϕ a literal
$y \simeq t$ where t contains a universally quantified variable, and $\vec{x}$ is non-empty
or ϕ is of the form $\phi = \forall \vec{x}'.\phi'$. If y is of sort S, then $\mathcal{F}' \subseteq \mathcal{F}$ is the set of
function symbols of sort $S_1, \ldots, S_n \to S$.
Ex2: $\forall \vec{x}.\phi \rightarrowtail \bigwedge_{f \in \mathcal{F}'} \forall \vec{x}, \vec{x}_f.y \not\simeq f(\vec{x}_f) \vee \phi\{y \mapsto f(\vec{x}_f)\}$
if y is free in ϕ, no other rule can be applied, there is in ϕ a literal $y \simeq t$ or $y \not\simeq t$
where t contains an existentially quantified variable, and $\vec{x}$ is non-empty. If y
is of sort S, then $\mathcal{F}' \subseteq \mathcal{F}$ is the set of function symbols of sort $S_1, \ldots, S_n \to S$.

Figure 3.2: Rules of the Calculus PDU for all Sorts

3.2 Disunification

Periodic Reduction:
  PR: $A[s^l(t)]_p \twoheadrightarrow A[s^k(t)]_p$
  if A is an atom and $s^l(t)$ belongs to an ultimately periodic sort of type (k,l).

Periodic Decomposition:

PD1: $s(t) \simeq s(t') \twoheadrightarrow \begin{cases} t \simeq t' & \text{if } t \text{ and } t' \text{ are ground} \\ t \simeq s^{k-1}(0) \vee t \simeq s^{l-1}(0) & \text{if } t \text{ is not ground} \\ & \text{and } s(t') = s^k(0) \\ t \simeq t' & \text{if } t \text{ is not ground} \\ & \text{and } t' \text{ is ground} \\ & \text{and } s(t') \neq s^k(0) \\ t \simeq t' \vee (t \simeq s^{k-1}(0) \wedge t' \simeq s^{l-1}(0)) & \text{if } t \text{ and } t' \\ \quad \vee (t \simeq s^{l-1}(0) \wedge t' \simeq s^{k-1}(0)) & \text{are not ground} \end{cases}$

PD2: $s(t) \not\simeq s(t') \twoheadrightarrow \begin{cases} t \not\simeq t' & \text{if } t \text{ and } t' \text{ are ground} \\ t \not\simeq s^{k-1}(0) \wedge t \not\simeq s^{l-1}(0) & \text{if } t \text{ is not ground} \\ & \text{and } s(t') = s^k(0) \\ t \not\simeq t' & \text{if } t \text{ is not ground} \\ & \text{and } t' \text{ is ground} \\ & \text{and } s(t') \neq s^k(0) \\ t \not\simeq t' \wedge (t \not\simeq s^{k-1}(0) \vee t' \not\simeq s^{l-1}(0)) & \text{if } t \text{ and } t' \\ \quad \wedge (t \not\simeq s^{l-1}(0) \vee t' \not\simeq s^{k-1}(0)) & \text{are not ground} \end{cases}$

  if $s(t)$ belongs to an ultimately periodic sort of type (k,l) and $s(t) \simeq s(t')$ is irreducible by PR.

  For $k = 0$, the atom $\bot$ replaces $t \simeq s^{k-1}(0)$ and $\top$ replaces $t \not\simeq s^{k-1}(0)$.

Periodic Clash Test:
  PC1: $s(t) \simeq 0 \twoheadrightarrow \begin{cases} t \simeq s^{l-1}(0) & \text{if } k = 0 \text{ and } t \text{ is not ground} \\ \bot & \text{if } k > 0 \text{ or } t \text{ is ground} \end{cases}$

  PC2: $s(t) \not\simeq 0 \twoheadrightarrow \begin{cases} t \not\simeq s^{l-1}(0) & \text{if } k = 0 \text{ and } t \text{ is not ground} \\ \top & \text{if } k > 0 \text{ or } t \text{ is ground} \end{cases}$

  if $s(t)$ belongs to an ultimately periodic sort of type (k,l) and $s(t) \simeq 0$ is irreducible by PR.

Periodic Occurrence:
  PO1: $x \simeq s^n(x) \twoheadrightarrow \begin{cases} x \simeq s^k(0) \vee \ldots \vee x \simeq s^{l-1}(0) & \text{if } l - k \text{ divides } n \\ \bot & \text{if } l - k \text{ does not divide } n \end{cases}$

  PO2: $x \not\simeq s^n(x) \twoheadrightarrow \begin{cases} x \not\simeq s^k(0) \wedge \ldots \wedge x \not\simeq s^{l-1}(0) & \text{if } l - k \text{ divides } n \\ \top & \text{if } l - k \text{ does not divide } n \end{cases}$

  if x and $s^n(x)$ belong to an ultimately periodic sort of type (k,l) and $n > 0$.

Periodic Sort Reduction:
  PS1: $\forall \vec{x}, x. \phi \twoheadrightarrow \forall \vec{x}. \phi\{x \mapsto 0\} \wedge \ldots \wedge \phi\{x \mapsto s^{l-1}(0)\}$
  PS2: $\exists \vec{x}. x. \phi \twoheadrightarrow \exists \vec{x}. \phi\{x \mapsto 0\} \vee \ldots \vee \phi\{x \mapsto s^{l-1}(0)\}$
  if x belongs to an ultimately periodic sort of type (k,l) and x occurs in ϕ.

Figure 3.3: Rules of the Calculus PDU for Ultimately Periodic Sorts

Proof. For free sorts and all rules but Ex1, this has been proved by Comon and Delor (1994, Proposition 1). For any sort, correctness of Ex1 has been shown by Comon and Lescanne (1989, Proposition 3). For ultimately periodic sorts, correctness of all the rules in Figures 3.1 and 3.2 and Periodic Sort Reduction follows easily.

Periodic Reduction is correct because $\mathcal{I} \models s^l(x) \simeq s^k(x)$ implies that $\mathcal{I} \models A[s^l(t)]_p \sigma$ holds if, and only if, $\mathcal{I} \models A[s^k(t)]_p \sigma$ holds.

For *Periodic Decomposition*, let $\mathcal{I} \models (s(t) \simeq s(t'))\sigma$. For free sorts, this is equivalent to $\mathcal{I} \models (t \simeq t')\sigma$, but for periodic sorts, it is also possible that $s(t)\sigma \simeq s(t')\sigma \simeq s^k(0)$ and $t\sigma \not\simeq t'\sigma$, namely if $t\sigma \simeq s^{l-1}(0)$ and $t'\sigma \not\simeq s^{l-1}(0)$ or vice versa. In this case, $t'\sigma$ (or $t\sigma$, respectively) must be equal to $s^{k-1}(0)$ in $\mathcal{I}$. On the other hand, it is easy to verify that every solution of the reduct is also a solution of $s(t) \simeq s(t')$: If, e.g., $\mathcal{I} \models (t \simeq s^{k-1}(0) \wedge t' \simeq s^{l-1}(0))\sigma$, then $\mathcal{I} \models s(t) \simeq s^k(0) \simeq s^l(0) \simeq s(t')$.

For *Periodic Clash Test*, assume that $\mathcal{I} \models (s(t) \simeq 0)\sigma$. This is equivalent to $s(t)\sigma \rightarrow^*_E 0$. For $k \neq 0$, such a reduction is not possible. For $k = 0$, $s^l(0) \rightarrow_E 0$ implies that $\mathcal{I} \models (s(t) \simeq 0)\sigma$ is equivalent to $\mathcal{I} \models (s(t) \simeq s^l(0))\sigma$. The equivalence with $\mathcal{I} \models (t \simeq s^{l-1}(0))\sigma$ follows as for PD, using $k = 0$.

If *Periodic Occurrence* is applicable to a literal $x \dot\simeq s^n(x)$, $n \geq 0$, then any ground instance of the literal must be of the form $s^m(0) \dot\simeq s^{n+m}(0)$. Then $s^m(0) \leftrightarrow^*_E s^{n+m}(0)$ if, and only if, $l - k$ divides n and $m \geq k$. ◇

To prove the termination of the system, I will use many ideas of the termination proof for DU from (Comon and Delor, 1994). However, the original course of action makes extensive use of symmetries in the rules and cannot be taken over because the generalized Explosion creates an asymmetry.

The proof consists of two steps: First I prove that the number of rule applications between two successive applications of the Explosion rules is finite, then I show that the number of applications of the Explosion rules is also finite. Both parts of the proof rely on a transformation of formulas, during which variable occurrences are annotated by two values: The number of ∀∃ quantifier alternations above the binding position and the number of variables bound by the same quantifier.

Definition 3.7 ($N_\phi(x), sl_\phi(x)$)

Let ϕ be a formula in which each variable is bound at most once and let x be a variable occurring in ϕ. Associate to x and ϕ two integers $N_\phi(x)$ and $sl_\phi(x)$: If x is free in ϕ, define $sl_\phi(x)$ to be the number of free variables in ϕ and $N_\phi(x) = 0$. If x is bound in ϕ at position p, define $sl_\phi(x)$ to be the number of variables bound at the same position of ϕ, and $N_\phi(x)$ is one plus the number of ∀∃ quantifier alternations in ϕ above p.

3.2 Disunification

This definition of $N_\phi(x)$ is different from the one in (Comon and Delor, 1994), where both $\forall\exists$ and $\exists\forall$ quantifier alternations are counted. This difference is negligible for rules that do not introduce any quantifiers because $N_\phi(x)$ (non-strictly) decreases for all variables with respect to both definitions. However, the difference is crucial when the generalized Explosion rule Ex1 is considered.

Definition 3.8 ($\succ_I$)
For a given signature $\Sigma = (\mathcal{S}, \mathcal{P}, \mathcal{F}, \mathcal{X}, \tau)$, let

$$\mathcal{F}' = \mathcal{F} \cup \mathcal{P} \cup \{\simeq, \not\simeq, \exists, \top, \bot, \wedge, \vee, \neg, g, h, a\}$$

be an extension of $\mathcal{F}$ and $\mathcal{P}$ by fresh symbols. All elements of $\mathcal{F}'$ are considered as function symbols over a single sort S. The symbols $\top, \bot, a$ are constants, $\exists, \neg, h$ are unary, and $\simeq, \not\simeq, \wedge, \vee, g$ are binary. For a formula ϕ over Σ, that is assumed to be renamed such that each variable is bound at most once in ϕ, inductively define a function $I_\phi(.)$ from formulas over Σ and terms over $\mathcal{F}$ to terms over $\mathcal{F}'$ as follows. First every universal quantifier occurrence $\forall \vec{x}.\psi'$ in the argument is replaced by $\neg \exists \vec{x}.\neg \psi'$ and the result is normalized by the Normalization rules from Figure 3.2 except $\neg(\exists \vec{x}.\phi) \not\to \forall \vec{x}.\neg\phi$. Finally

$$\begin{aligned}
I_\phi(\psi_1 \circ \psi_2) &= I_\phi(\psi_1) \circ I_\phi(\psi_2) & \text{for } \circ \in \{\wedge, \vee\} \\
I_\phi(\exists x_1, \ldots, x_n.\psi) &= \exists^n(I_\phi(\psi)) \\
I_\phi(\neg P(\vec{t})) &= I_\phi(P(\vec{t})) \\
I_\phi(\neg\psi) &= \neg I_\phi(\psi) & \text{if } \psi \text{ is not an atom} \\
I_\phi(\circ(t_1, \ldots, t_n)) &= \circ(I_\phi(t_1), \ldots, I_\phi(t_n)) & \text{for } \circ \in \mathcal{F} \cup \mathcal{P} \cup \{\top, \bot, \simeq, \not\simeq\} \\
I_\phi(x) &= g(h^{N_\phi(x)}(a), h^{\mathrm{sl}_\phi(x)}(a))
\end{aligned}$$

Assume the partial ordering $\neg \succ g \succ h \succ f \succ a \succ \simeq \succ \not\simeq \succ P \succ \top \succ \bot \succ \exists \succ \wedge \succ \vee$ on $\mathcal{F}'$ (for all $f \in \mathcal{F}$ and $P \in \mathcal{P}$), and symbols within $\mathcal{F}$ and within $\mathcal{P}$, respectively, are incomparable. The symbols $\wedge, \vee, \simeq, \not\simeq$ have multiset status and g and all symbols in $\mathcal{F}$ and $\mathcal{P}$ have lexicographic status. Define a strict partial ordering $\succ_I$ by $\phi \succ_I \phi' \iff I_\phi(\phi) \succ_{\mathrm{apo}} I_{\phi'}(\phi')$.

Example 3.9
If t is a term that contains at least one variable and t' is a ground term, then $I_\phi(t) \succ_{\mathrm{apo}} I_{\phi'}(t')$ for any formulas ϕ, ϕ'. In fact, $I_\phi(t)$ contains a subterm of the form $g(h^n(a), h^m(a))$ which is already greater than $I_{\phi'}(t')$ because the latter term contains only symbols from $\mathcal{F} \cup \{\simeq, \not\simeq\}$ and g is greater than all these symbols.

Chapter 3: Disunification and Predicate Completion

I will show that the combination of a rule application and the following normalization decreases $\succ_I$ for all rules except Explosion. Since normalization is obviously terminating, this implies that only a finite number of transformation steps can occur between two successive explosions.

Proposition 3.10 (Termination of PDU without Explosion)
There is no infinite chain $\phi_1, \phi_2, \ldots$ of formulas such that $\phi_1 \twoheadrightarrow_{\text{PDU}} \phi_2 \twoheadrightarrow_{\text{PDU}} \cdots$ and none of the steps is an Explosion.

Proof. I will show that $\phi \succ_I \phi'$ holds whenever $\phi \twoheadrightarrow_{\text{PDU}} \phi'$ by application of a non-Explosion rule. The proposition follows because, as an associative path ordering, $\succ_I$ is well-founded.

For the rules in Figure 3.2, $\phi \succ_I \phi'$ was proved by Comon and Delor (1994, Lemmas 3–9). *Periodic Sort Reduction* is a syntactic variation of Finite Sort Reduction, so the proofs for both rules are identical.

For *Periodic Reduction* $A[t] \to A[t']$, note that $N_\phi(x) = N_{\phi'}(x)$ and $sl_\phi(x) = sl_{\phi'}(x)$. This implies that $I_{\phi'}(t')$ is a strict subterm of $I_\phi(t)$. So $I_\phi(t) \succ_{\text{apo}} I_{\phi'}(t')$, i.e. $I_\phi(\phi) \succ_{\text{apo}} I_{\phi'}(\phi')$ by monotonicity of $\succ_{\text{apo}}$.

For *Periodic Clash Test* and $k > 0$ or ground t, the proposition follows from the ordering $\dot{\simeq} \succ \top, \bot$ on the top symbols and monotonicity of $\succ_{\text{apo}}$. For $k = 0$ and non-ground t, consider the rewriting $s(t) \dot{\simeq} 0 \to t \dot{\simeq} s^{l-1}(0)$. By monotonicity of $\succ_{\text{apo}}$, it suffices to show that $I_\phi(s(t) \dot{\simeq} 0) \succ_{\text{apo}} I_{\phi'}(t \dot{\simeq} s^{l-1}(0))$, which reduces after application of the definition of I to $s(I_\phi(t)) \dot{\simeq} 0 \succ_{\text{apo}} I_{\phi'}(t) \dot{\simeq} s^{l-1}(0)$. Again, N and sl do not change in this step, and so $I_\phi(t) = I_{\phi'}(t)$. By definition of $\succ_{\text{apo}}$, it suffices to show that $s(I_\phi(t)) \dot{\simeq} 0 \succ_{\text{apo}} I_\phi(t)$ and $s(I_\phi(t)) \dot{\simeq} 0 \succ_{\text{apo}} s^{l-1}(0)$ and $\{s(I_\phi(t)), 0\} \succ^{mul}_{\text{apo}} \{I_\phi(t), s^{l-1}(0)\}$. All three relations follow from $s(I_\phi(t)) \succ_{\text{apo}} s^{l-1}(0)$ (c.f. Example 3.9), and the subterm property of $\succ_{\text{apo}}$.

For *Periodic Decomposition*, it suffices to show $I_\phi(s(t) \dot{\simeq} s(t')) \succ_{\text{apo}} I_{\phi'}(A)$ for all newly introduced atoms A (remember that $\dot{\simeq} \succ \wedge$ and $\dot{\simeq} \succ \vee$). Clearly $I_\phi(s(t) \dot{\simeq} s(t')) \succ_{\text{apo}} I_{\phi'}(t \dot{\simeq} t')$ holds by the subterm property of $\succ_{\text{apo}}$. For all other atoms, the relation $I_\phi(s(t) \dot{\simeq} s(t')) \succ_{\text{apo}} I_{\phi'}(A)$ follows as in the case of Periodic Clash Test and $k = 0$.

For *Periodic Occurrence*, the proposition follows from monotonicity and the ordering $\dot{\simeq} \succ \top, \bot$ on the top symbols if the literal is replaced by $\top$ or $\bot$; the argument is analogous to the one for Periodic Decomposition if the literal is replaced by a conjunction or disjunction. ◇

An application of Explosion to a formula does not reduce the formula with respect to $\succ_I$. Because of this, a different ordering is needed to handle explosions. This ordering will be a lexicographic combination of orderings based on $I_\phi(\psi)$.

3.2 Disunification

Lemma 3.11 (Decreasing Number of $\forall\exists$ Quantifier Alternations)
For a formula ϕ, let $H(\phi)$ be one plus the maximal number of $\forall\exists$ quantifier alternations along a path in ϕ. Then every application of a rule in PDU non-strictly decreases H.

Proof. The only rules that can add new quantifier symbols to a formula are Q1/2 and the Sort Reduction, Distribution and Explosion rules. Q1/2, Sort Reduction and Distribution only duplicate existing quantifiers and cannot introduce new quantifier alternations. Both Ex1 applied at an existential quantifier position and Ex2 obviously also do not introduce a new quantifier alternation. Because Explosion only applies to a formula to which the rule P1 is not applicable, Ex1 also does not introduce a new $\forall\exists$ quantifier alternation if it is applied to at a universal quantifier position. ◇

Definition 3.12 ($\succ_\omega$)
Let ϕ, ψ be formulas over the signature $\Sigma = (\mathcal{S}, \mathcal{P}, \mathcal{F}, \mathcal{X}, \tau)$, let ω be a new function symbol, and let $i \geq 1$. Define the formula $\Omega_{\phi,i}(\psi)$ as the normal form of ψ under the following rewrite system that is confluent modulo associativity and commutativity (Comon and Delor, 1994, Lemma 12):

$$\circ(\omega, \ldots, \omega) \twoheadrightarrow \omega \qquad \text{if } \circ \in \mathcal{F} \cup \mathcal{P} \cup \{\simeq, \not\simeq, \vee, \neg\}$$
$$x \twoheadrightarrow \omega \qquad \text{if } N_\phi(x) < i$$
$$\psi_1 \wedge \omega \twoheadrightarrow \omega$$
$$\neg\psi_1 \vee \omega \twoheadrightarrow \neg\psi_1$$
$$\forall \vec{x}.\psi_1 \twoheadrightarrow \neg\exists\vec{x}.\neg\psi_1$$
$$\exists x.\psi_1 \twoheadrightarrow \psi_1 \qquad \text{if } x \notin \text{var}(\psi_1)$$
$$(\exists x.\psi_1) \vee \omega \twoheadrightarrow \exists x.\psi_1 \qquad \text{if } \exists x.\psi_1 \text{ is irreducible}$$

Let $\Omega_i(\phi) = \Omega_{\phi,i}(\phi)$. Extend the previous strict partial ordering from Definition 3.8 by $\top \succ \omega \succ \exists$. Moreover, define strict partial orderings $\succ_i$ and $\succ_\omega$ by $\phi \succ_i \phi' \iff I_\phi(\Omega_i(\phi)) \succ_{\text{apo}} I_{\phi'}(\Omega_i(\phi'))$ and $\phi \succ_\omega \phi' \iff$ there is an index i such that $I_\phi(\Omega_j(\phi)) = I_{\phi'}(\Omega_j(\phi'))$ for all $j > i$ and $\phi \succ_i \phi'$.

Lemma 3.11 implies that $\Omega_j(\phi_n) = \omega$ holds for all formulas ϕ_n in a derivation $\phi_1 \to_{\text{PDU}} \phi_2 \to_{\text{PDU}} \cdots$ and all j above the fixed boundary $H(\phi_1)$. Hence $\succ_\omega$ is well-founded on $\{\phi_1, \phi_2, \ldots\}$ as a lexicographic combination of the well-founded partial orderings $\succ_{H(\phi_1)}, \ldots, \succ_2, \succ_1$.

Lemma 3.13 (Non-Explosion Rules are Non-Strictly Decreasing)
Let $\phi \to \phi'$ not be an Explosion. Then $\phi \succeq_i \phi'$ for all $i \geq 1$.

Chapter 3: Disunification and Predicate Completion

Proof. For the rules in Figure 3.2, this was proved by Comon and Delor (1994, Lemma 15).

For *Periodic Reduction* $A[t]_p \twoheadrightarrow A[t']_p$, it holds that $N_x(\phi) = N_x(\phi')$ and hence $\Omega_{\phi',i}(t')$ is a subterm of $\Omega_{\phi,i}(t)$.

For *Periodic Clash Test* and $k > 0$ or ground t, note that the top symbol of the subterm $\Omega_{\phi,i}(s(t)\dot{\simeq}0)$ of $\Omega_{\phi,i}(\phi)$ is either $\dot{\simeq}$ or ω, and both are larger than $\bot$. For $k = 0$ and non-ground t, consider the rewriting $s(t)\dot{\simeq}0 \twoheadrightarrow t\dot{\simeq}s^{l-1}(0)$. Again, N does not change in this step, and so applying $\Omega_{\phi,i}$ and $\Omega_{\phi',i}$, respectively, yields the normal form ω for both sides if t reduces to ω, and the literals $s(t')\dot{\simeq}\omega$ and $t'\dot{\simeq}\omega$ if t reduces to some other term t'. In both cases, $I_\phi(\Omega_{\phi,i}(s(t)\dot{\simeq}0)) \succeq_{\text{apo}} I_{\phi'}(\Omega_{\phi',i}(t\dot{\simeq}s^{l-1}(0)))$.

For *Periodic Decomposition*, let $\psi = s(t)\dot{\simeq}s(t')$ reduce to ψ'. If t and t' are ground, then $\Omega_{\phi,i}(\psi) = \Omega_{\phi',i}(\psi') = \omega$. So let t not be ground. It suffices to show that $I_\phi(\Omega_{\phi,i}(\psi))$ is at least as large as $I_\phi(\Omega_{\phi,i}(A)) = I_{\phi'}(\Omega_{\phi',i}(A))$ for all newly introduced literals A.

By definition of recursive path orderings, $I_\phi(\Omega_{\phi,i}(\psi)) \succeq_{\text{apo}} I_\phi(\Omega_{\phi,i}(t\dot{\simeq}t'))$ follows from the relations $I_\phi(\Omega_{\phi,i}(\psi)) \succeq_{\text{apo}} I_\phi(\Omega_{\phi,i}(t))$ and $I_\phi(\Omega_{\phi,i}(\psi)) \succeq_{\text{apo}} I_\phi(\Omega_{\phi,i}(t'))$ and $\{I_\phi(\Omega_{\phi,i}(s(t))), I_\phi(\Omega_{\phi,i}(s(t')))\} \succeq^{mul}_{\text{apo}} \{I_\phi(\Omega_{\phi,i}(t)), I_\phi(\Omega_{\phi,i}(t'))\}$, that all hold by the subterm property of $\succ_{\text{apo}}$.

The ground term $s^{l-1}(0)$ reduces to the minimal term ω, and so finally $I_\phi(\Omega_{\phi,i}(\psi)) \succeq_{\text{apo}} I_\phi(\Omega_{\phi,i}(t\dot{\simeq}t')) \succeq_{\text{apo}} I_\phi(\Omega_{\phi,i}(t\dot{\simeq}s^{l-1}(0)))$. The same holds for the three literals $t'\dot{\simeq}s^{l-1}(0)$, $t\dot{\simeq}s^{k-1}(0)$, and $t'\dot{\simeq}s^{k-1}(0)$.

For *Periodic Occurrence*, the proposition follows from $\Omega_{\phi',i}(\top) = \Omega_{\phi',i}(\bot) = \omega$ and the ordering $\dot{\simeq}, \omega \geq \omega$ if the literal is replaced by $\top$ or $\bot$; otherwise it follows as for Periodic Decomposition. $\diamond$

The strict partial ordering $\succ_\omega$ is still not strong enough to show directly that the Explosion rules are decreasing in some sense. In fact, if $\phi \to_{\text{Ex1/2}} \phi'$, then $\phi' \succ_\omega \phi$. However, the non-Explosion rule applications following such a step revert this increase. The proofs of the following Lemmas 3.15–3.17 are almost identical to the respective proofs for DU (Comon and Delor, 1994, Lemmas 16–18); they are presented anyway because it is there that the difference in definitions of $N_\phi(x)$ is of importance.

Definition 3.14 (Explosion Level L_ϕ)
Let $\phi \to_{\text{Ex1/2}} \phi'$ be an explosion using the literal $y\dot{\simeq}t[z]$. The *explosion level* L_ϕ is defined as $L_\phi = N_\phi(z)$.

By the control on Ex1/2, it holds that $N_\phi(z) \geq N_\phi(y)$.

Lemma 3.15
Let $\phi \to_{\text{Ex1}} \bigvee_f \phi_f$ or $\phi \to_{\text{Ex2}} \bigwedge_f \phi_f$ be an explosion at the root position of ϕ

3.2 Disunification

and let $\phi_f \twoheadrightarrow^*_{\text{PDU}\setminus\{\text{Ex1},\text{Ex2}\}} \psi_f$ such that every ψ_f is irreducible with respect to PDU $\setminus$ {Ex1, Ex2}. Then for every f there is an index $i \geq L_\phi$ such that
(i) $I_{\phi_f}(\Omega_j(\phi_f)) = I_{\psi_f}(\Omega_j(\psi_f))$ for every $j > i$ and
(ii) $\phi_f \succ_i \psi_f$.

Proof. Let i be the largest index such that $I_{\phi_f}(\Omega_i(\phi_f)) \neq I_{\psi_f}(\Omega_i(\psi_f))$. The side conditions of Ex1/2 guarantee that i exists and $i \geq L_\phi$. By Lemma 3.13, $I_{\phi_f}(\Omega_i(\phi_f)) \geq I_{\psi_f}(\Omega_i(\psi_f))$ and since, by definition of i, they are distinct, $\phi_f \succ_i \psi_f$ follows. ◊

Lemma 3.16

Let $\phi \twoheadrightarrow_{\text{Ex1}} \bigvee_f \phi_f$ or $\phi \twoheadrightarrow_{\text{Ex2}} \bigwedge_f \phi_f$ be an explosion at the root position of ϕ and let $\bigvee_f \phi_f \twoheadrightarrow^*_{\text{PDU}\setminus\{\text{Ex1},\text{Ex2}\}} \psi$, or $\bigwedge_f \phi_f \twoheadrightarrow^*_{\text{PDU}\setminus\{\text{Ex1},\text{Ex2}\}} \psi$, respectively, such that ψ is irreducible with respect to PDU $\setminus$ {Ex1, Ex2}. Then it holds that $\phi \succ_\omega \psi$.

Proof. I show the proposition for Ex1; the case of Ex2 is analogous. By definition of Ω and L_ϕ, $I_\phi(\Omega_i(\phi)) = I_{\phi_f}(\Omega_i(\phi_f))$ for every f and every $i \geq L_\phi$. Note that for Ex1, this does not hold for the original definition of $N_\phi(x)$ by Comon and Delor, because an additional quantifier level may have been introduced. No rule can affect two disjuncts at the same time unless one becomes equal to $\top$ and the whole problem reduces to $\top$ and hence obviously decreases with respect to $\succ_\omega$. So let $\psi = \bigvee_f \psi_f$ and $\phi_f \twoheadrightarrow^*_{\text{PDU}\setminus\{\text{Ex1},\text{Ex2}\}} \psi_f$. Then $\phi \succ_\omega \psi_f$ for every f because of Lemma 3.15. Let i_f be the index from this lemma for ϕ_f and let i be the maximum of the i_f. The top symbol of ϕ can only be a quantifier, i.e. the top of $I_\phi(\Omega_i(\phi))$ is either $\exists\neg$ or $\neg$ and hence greater than the top symbol of $I_\psi(\Omega_i(\psi))$. Hence $\phi \succ_\omega \psi$. ◊

Lemma 3.17

Let $\phi \twoheadrightarrow_{\text{Ex1/2}} \phi' \twoheadrightarrow^*_{\text{PDU}\setminus\{\text{Ex1},\text{Ex2}\}} \psi \twoheadrightarrow_{\text{Ex1/2}} \cdots$. Then it holds that $\phi \succ_\omega \psi$.

Proof. Lemma 3.16 shows this when Ex1 or Ex2 is applied at the top position of ϕ. At other positions, no rule can modify the context of the exploded subformula, unless this subformula itself reduces to $\top$ or $\bot$. But if this happens, the part which disappears is deeper than the part which is modified and $\phi \succ_\omega \psi$. ◊

Theorem 3.18 (Termination)

There is no infinite chain $\phi_1, \phi_2, \ldots$ of formulas such that $\phi_1 \twoheadrightarrow_{\text{PDU}} \phi_2 \twoheadrightarrow_{\text{PDU}} \cdots$.

Proof. Because of Lemma 3.17, each chain can only contain a finite number of Explosion steps. Because of Proposition 3.10, there can also only be finitely many successive non-Explosion steps.

◊

3.3 Predicate Completion

3.3.1 The Predicate Completion Algorithm PC

When an interpretation is given as a minimal model $\mathcal{I}_N$ of a set N of clauses, it is often of interest to enrich N to a set N' in such a way that N' does not have any Herbrand models other than $\mathcal{I}_N$. The key to this enrichment is the so-called *completion* of predicates (Clark, 1977): For each predicate P, the set N' has to describe for which arguments P does *not* hold in $\mathcal{I}_N$.

Example 3.19 (Completion of the Even Predicate)
If $N_{\text{Even}} = \{\text{Even}(0), \text{Even}(x) \to \text{Even}(s(s(x)))\}$ describes the even numbers over the single-sorted signature $\Sigma_{\text{Even}} = (\{\text{Even}\}, \{s, 0\})$, with Even : Nat, s : Nat $\to$ Nat and 0 : Nat, then $\text{Even}(s^n(0))$ holds in the minimal model $\mathcal{I}_{N_{\text{Even}}}$ if, and only if, n is an even number. Let N'_{Even} contain N_{Even} and the additional clauses $\text{Even}(s(0)) \to$ and $\text{Even}(s(s(x))) \to \text{Even}(x)$. Then $\mathcal{I}_{N_{\text{Even}}}$ is the only Herbrand model of N'_{Even} over Σ_{Even}.

For predicative clause sets N, $\simeq$ is interpreted as syntactic equality in $\mathcal{I}_N$. Comon and Nieuwenhuis (2000, Section 7.3) used this fact to develop a predicate completion procedure for predicative and universally reductive Horn clause sets based on a disunification algorithm. They did not, however, give a formal proof of the correctness of the procedure. In this section, I will extend the predicate completion algorithm to clause sets describing ultimately periodic interpretations and prove its correctness and termination.

Definition 3.20 (PC)
Let $\Sigma = (\mathcal{S}, \mathcal{P}, \mathcal{F}, \mathcal{X}, \tau)$ be a signature and let $\succ$ be a well-founded strict reduction ordering that is total on ground terms. Let $\mathcal{I}_{N \cup E}$ be an ultimately periodic interpretation over Σ as in Definition 3.2 (in particular, all clauses in N with non-empty succedent have a unique strictly maximal positive literal occurrence).

The *Predicate Completion Algorithm* PC works as follows:

(i) For every $P \in \mathcal{P}$, let $N_P \subseteq N$ be the set of all clauses in N of the form $\Gamma \to \Delta, P(\vec{t})$, where $P(\vec{t})$ is a strictly maximal literal occurrence. Combine all these clauses into the single formula $\forall \vec{x}.(\phi_P \to P(\vec{x}))$ where

$$\phi_P = \exists \vec{y}. \bigvee_{\Gamma \to \Delta, P(\vec{t}) \in N_P} (x_1 \simeq t_1 \wedge \ldots \wedge x_n \simeq t_n \wedge \bigwedge_{A \in \Gamma} A \wedge \bigwedge_{B \in \Delta} \neg B),$$

the y_i are the variables appearing in N_P, and the x_j are fresh variables. In particular if N_P is empty, then $\phi_P = \bot$.

(ii) In the interpretation $\mathcal{I}_N$, the formula $\forall \vec{x}.(\phi_P \to P(\vec{x}))$ is equivalent to the formula $\forall \vec{x}.(\neg \phi_P \to \neg P(\vec{x}))$. Transform $\neg \phi_P$ using the algorithm PDU for E into an equivalent formula ϕ'_P that does not contain any universal quantifiers.

(iii) Write the formula $\forall \vec{x}.(\phi'_P \to \neg P(\vec{x}))$ as a set finite N'_P of clauses.

(iv) Let N' be the union of $N \cup E$ and all sets N'_P, $P \in \mathcal{P}$.

The idea of the algorithm was already introduced by Clark in 1977, who executed steps (ii) and (iii) by hand and did not discuss the question if they can be automatized. He showed that, given that the transformation of $\neg \phi_P$ to ϕ'_P is correct and $\forall \vec{x}.(\phi'_P \to \neg P(\vec{x}))$ does correspond to a set of clauses, N' is a completion of N. So the critical steps are (ii) and (iii): It is neither obvious that the universal quantifiers can be eliminated from $\neg \phi_P$, nor is it obvious that, once the universal quantifiers are gone, the result can be written as a finite set of clauses.

3.3.2 Disunification-based Quantifier Elimination

To prove that the universal quantifiers can in fact be eliminated from $\neg \phi_P$, I will examine an invariant that holds for $\neg \phi_P$ (Lemma 3.23), is preserved during the application of PDU (Lemma 3.24), and holds only for such normal forms that do not contain universal quantifiers (Lemma 3.27).

In this section, I always implicitly assume a set E of ultimate periodicity equations to be given.

Invariant 3.21

Let $\phi \downarrow$ be the normal form of a formula ϕ under the Normalization rules, Decomposition, Periodic Decomposition and Distribution. Consider the following properties of ϕ:

(1) No subformula of $\phi \downarrow$ of the form $\forall \vec{x}.\phi'$, where the top symbol of ϕ' is not a universal quantifier, contains a quantifier.

(2) Universally quantified variables occur in $\phi \downarrow$ only in predicative literals or in disequations $t[x] \not\doteq t'$ where all variables in t' are free or existentially quantified.

For every predicative literal occurrence A_x in $\phi \downarrow$ containing a universally quantified variable x, there is a subformula of $\phi \downarrow$ of the form $A_x \vee B_x \vee \phi_x$ where B_x is a disequation containing x.

Chapter 3: Disunification and Predicate Completion

Condition (1) in Invariant 3.21 is obviously always fulfilled if ϕ does not contain nested quantifiers:

Definition 3.22 (Nested Quantifiers)
A formula ϕ contains *nested quantifiers* if either
  (i) $\phi = \phi[\forall x.\phi_1[\exists y.\phi_2]_p]_q$ or $\phi = \phi[\exists x.\phi_1[\forall y.\phi_2]_p]_q$, or
  (ii) $\phi = \phi[\exists x.\phi_1[\exists y.\phi_2]_p]_q$ or $\phi = \phi[\forall x.\phi_1[\forall y.\phi_2]_p]_q$ and the top symbol of ϕ_1 is not a quantifier.

Lemma 3.23 (Invariant Holds Initially)
Let N be a universally reductive clause set and let ϕ_P be defined as in Definition 3.20. Then Invariant 3.21 holds for $\neg\phi_P$.

Proof. The normal form $(\neg\phi_P)\downarrow$ of $\neg\phi_P$ is

$$(\neg\phi_P)\downarrow = \forall \vec{y}. \bigwedge_{\Gamma \to \Delta, P(\vec{t}) \in N_P} (x_1 \not\simeq t_1 \vee \ldots \vee x_n \not\simeq t_n \vee \bigvee_{A \in \Gamma} \neg A \vee \bigvee_{B \in \Delta} B) .$$

Invariant 1 holds because there are no nested quantifiers in $(\neg\phi_P)\downarrow$. Invariant 2 holds because all clauses in N are universally reductive, and so every variable that occurs in a predicative literal A or B also occurs in one of the disequations $x_i \not\simeq t_i$ in the same conjunct of $(\neg\phi_P)\downarrow$. ◊

Lemma 3.24 (Invariant is Preserved)
Let $\phi \to_{\text{PDU}} \phi'$. If ϕ satisfies Invariant 3.21 then so does ϕ'.

Proof. Invariant 1: The only rule to introduce a possibly critical quantifier symbol is the rule Ex1 applied to a subformula of the form $\forall \vec{x}.\psi'$:

$$\phi[\forall \vec{x}.\psi']_p \to \phi[\bigvee_{f \in \mathcal{F}'} \exists \vec{x}_f. y \simeq f(\vec{x}_f) \wedge \forall \vec{x}.\psi'\{y \mapsto f(\vec{x}_f)\}]_p$$

If the new existential quantifier $\exists \vec{x}_f$ is in the scope of a universal quantifier in ϕ' and $\phi'\downarrow$, then so was the original universal quantifier $\forall \vec{x}$ in ϕ and $\phi\downarrow$.
Invariant 2: This invariant can only be destroyed by

- introducing new universally quantified variables into a literal,
- disconnecting A_x and B_x, or
- altering a disequation B_x.

It is easy to see that all rules that do not replace variables or reduce B_x preserve the invariant.

If C2, O2, PC2 or PO2 reduces B_x to $\top$, then the whole subformula $A_x \vee B_x \vee \phi_x$ is reduced to $\top$ by the normalization rules, i.e. the invariant is maintained.

3.3 Predicate Completion

Alternatively, PC2 can alter B_x by $s(t[x]) \not\simeq 0 \twoheadrightarrow t \not\simeq s^{l-1}(0)$. By PD2 and Normalization, this literal either reduces to $\top$ or to a formula ψ consisting of disjunctions, conjunctions and literals such that ψ contains x in disequations $t''[x] \not\simeq t'$ as required for the invariant. In the former case, the whole disjunction $A_x \lor \psi \lor \phi_x$ reduces to $\top$; in the latter, the distribution rule is applicable because the disequation is in the scope of a universal quantifier and Invariant 1 guarantees that there is no existential quantifier in between. Distribution brings $A_x \lor \psi \lor \phi_x$ into the form $\psi'_1 \land \ldots \land \psi'_n$ where each ψ'_i is of the form $A_x \lor x \not\simeq t' \lor \psi''_i$, i.e. the invariant is preserved.

PO2 is not applicable to a disequation B_x because one side contains a universal quantifier and the other one does not.

The Sort Reduction rules only replace variables by ground terms and thus are harmless.

If Q5: $\phi[\forall \vec{x}, x.x \not\simeq t \lor \psi]_p \twoheadrightarrow \phi[\forall \vec{x}.\psi\{x \mapsto t\}]_p$ works on a universally quantified variable x (and B_x may or may not be $x \not\simeq t$), then every occurrence of x is replaced by a term that, by Invariant 1, does not contain any universally quantified variables, which maintains the invariant.

When Q6: $\phi[\exists \vec{y}, y.y \simeq t \land \psi]_p \twoheadrightarrow \phi[\exists \vec{y}.\psi\{y \mapsto t\}]_p$ is applied, then t contains only free or existentially quantified variables because of Invariant 1. Again, the invariant is not affected.

An Explosion Ex1: $\phi[\exists \vec{x}.\psi]_p \twoheadrightarrow \phi[\bigvee_{f \in \mathcal{F}'} \exists \vec{x}, \vec{x}_f.y \simeq f(\vec{x}_f) \land \psi\{y \mapsto f(\vec{x}_f)\}]_p$ replaces a variable y that is free in ψ. By Invariant 1, this variable is existentially quantified or free in ϕ and the replacement $f(\vec{x}_f)$ contains only existentially quantified variables. The same holds for the second version of Ex1.

An Explosion Ex2: $\phi[\forall \vec{x}.\psi]_p \twoheadrightarrow \phi[\bigwedge_{f \in \mathcal{F}'} \forall \vec{x}, \vec{x}_f.y \not\simeq f(\vec{x}_f) \lor \psi\{y \mapsto f(\vec{x}_f)\}]_p$ cannot be executed because it relies on the existence of a variable that is existentially quantified in ψ, which is excluded by Invariant 1. ◇

Lemma 3.25 (Irreducibility of Subformulas)
Let ϕ be a formula that is irreducible by PDU. Then every subformula ψ of ϕ is also irreducible by PDU.

Proof. The proof of this proposition is identical to the proof of the corresponding lemma for DU (Comon and Delor, 1994, Lemma 21):

The only contextual conditions in the control part of the rules are irreducibility conditions; the only situations where the control can prevent a reduction $\phi[\psi]_p \twoheadrightarrow_{\text{PDU}} \phi[\psi']_p$ when $\psi \twoheadrightarrow_{\text{PDU}} \psi'$ are such that there is another redex in ϕ. ◇

Lemma 3.26 (Normal Forms and Nested Quanfitiers)
Normal forms with respect to PDU do not contain nested quantifiers.

Chapter 3: Disunification and Predicate Completion

Proof. Comon and Delor showed that normal forms with respect to DU do not contain nested quantifiers (Comon and Delor, 1994, Lemma 22). Because PDU contains DU, every well-sorted formula that is reducible by DU is also reducible by PDU. ◊

Lemma 3.27 (Normal Forms Without Universal Quantifiers)
A normal form ϕ with respect to PDU that
 (i) fulfills Invariant 3.21 or
 (ii) does not contain any predicative literals
is free of universal quantifiers.

Proof. Consider a formula that fulfills the invariant or does not contain any predicative atoms, but that contains a subformula $\forall \vec{x}.\phi$. Assume that the whole formula and hence, by Lemma 3.25, $\forall \vec{x}.\phi$ is irreducible by PDU. This will result in a contradiction.

By Lemma 3.26, ϕ can only be a disjunction, a conjunction, or a literal. If it is a conjunction, then Q2 is applicable. The case that ϕ is a literal arises as the special case of a disjunction with only one disjunct. So let ϕ be a disjunction. If a disjunct contains a variable from $\vec{x}$, then it must be a literal: If it is a conjunction, then rule N2 applies and the top symbol cannot be a quantifier because of Lemma 3.26.

So ϕ can be written as $\phi = \phi_1 \lor \ldots \lor \phi_n \lor \phi'$, where the ϕ_i are literals containing universal variables and ϕ' does not contain any universal variables. Because of the Normalization rules, each ϕ_i can only be a predicative literal or an equational literal.

ϕ_i cannot be a disequation: Because of the decomposition rules, it would be either $x \not\simeq t$ or $y \not\simeq t[x]$ where $x \in \vec{x}$ and y is free in ϕ. In the former case, Q5 is applicable, in the latter Ex1.

ϕ_i can only be predicative in variant (i) of the lemma, and then Invariant 2 requires that one of the other ϕ_j is a disequation containing a variable from $\vec{x}$. This possibility has already been refuted.

If ϕ_i is an equation, the decomposition rules only leave the possibilities $x \simeq t$ and $y \simeq t[x]$ where $x \in \vec{x}$ and y is free in ϕ. In the latter case, Ex1 applies, so only $x \simeq t$ is possible.

All in all, ϕ is of the form $\phi = x_{i_1} \simeq t_1 \lor \ldots \lor x_{i_n} \simeq t_n \lor \phi'$ and Q6 applies. ◊

Corollary 3.28 (Universal Quantifier Elimination)
Let N be a universally reductive clause set and let ϕ_P be defined as in Definition 3.20 and let ϕ'_P be a normal form of $\neg \phi_P$ with respect to PDU. Then ϕ'_P does not contain any universal quantifiers.

Proof. This corollary is a straightforward combination of the preceding Lemmas 3.23, 3.24, and 3.27(i). ◊

3.3 Predicate Completion

Quantifier Elimination:
Q1: $\exists \vec{x}.\phi_1 \vee \phi_2 \twoheadrightarrow (\exists \vec{x}.\phi_1) \vee (\exists \vec{x}.\phi_2)$ if $\vec{x} \cap \mathrm{var}(\phi_1, \phi_2) \neq \emptyset$
Q6: $\exists \vec{x}, x.x \simeq t \wedge \phi \twoheadrightarrow \exists \vec{x}.\phi\{x \mapsto t\}$ if $x \notin \mathrm{var}(t)$
All formulas are kept normalized with respect to Q1.

Distribution:
N2': $\phi_0 \wedge (\phi_1 \vee \phi_2) \twoheadrightarrow (\phi_0 \wedge \phi_1) \vee (\phi_0 \wedge \phi_2)$

Replacement and Merging:
R: $\exists \vec{x}.x \simeq t \wedge \phi \twoheadrightarrow \exists \vec{x}.x \simeq t \wedge \phi\{x \mapsto t\}$ if x is free and $x \notin \mathrm{var}(t)$
                                                                                         and if $t \in \mathcal{X}$ then $t \in \mathrm{var}(\phi)$
M: $x \simeq t_1 \wedge x \simeq t_2 \twoheadrightarrow x \simeq t_1 \wedge t_1 \simeq t_2$ if t_1 is not a variable
                                                                                          and $|t_1| \leq |t_2|$

Figure 3.4: Solved Form Conversion Rules

3.3.3 Solved Form Computation

To address the second issue of transforming the formula $\forall \vec{x}.(\phi'_P \to \neg P(\vec{x}))$ into a set of clauses, I will make use of the fact that certain normal forms with respect to PDU can be transformed into a particularly simple form:

Definition 3.29 (Solved Forms)
Let $\mathcal{I}$ be an ultimately periodic interpretation. A formula ϕ is a *solved form with respect to* $\mathcal{I}$ if $\phi = \top$, $\phi = \bot$, or ϕ is a disjunction $\phi = \phi_1 \vee \ldots \vee \phi_m$ and each ϕ_j is of the shape

$$\phi_j = \exists \vec{y}.x_{i_1} \simeq t_1 \wedge \ldots \wedge x_{i_n} \simeq t_n \wedge A_1 \wedge \ldots \wedge A_k \wedge \neg B_1 \wedge \ldots \wedge \neg B_{k'} \wedge z_1 \not\simeq t'_1 \wedge \ldots \wedge z_l \not\simeq t'_l,$$

where $x_{i_1}, \ldots, x_{i_n}$ occur only once in ϕ_j, the A_i and B_i are predicative atoms, the z_i are variables and $z_i \neq t'_i$, and ϕ_j is irreducible by Periodic Reduction.

The transformation into a solved form is again performed using a rewrite system:

Definition 3.30 (SF)
Let E be a set of ultimate periodicity equations. The *Solved Form Transformation Algorithm* **SF** *for* E consists of the Normalization rules of Figure 3.1, the (regular and periodic) rules Decomposition, Clash and Occurrence rules as well as the rule Periodic Reduction from Figures 3.2 and 3.3 and the rules of Figure 3.4.

This calculus is an extension of a corresponding calculus used by Comon and Delor (1994, Section 6.3). The proofs of the following lemmas are almost

Chapter 3: Disunification and Predicate Completion

identical (in the case of Lemma 3.31) or based on the proof ideas for their calculus (in the case of Lemma 3.32).

Lemma 3.31 (SF Produces Solved Forms)
Let $\phi = \bigvee_{i \in I} \exists \vec{x}_i.\phi_i$ be a formula where the ϕ_i are quantifier-free conjunctions. If ϕ is normal form with respect to SF, then ϕ is a solved form.

Proof. Because of the (normal and Periodic) Decomposition and Clash rules, each equational literal must be of the form $x \doteq t$. So each disjunct is of the form

$$\exists \vec{y}. x_{i_1} \doteq t_1 \wedge \ldots \wedge x_{i_n} \doteq t_n \wedge A_1 \wedge \ldots \wedge A_k \wedge \neg B_1 \wedge \ldots \wedge \neg B_{k'} \wedge z_1 \not\doteq t'_1 \wedge \ldots \wedge z_l \not\doteq t'_l$$

where the x_i, y_i and z_i are variables and the A_i and B_i are predicative atoms. Because of Q6, the x_i must be free variables. Moreover, each x_i occurs only once: Either t_i is not a free variable and x occurs only once because of R, O1 and PO1, or t_i is a free variable, in which case R guarantees that one of x_i and t_i occurs only once; by symmetry, this variable is without loss of generality x_i. Finally, $z_i \neq t'_i$ is guaranteed by O2 and PO2 and ϕ is irreducible by Periodic Reduction by definition. ◇

Lemma 3.32 (Termination of SF)
Let $\phi = \bigvee_{i \in I} \exists \vec{x}_i.\phi_i$ be a formula where the ϕ_i are quantifier-free conjunctions. Then SF terminates on ϕ.

Proof. Note that, because formulas are kept in normal form with respect to Q1 and the Normalization rules, they always stay in the given shape (where any $\vec{x}_i$ may be empty and the main disjunction and the subordinate conjunctions may degenerate to ranging only over one or zero elements).

To prove that SF terminates, I show that it is decreasing for a well-founded strict ordering $\succ_{\text{SF}}$ on formulas of the given form. To define this ordering, let $I_{\text{SF}}(\bigvee_{i \in I} \exists \vec{x}_i.\phi_i)$, where ϕ_i is quantifier-free, be the multiset

$$\{(I_1(\exists \vec{x}_i.\phi_i), I_2(\exists \vec{x}_i.\phi_i), I_3(\exists \vec{x}_i.\phi_i), I_4(\exists \vec{x}_i.\phi_i), I_5(\exists \vec{x}_i.\phi_i)) \mid i \in I\} ,$$

where the five components of each tuple are defined as follows:

(i) $I_1(\exists \vec{x}_i.\phi_i)$ is the number of variables in $\vec{x}_i$.

(ii) $I_2(\exists \vec{x}_i.\phi_i)$ is the number of variables in ϕ_i that are not solved; a variable x in ϕ_i is *solved* if $\phi_i = x \doteq t \wedge \phi'_i$ and x occurs only once in ϕ_i, and *unsolved* otherwise.

(iii) $I_3(\exists \vec{x}_i.\phi_i)$ is a term over the set $\mathcal{F}_3 = \{\vee, \wedge, g, f, a, \top, \bot\}$ of function symbols, inductively defined by

74

3.3 Predicate Completion

- $I_3(\exists \vec{x}_i.\phi_i) = I_3(\phi_i)$
- $I_3(\psi_1 \vee \psi_3) = I_3(\psi_1) \vee I_3(\psi_3)$
- $I_3(\psi_1 \wedge \psi_3) = I_3(\psi_1) \wedge I_3(\psi_3)$
- $I_3(t_1 \dot{\simeq} t_3) = g(f^{\max\{|t_1|,|t_3|\}}(a))$ if t_1 and t_3 are not ground
  $I_3(t_1 \dot{\simeq} t_3) = f^{\max\{|t_1|,|t_3|\}}(a)$ if t_1 and t_3 are ground,
  $I_3(t_1 \dot{\simeq} t_3) = g(f^{|t_1|}(a))$ if t_1 is not ground and t_3 is ground
- $I_3(P(\vec{t})) = I_3(\neg P(\vec{t})) = a$ if P is a predicate symbol.
- $I_3(\top) = \top$ and $I_3(\bot) = \bot$

(iv) $I_4(\exists \vec{x}_i.\phi_i)$ is the number of redexes for PR in $\exists \vec{x}_i.\phi_i$.

(v) $I_5(\exists \vec{x}_i.\phi_i)$ is the number of redexes for M in $\exists \vec{x}_i.\phi_i$.

Terms over $\mathcal{F}_3$ are ordered by the associative path ordering $\succ_3$ extending the strict ordering $g \succ f \succ a \succ \wedge \succ \vee \succ \top \succ \bot$. The function symbol g serves as a marker for non-ground equations that makes such equations larger than all ground equations. The other components are ordered by the usual ordering on $\mathbb{N}$. Let $\phi \succ_{\mathsf{SF}} \psi$ if, and only if, $I_{\mathsf{SF}}(\phi)$ is greater than $I_{\mathsf{SF}}(\psi)$ with respect to the multiset extension of the lexicographic combination of the five orderings on the components. SF is indeed decreasing with respect to this ordering:

- If $\psi \twoheadrightarrow_{\text{Normalize}} \psi$ or $\psi \twoheadrightarrow_{\text{C1/2}} \psi$ or $\psi \twoheadrightarrow_{\text{O1/2}} \psi$, then the numbers of quantified and unsolved variables cannot increase and the strict decrease in the third component is obvious because $\top$ and $\bot$ are minimal with respect to $\succ_3$.

- If $\psi \twoheadrightarrow_{\text{D1/2}} \psi$, then the first two components are unaffected. Since every term on the right hand side of D1/2 is has a smaller size than the maximal term on the left hand side, and they can only contain variables if the left hand side does, the third component decreases strictly.

- If $\psi \twoheadrightarrow_{\text{PD1/2}} \psi$, then the first component is unaffected, the second one cannot increase, and the third one strictly decreases:

  - If $s(t) \dot{\simeq} s(t') \twoheadrightarrow t \dot{\simeq} t'$ then the decrease follows from the subterm property of the associative path ordering $\succ_3$.
  - If t is not ground and $s(t') = s^k(0)$ then $I_3(s(t) \dot{\simeq} s(t')) = g(f^{1+|t|}(a))$ as well as $I_3(t \dot{\simeq} s^n(0)) = g(f^{|t|}(a))$, so the left hand side is larger than every atom on the right hand side, and the strict decrease follows from $g \succ \wedge$ and $g \succ \vee$ as in the previous proofs that used associative path orderings.

Chapter 3: Disunification and Predicate Completion

- If both t and t' are not ground, the same argument applies again because the term $I_3(s(t)\tildeeq s(t')) = g(f^{1+max\{|t|,|t'|\}}(a))$ is larger than $I_3(t\tildeeq s^n(0)) = g(f^{|t|}(a))$ and $I_3(t'\tildeeq s^n(0)) = g(f^{|t'|}(a))$.

- If $\psi \twoheadrightarrow_{PC1/2} \psi$ or $\psi \twoheadrightarrow_{PO1/2} \psi$, then again the first component is unaffected, the second one cannot increase, and the third one strictly decreases because of the same argumentation as either for C1/2 and O1/2 or for PD1/2, depending on whether or not the reduct equals $\top$ or $\bot$.

- If $\psi \twoheadrightarrow_{PR} \psi$, then none of the first three components can increase and the fourth one strictly decreases.

- If $\psi \twoheadrightarrow_{Q1} \psi$, then one component $\exists \vec{x}_i.\phi_i$ of ϕ is split into two components and each of the resulting components is obviously smaller than $\exists \vec{x}_i.\phi_i$ (the first component is unaffected, the second does not increase, the third one decreases because of the subterm property of the associative path ordering $\succ_3$).

- If $\psi \twoheadrightarrow_{Q6} \psi$, then the number of existential variables decreases by one. So the first component is strictly decreasing.

- If $\psi \twoheadrightarrow_{N2'} \psi$ and the result is normalized with Q1, then the first component is unaffected, the second one cannot increase and the third component decreases because of the subterm property of the associative path ordering $\succ_3$).

- If $\psi \twoheadrightarrow_R \psi$, then the number of existentially quantified variables decreases by one.

- If $\psi \twoheadrightarrow_M \psi$, then the first component is unaffected. The number of unsolved variables cannot increase because t_1 is not a variable. The third component does not change if t_2 is non-ground, it non-strictly decreases if t_2 is ground while t_1 is not (because $I_3(x\tildeeq t_2) = g(f^{|t_2|}(a)) \succeq_3 g(f^{|t_1|}(a)) = I_3(t_1\tildeeq t_2)$), and it strictly decreases if both t_1 and t_2 are ground (because $I_3(x\tildeeq t_2) = g(a) \succ_3 f^{|t_2|}(a) = I_3(t_1\tildeeq t_2)$). The fourth component is not increased because no new terms are introduced. In any case, the last component strictly decreases. ◊

Corollary 3.33 (Equivalence to Solved Forms)
Let $\mathcal{I}$ be an ultimately periodic interpretation and let ϕ be a formula in negation normal form that does not contain any universal quantifiers. Then ϕ can be transformed into an equivalent solved form. If furthermore ϕ is irreducible by PDU, then all bound variables of the solved from are of infinite sorts.

3.3 Predicate Completion

The second part of this corollary is not relevant to the current considerations, but it will be used in Section 3.4.

Proof. Using Q1, N2' and the rule $(\exists x.\psi_1) \wedge \psi_2 \twoheadrightarrow \exists x.(\psi_1 \wedge \psi_2)$, where x is renamed if it occurs in ψ_2 to avoid capturing (this rule is well-known to be correct for any interpretation), ϕ can be transformed into a disjunction of formulas of the form $\exists \vec{x}. \bigwedge L_i$ with literals L_i.

By the preceding Lemmas 3.31 and 3.32, the calculus SF transforms this formula into a solved form. The algorithm preserves the solutions of a formula with respect to every interpretation $\mathcal{I}$: The correctness of the all rules except Replacement and Merging follows from the correctness of PDU (Theorem 3.6; the correctness of N2 is independent of the constraint on the context) and the correctness of the remaining two rules is obvious because they replace equals by equals.

If ϕ is irreducible by PDU, then it is in particular irreducible by Finite and Periodic Sort Reduction and does not contain any bound variables of a finite free or ultimately periodic sort. Since the transformation algorithm does not introduce any new quantifier symbols, this invariant is preserved throughout the transformation. ◇

So the formula ϕ'_P appearing in the predicate completion procedure (Definition 3.20) can be transformed into a solved form, and the formula $\forall \vec{x}.(\phi'_P \to \neg P(\vec{x}))$ is equivalent to either

- $\top$, i.e. to the empty clause set, or to
- $\forall x.\neg P(\vec{x})$, i.e. to the singleton clause set $\{P(\vec{x}) \to\}$, or to
- $\forall \vec{x}. \bigwedge_j (\phi'_j \to \neg P(\vec{x}))$, and each conjunct can equivalently be written as a clause of the form

$$A_1, \ldots, A_k, P(\vec{x})\{x_{i_1} \mapsto t_1, \ldots, x_{i_n} \mapsto t_n\} \to B_1, \ldots, B_k, z_1 \simeq t'_1, \ldots, z_l \simeq t'_l.$$

Corollary 3.28 states that PDU eliminates the universal quantifiers from $\neg \phi_P$. Together with Corollary 3.33 and the correctness and termination of disunification (Theorems 3.6 and 3.18), this implies the applicability and the termination of the predicate completion algorithm PC.

Theorem 3.34 (Predicate Completion)
Let $\mathcal{I}_{N \cup E}$ be an ultimately periodic interpretation over Σ as in Definition 3.2. Then PC terminates on $\mathcal{I}_{N \cup E}$ with a completion of N.

Example 3.35 (Completion of the Even Predicate)
For Example 3.19, ϕ_{Even} is given by $\phi_{\text{Even}} = x \simeq 0 \vee \exists y.y \simeq s(s(x)) \wedge \text{Even}(y)$ and

a normal form of $\neg\phi_{\text{Even}}$ with respect to PDU and an equation $E = \{s^l(x) \simeq x\}$ is

$$\phi'_{\text{Even}} = \begin{cases} x \not\simeq s^{l-1}(0) \wedge \neg\text{Even}(x) & \text{for } l \in \{1,2\} \\ (x \simeq s(0) \wedge \neg\text{Even}(s^{l-1}(0))) \\ \quad \vee (\exists z. x \simeq s(s(z)) \wedge \neg\text{Even}(z) \wedge z \not\simeq s^{l-2}(0)) & \text{for } l > 2 \end{cases}.$$

This formula corresponds to the following clauses in N'_{Even}:

$$\begin{cases} \text{Even}(x) \to \text{Even}(x), x \simeq s^{l-1}(0) & \text{for } l \in \{1,2\} \\ \text{Even}(s(0)) \to \text{Even}(s^{l-1}(0)) \\ \text{and } \text{Even}(s(s(z))) \to \text{Even}(z), z \simeq s^{l-2}(0) & \text{for } l > 2 \end{cases}$$

3.3.4 Predicate Completion and Unique Herbrand Models

Comon and Nieuwenhuis (2000, Lemma 47) showed that the minimal model of a satisfiable universally reductive and predicative Horn clause set is the unique Herbrand model of its completion:

Lemma 3.36 (Completions of Horn Clause Sets)
Let N be a satisfiable universally reductive predicative Horn clause set over Σ and let N' be a completion of N. Then the minimal model of N (with respect to set inclusion) is the unique Herbrand model of N' over Σ in which $\simeq$ is interpreted as syntactic equality (i.e. $t_1 \simeq t_2$ holds if, and only if, $t_1 = t_2$) on non-predicative terms.

The previous result also extends to some classes of non-Horn clause sets. Non-Horn clause sets may have more than one minimal model, a simple example being $\{\to P, Q\}$ with minimal models $\{P\}$ and $\{Q\}$. Given a well-founded strict reduction ordering $\succ$ that is total on ground terms, one of them can be distinguished using the construction of Definition 2.35. This Herbrand interpretation is called $\mathcal{I}_N^{\succ}$. It turns out that, whenever it is applicable, completion singles out the same interpretation:

Lemma 3.37 (Completions of Universally Reductive Saturated Clause Sets)
Let $\succ$ be a well-founded strict reduction ordering that is total on ground terms. Let $N \cup E$ as in Definition 3.2 be saturated with respect to a refutationally complete calculus and let $\mathcal{M}$ be a Herbrand model of the completion N' of $N \cup E$. If $\simeq$ is interpreted in $\mathcal{M}$ as E-equality (i.e. $\mathcal{M} \models t_1 \simeq t_2$ if, and only if, $t_1 =_E t_2$) on non-predicative terms, then $\mathcal{M}$ equals $\mathcal{I}_{N \cup E}^{\succ}$.

Proof. Because $N \cup E$ is saturated, $\mathcal{I}_{N \cup E}^{\succ}$ is a minimal model of $N \cup E$ with respect to set inclusion (Lemma 2.36) and $\mathcal{M}$ cannot be a strict subset of $\mathcal{I}_{N \cup E}^{\succ}$.

Assume, contrary to the proposition, that $\mathcal{M} \setminus \mathcal{I}_{N \cup E}^{\succ} \neq \emptyset$ and let $P(\vec{s}) \in \mathcal{M} \setminus \mathcal{I}_{N \cup E}^{\succ}$ be minimal with respect to $\succ$. Because $\mathcal{M}$ is a model of the completion and the algorithms PDU and SF are correct, the formula $\forall \vec{x}.P(\vec{x}) \to \phi_P$ holds in $\mathcal{M}$. In particular, $\mathcal{M} \models \phi_P\{\vec{x} \mapsto \vec{s}\}$. This formula has the following shape:

$$\phi_P\{\vec{x} \mapsto \vec{s}\} = \exists \vec{y}. \bigvee_{\Gamma \to \Delta, P(\vec{t}) \in N_P} (s_1 \simeq t_1 \wedge \ldots \wedge s_n \simeq t_n \wedge \bigwedge_{A \in \Gamma} A \wedge \bigwedge_{B \in \Delta} \neg B)$$

Because the equality predicate is interpreted as E-equality, each of the disjuncts can only hold in $\mathcal{M}$ if $\vec{s} =_E \vec{t}$. The remaining literals are by definition strictly smaller (with respect to $\succ$) than $P(\vec{t})$ and hence also strictly smaller than $P(\vec{s})$. By minimality of $P(\vec{s})$, they all hold in $\mathcal{M}$ if, and only if, they hold in $\mathcal{I}_{N \cup E}^{\succ}$. Because $\simeq$ is interpreted as E-equality on non-predicative terms in $\mathcal{I}_{N \cup E}^{\succ}$ as well, it follows that $\mathcal{I}_{N \cup E}^{\succ} \models \phi_P\{\vec{x} \mapsto \vec{s}\}$. Because $\mathcal{I}_{N \cup E}^{\succ} \models N$, the formula $\forall \vec{x}.\phi_P \to P(\vec{x})$ also holds in $\mathcal{I}_{N \cup E}^{\succ}$. This implies $\mathcal{I}_{N \cup E}^{\succ} \models P(\vec{s})$, which contradicts the choice of $P(\vec{s})$. Hence $\mathcal{M} \subseteq \mathcal{I}_N^{\succ}$, i.e. $\mathcal{M} \subseteq \mathcal{I}_N^{\succ}$. ◊

Note that this means that $\mathcal{I}_{N \cup E}^{\succ}$ agrees with all Herbrand models of N' over Σ on the validity of predicative atoms (and formulas), i.e. minimal model and fixed domain validity coincide:

Theorem 3.38
Let Σ be a signature and let $\succ$ be a well-founded strict reduction ordering that is total on ground terms. Moreover, let $N \cup E$ as in Definition 3.2 be saturated with respect to a refutationally complete calculus and let A be a predicative atom. Then $\mathcal{I}_{N \cup E}^{\succ} \models A$ if, and only if, $\mathcal{M} \models A$ for every Herbrand model $\mathcal{M}$ of $N \cup E$.

Further examples of the completion of non-Horn clause sets will occur in Chapter 5 (especially in Example 5.17).

3.4 Decidability of the Satisfiability of Equational Formulas

It is obvious that the decidability of the satisfiability of equational formulas in models over free sorts implies the decidability of the satisfiability of equational formulas in models over both free and ultimately periodic sorts: As there are only finitely many non-equivalent terms of each ultimately periodic sort, variables of such sorts can be eliminated by immediate grounding of quantified variables (e.g. with the rules PS1, PS2) and free variables (by the transformation $\phi \twoheadrightarrow \phi\{x \mapsto 0\} \vee \ldots \vee \phi\{x \mapsto s^{l-1}(0)\}$) in both model description and query formula. If then every term of an ultimately periodic sort is replaced by a unique representative of its equivalence class, the original disunification algorithm decides satisfiability.

The eager grounding leads, however, to a huge blow-up of both the set N of clauses describing the model and the query formula. The combination of the results of the previous sections provides a more flexible decision procedure for the satisfiability of an equational formula ϕ in a given ultimately periodic interpretation $\mathcal{I}$ that allows to postpone grounding and thus improve the practical efficiency of the decision procedure:

Lemma 3.39 (Satisfiability of Solved Forms)
Let $\mathcal{I}$ be an ultimately periodic interpretation and let $\phi \neq \bot$ be a solved form in which all variables are of infinite sorts and all atoms are equational. Then ϕ has at least one solution in $\mathcal{I}$.

Proof. For $\phi = \top$, this is trivial. Otherwise consider a disjunct as in Definition 3.29. Since all variables appearing in $z_1 \not\doteq t'_1 \wedge \ldots \wedge z_l \not\doteq t'_l$ are of infinite sorts, these disequations have a common solution σ (cf. e.g. Comon and Delor, 1994, Lemma 2). Then the substitution $\{x_{i_1} \mapsto t_1\sigma, \ldots, x_{i_n} \mapsto t_n\sigma\}$ is a solution of the considered disjunct (and hence also of ϕ) with respect to $\mathcal{I}$ and the variables $x_{i_1}, \ldots, x_{i_n}$. This solution can trivially be extended to a solution for all free variables of ϕ. ◇

Theorem 3.40 (Decidability of Satisfiability)
Let $\mathcal{I}$ be an ultimately periodic interpretation over the signature Σ. Then satisfiability in $\mathcal{I}$ of an equational formula ϕ over Σ is decidable.

Proof. Let $\vec{x}$ be the free variables in ϕ of finite (e.g. ultimately periodic) sorts. Then ϕ is satisfiable in $\mathcal{I}$ if, and only if, $\exists \vec{x}.\phi$ is. Using PDU, $\exists \vec{x}.\phi$ can be transformed into an equivalent normal form ϕ'. Because ϕ does not contain any predicative atoms, neither does ϕ'. Lemma 3.27(ii) implies that ϕ' is free of universal quantifiers and Corollary 3.33 states that it can be transformed into an equivalent solved form. By Lemma 3.39, it is decidable whether this solved form (and hence also ϕ) has a solution in $\mathcal{I}$. ◇

The same does not hold for formulas containing predicative atoms, as e.g. $\forall y.P(y)$ is a normal form with respect to PDU if y is of a free and infinite sort.

3.5 Implementation

I have implemented a single-sorted version of the presented algorithms on top of the automated theorem prover SPASS (Weidenbach et al., 2009). SPASS is a theorem prover for full first-order logic with equality and a number of non-classical logics and provides support for first-order formulas with both equational and predicative atoms.

I represent the ultimate periodicity equation describing an ultimately periodic sort using a globally accessible data structure that provides constant-time access to the values k and $l - k$, the constructors of the ultimately periodic sort (e.g. s and 0) and the regularly needed terms $s^{k-1}(0)$ and $s^{l-1}(0)$:

```
typedef struct upi_info {
    int    stick_length;   /* length of the non-periodic part */
    int    loop_length;    /* length of a minimal loop */
    SYMBOL state_start;    /* the constant constructor */
    SYMBOL state_iter;     /* the unary constructor */
    TERM   stick;          /* succ^{stick_length-1}(0) */
    TERM   sticknloop;     /* succ^{stick_length+loop_length-1}(0) */
} UPI_INFO;
```

Formulas are represented using the term module of SPASS. To improve the efficiency of the implementation of PDU, I adapted the data structures to grant instant access to regularly needed information. In particular, I used parent links to efficiently navigate through formulas. Since some rules like Q5/6, Sort Reduction and Explosion perform non-local changes in the formula, it is not possible to normalize the formula in one run, e.g. bottom up, but multiple successive runs are needed. To keep track of which subformulas are normalized, every subformula is additionally equipped with a normality marker. This marker is set when the subformula is normalized and only reset for subformulas in which a replacement takes place. This avoids multiply traversing subformulas where all reduction steps have already been performed.

The nondeterminism of PDU allows for a wide variety of normalization strategies. In my concrete implementation, I made the following decisions:

I traverse the formula in a depth search pattern. The reason is that this allows me to early decompose equations deep in the formula which then often lead to a $\top$ or $\bot$ literal that can directly be propagated far up in the formula tree and considerably reduces the size of the formula. It also allows me to effectively update and use the normality marker.

The rules that are most critical for the size of the formula (because subformulas are duplicated) are the Sort Reduction, Distribution and Explosion rules. To delay the blow-up that is induced by them as long as possible, I only apply those rules to terms that are normalized with respect to all other rules.

Chapter 3: Disunification and Predicate Completion

According to the side conditions of the Explosion rules, they must only be applied to terms that are normalized by all other rules. Nevertheless, the Sort Reduction rules are even postponed until after Explosion in the implementation. I have not explicitly proved in this chapter that this is uncritical for the termination of the algorithm, but the proof is not complicated. Delaying the application of Sort Reduction in this way has led to a considerable speed-up and predominantly more compact normal forms.

The disunification algorithm by Comon and Lescanne (1989) restricts its version of the Quantifier Elimination rules to quantifier-free formulas. Although this is done to simplify the termination proof and not as a speed-up technique, I temporarily mimicked this approach by performing rewritings on quantifier-free formulas before rules on subformulas with quantifiers. To make the information on the existence of quantifiers efficiently available, I used a marker indicating whether a subformula is quantifier-free. This marker was updated on the go, similar to the normalization marker. Experimental experience showed, however, a slowdown when this strategy was applied. This may be due to an increased number of passes through the formula that is not sufficiently compensated by a decreased formula size. Hence I do not use this strategy any more. Since Normalization is the only rule where quantifiers in arguments must be avoided to guarantee termination, quantifier-freeness is now simply checked on demand and the marker has been dropped.

Further improvements might include the precomputation of more regularly needed information, like the result of a Periodic Occurrence rewriting or a template for the result of a Periodic Decomposition inference on a (dis-)equation $s(t)\tilde{=}s(t')$ between two non-ground terms. Moreover, an extension to explicit many-sorting is of course possible.

The implementation of PC consists of several steps: First the input is parsed, the ultimate periodicity information extracted and the input clauses partitioned with respect to the predicate of their maximal succedent atom. For each predicate, the formula ϕ_P is then created and the implementation of PDU is used to compute a normalization of $\neg \phi_P$. The solved form computation of SF is performed by the same implementation in a post-processing step. Finally, the resulting completion is extracted in a straightforward way.

Since the completed clause set can directly be used as an input for SPASS, this implementation effectively allows SPASS to perform minimal model reasoning with a first-order machinery. The implementation has been tested on and optimized with the help of the problems in the TPTP library (Sutcliffe, 2009). To be able to use a broad range of problems from the different problem classes in this library, I allowed every first-order problem from this library as an input. To make them match the applicability restrictions of PC,

3.5 Implementation

I eliminated those clauses in each problem that were not obviously universally reductive or that contained equations. The implementation is available from the SPASS homepage (www.spass-prover.org/prototypes/).

Example 3.41
To complete the Even predicate as in Example 3.35 with the equation $E = \{s^3(0) \simeq 0\}$, a file even.dfg containing the following input is given to SPASS:

```
begin_problem(X).
list_of_descriptions.
name({*PC Example*}).
author({*Matthias Horbach*}).
status(satisfiable).
description({*Demonstrates Predicate Completion for Even*}).
end_of_list.

list_of_symbols.
predicates[(Even,1)].
functions[(s,1),(0,0)].
end_of_list.

list_of_formulae(axioms).
formula(Even(0)).
formula(forall([x],implies(Even(x),Even(s(s(x)))))).
formula(equal(s(s(s(0))),0)).
end_of_list.

list_of_settings(SPASS).
{*
set_flag(PComp,1).
*}
end_of_list.
end_problem.
```

The list_of_descriptions contains some information on the problem. In the following list_of_symbols, the signature is fixed to Σ_{Even}, and the clauses describing the ultimately periodic interpretation, i.e. the Even predicate and the periodicity equation, are given in the list_of_formulae. Finally, SPASS is told in the list_of_settings to apply the predicate completion algorithm to the input. The output of SPASS when run on this input begins with the following lines:

```
Perfect SPASS: Input completed.
------------------------SPASS-START-----------------------------
```

This states that predicate completion was successful and SPASS is ready to work with the completed clause set. Then the completion is output:

83

Chapter 3: Disunification and Predicate Completion

```
Input Problem:
1[0:Inp]  ||   -> Even(0)*.
2[0:Inp]  || Even(U) -> Even(s(s(U)))*.
3[0:Inp]  ||   -> equal(s(s(s(0))),0)**.
4[0:Inp]  || Even(s(0)) -> Even(s(s(0)))*.
5[0:Inp]  || Even(s(s(0)))* -> Even(0).
```

The clauses with numbers 1–3 are the clauses describing the interpretation, and clauses 4 and 5 complete the Even predicate. Note that the completion procedure found a completion that is different from the one in Example 3.35 due to a different normalization strategy. The clause list is followed by some output indicating SPASS' analysis of the completed clause set:

```
This is a first-order Horn problem containing equality.
This is a problem that contains sort information.
Axiom clauses: 5 Conjecture clauses: 0
Inferences: IEmS=1 ISoR=1 ISpR=1 ISpL=1 IORe=1
Reductions: RFRew=1 RBRew=1 RFMRR=1 RBMRR=1 RObv=1 RUnC=1 RTaut=1
            RSSi=1 RFSub=1 RBSub=1 RCon=1
Extras     : Input Saturation, Dynamic Selection, No Splitting,
             Full Reduction, Ratio: 5, FuncWeight: 1, VarWeight: 1
Precedence: s > nequal > div > id > Even > 0
Ordering   : KBO
```

In the end, SPASS by default computes a saturation of the completed clause set:

```
Processed Problem:

Worked Off Clauses:

Usable Clauses:
1[0:Inp]  ||   -> Even(0)*.
2[0:Inp]  ||   -> equal(s(s(s(0))),0)**.
3[0:Inp] Even(U) ||   -> Even(s(s(U)))*.
4[0:Inp]  || Even(s(0)) -> Even(s(s(0)))*.
         Given clause: 1[0:Inp]  ||   -> Even(0)*.
         Given clause: 2[0:Inp]  ||   -> equal(s(s(s(0))),0)**.
         Given clause: 3[0:Inp] Even(U) ||   -> Even(s(s(U)))*.
         Given clause: 4[0:Inp]  ||   -> Even(s(s(0)))*.
         Given clause: 7[0:SpR:2.0,3.1]  ||   -> Even(s(0))*.
SPASS V 3.5c
SPASS beiseite: Completion found.
Problem: even.dfg
SPASS derived 1 clauses, backtracked 0 clauses, performed -1 splits
        and kept 4 clauses.
```

84

```
SPASS allocated 28364 KBytes.
SPASS spent    0:00:00.13 on the problem.
               0:00:00.01 for the input.
               0:00:00.01 for the FLOTTER CNF translation.
               0:00:00.00 for the input completion.
               0:00:00.00 for inferences.
               0:00:00.00 for the backtracking.
               0:00:00.00 for the reduction.

-------------------------SPASS-STOP---------------------------
```

A description of the implementation of disunification and predicate completion has been published as (Horbach, 2011b).

3.6 Conclusion

In this chapter, I have presented the disunification algorithm PDU for ultimately periodic interpretations, proved its correctness and termination, and used the algorithm to establish the decidability of satisfiability for equational formulas in such interpretations. I have also presented the disunification-based predicate completion algorithm PC for ultimately periodic interpretations defined by universally reductive clauses and generalized a unique model result for predicate completion to saturated non-Horn clause sets. This extends work by Comon and Lescanne (1989), Comon and Delor (1994) and Comon and Nieuwenhuis (2000). An instance of both PDU and PC has been implemented as part of a predicate completion procedure on top of the first-order theorem prover SPASS (Weidenbach et al., 2009).

The approach of widening the scope of disunification that is most closely connected to mine is the one by Comon (1988), who adapted a predecessor of the algorithm by Comon and Delor to interpretations $\mathcal{T}(\Sigma)/_E$ where E is a so-called quasi-free or compact axiomatization. This approach only results in a terminating procedure if (among other conditions) all equations have at most depth 1.

Another way to extend disunification is by considering not only term algebras but more general structures. Maher (1988) and Comon and Lescanne (1989) considered rational tree algebras and Comon and Delor (1994) extended disunification to classes of non-regular tree algebras.

In later chapters, I will use disunification to decide the coverage of sets of constraints (Section 4.2.2) and I will exploit the unique model property of completed clause sets to link reasoning with respect to fixed domains and to minimal models (Section 5.3) and to transform totality problems into better understood emptiness problems (Section 6.4). This will result in a number of decidability results for minimal model validity.

Another possible application of both disunification for ultimately periodic interpretations in general and predicate completion in particular is saturation-based theorem proving for propositional linear time temporal logic: Ultimately periodic interpretations appear naturally in this setting as minimal models of formula sets (Ludwig and Hustadt, 2009) and methods based on the mentioned calculi developed later on might be useful in this context. The pursuit of this relationship is subject to further work.

4 A Superposition Calculus for Fixed Domains

4.1 Introduction

In this Chapter, I will generalize superposition to a sound and refutationally complete calculus for $\models_\Sigma$. The algorithm can handle equality and is not restricted to clauses of any special syntactic form. Based on an additional induction rule, I further extend the calculus to reason over $\models_{Ind}$.

The basis for the calculus has been formed in Chapters 2 and 3: As explained in the introduction, existential variables cannot be eliminated by Skolemization in the context of reasoning over a fixed domain. Instead, constrained clauses (Section 2.2.2) will be used to handle existential variables. Disunification (Section 3.2) then provides a means to decide whether a saturated set of clauses provides a contradiction.

In Section 4.2, I will first explain how the semantics of constrained clauses supports reasoning over fixed domains and introduce the superposition calculus for fixed domains SFD. I will prove its refutational completeness and soundness and show how, in case of termination, it can be used to decide queries of the form $N \models_\Sigma \forall^* \exists^* \phi$. In Section 4.3, I will shift the focus to minimal model reasoning. I will analyze when minimal model validity corresponds to first-order or fixed domain validity. Then I present an extension of SFD by an induction rule and examples where this extension makes saturation terminate and allows for the derivation of minimal model validity results.

The results in this chapter have been published as (Horbach and Weidenbach, 2008, 2009e, 2010).

4.2 First-Order Reasoning in Fixed Domains

In this section, I will present a saturation procedure for sets of constrained clauses over a signature Σ and show how it is possible to decide whether a saturated set of positively constrained clauses possesses a Herbrand model over Σ. The calculus extends the superposition calculus of Bachmair and Ganzinger (1994).

Chapter 4: A Superposition Calculus for Fixed Domains

Before I come to the actual inference rules, I want to shortly review the semantics of constrained clauses by means of a simple example. Consider the constrained clause set

$$\{ \quad \| \quad \to GT(s(x),0) \; , \\ u{\simeq}x, v{\simeq}y \quad \| \; GT(x,y) \; \to \quad \}$$

over the signature $\Sigma_{GT} = (\{GT\}, \{s, 0\})$. This constrained clause set corresponds to the formula $\exists u, v.(\forall x.GT(s(x),0)) \land \neg GT(u,v)$. In each Herbrand interpretation over Σ_{GT}, this formula is equivalent to the formula

$$\exists u, v.(\forall x.GT(s(x),0)) \land \neg GT(u,v) \land (\forall x.u{\neq}s(x) \lor v{\neq}0) \; ,$$

which corresponds to the following constrained clause set:

$$\{ \quad \| \quad \to GT(s(x),0) \; , \\ u{\simeq}x, v{\simeq}y \quad \| \; GT(x,y) \; \to \quad , \\ u{\simeq}s(x), v{\simeq}0 \; \| \quad \Box \quad \}$$

Hence these two constrained clause sets are equivalent in every Herbrand interpretation over the signature Σ_{GT}.

An aspect that catches the eye is that, although the clausal part of the last constrained clause is empty, this does not mean that the constrained clause set is unsatisfiable over Σ_{GT}. The empty clause is constrained by $u{\simeq}s(x) \land v{\simeq}0$, which means that, for example, the clause set is not satisfiable under the instantiation $u \mapsto s(0)$ and $v \mapsto 0$. In fact, the instantiated formula $(\forall x.GT(s(x),0)) \land \neg GT(s(0),0) \land (\forall x.s(0){\neq}s(x) \lor 0{\neq}0)$ is unsatisfiable. On the other hand, the clause set is satisfiable under the instantiation $u \mapsto 0$ and $v \mapsto s(0)$.

Derivations using the calculus will usually contain multiple, potentially infinitely many, constrained clauses with empty clausal parts. I explore in Theorem 4.12 how the unsatisfiability of a saturated set of constrained clauses over Σ depends on a covering property of the constraints of constrained clauses with empty clausal part. In Theorem 4.6, I prove that this property is decidable for finite constrained clause sets. Furthermore, I show how to saturate a given set of constrained clauses (Theorem 4.16). Finally, I present in Section 4.2.3 an extension of the calculus that allows for the deduction of a wider range of Herbrand models of Σ-satisfiable constrained clause sets.

The calculus is refutationally complete only for sets of positively constrained clauses. This is not a problem because every formula of the form $\exists^*\forall^*\phi$ obviously corresponds to a set of positively constrained clauses and the calculus does not produce constraint disequations if they are not already present in the input. It would be possible to extend the calculus in order to be refutationally complete for clauses with arbitrary constraints, but the resulting calculus is very complicated and, due to an interference between equational clauses and constraint disequations, requires that much of the work of Bachmair and Ganzinger (1994) must be redone in the current setting. Since positively constrained clauses suffice for the current considerations anyway, I will avoid these complications. When the saturation of clauses with general constraints becomes important in Chapter 5, all clauses will be predicative and the difference will not be visible.

4.2.1 The Superposition Calculus for Fixed Domains SFD

To reason about positively constrained clauses, consider the inference rules presented in Figures 4.1 and 4.2, which are defined with respect to a reduction ordering $\succ$ on $\mathcal{T}(\Sigma, \mathcal{X})$ that is total on ground terms and with respect to a *selection function* that assigns to every clause a (possibly empty) set of literals in its antecedent. Most of the rules are quite similar to the usual superposition rules (Bachmair and Ganzinger, 1994), just generalized to positively constrained clauses. However, they require additional treatment of the constraints to avoid inferences like

$$\frac{v \simeq f(x) \parallel \to a \simeq b \quad v \simeq g(y) \parallel a \simeq c \to}{v \simeq f(x), v \simeq g(y) \parallel b \simeq c \to}$$

the conclusion of which contains the existential variable v more than once in its constraint and hence is not a constrained clause. In addition, there are two rules that rewrite constraints.

As usual, I consider the universal variables in different appearing premises to be renamed apart. If $\alpha_1 = v_1 \simeq s_1, \ldots, v_n \simeq s_n$ and $\alpha_2 = v_1 \simeq t_1, \ldots, v_n \simeq t_n$ are two positive constraints, I write $\alpha_1 \simeq \alpha_2$ for the equations $s_1 \simeq t_1, \ldots, s_n \simeq t_n$. Note that $\alpha_1 \simeq \alpha_2$ does not contain any existential variables. The notion of the most general unifier of two positive constraints has been formally introduced in Section 2.2.3.

Definition 4.1 (SFD)
Let $\succ$ be a well-founded strict reduction ordering on atoms over Σ that is total on ground terms. The *Superposition Calculus for Fixed Domains* SFD consists of the inference rules in Figures 4.1 and 4.2, where all (strict) maximality constraints have to be considered with respect to $\succ$.

Note that the maximality conditions in all rules do not consider the constraint part.

Chapter 4: A Superposition Calculus for Fixed Domains

Equality Resolution:
$$\frac{\alpha \,\|\, \Gamma, s{\simeq}t \to \Delta}{(\alpha \,\|\, \Gamma \to \Delta)\sigma}$$

where

(i) $\sigma = \mathrm{mgu}(s, t)$, and
(ii) either $s{\simeq}t$ is selected in the premise
or no literal is selected and $(s{\simeq}t)\sigma$ is maximal in $(\Gamma, s{\simeq}t \to \Delta)\sigma$.

Equality Factoring:
$$\frac{\alpha \,\|\, \Gamma \to \Delta, s{\simeq}t, s'{\simeq}t'}{(\alpha \,\|\, \Gamma, t{\simeq}t' \to \Delta, s'{\simeq}t')\sigma}$$

where

(i) $\sigma = \mathrm{mgu}(s, s')$,
(ii) no literal is selected in the premise
and $(s{\simeq}t)\sigma$ is maximal in $(\Gamma \to \Delta, s{\simeq}t, s'{\simeq}t')\sigma$, and
(iii) $t\sigma \not\succeq s\sigma$

Left Superposition:
$$\frac{\alpha_1 \,\|\, \Gamma_1 \to \Delta_1, l{\simeq}r \quad \alpha_2 \,\|\, \Gamma_2, s[l']_p{\simeq}t \to \Delta_2}{(\alpha_1, \alpha_2^{\not\simeq} \,\|\, \Gamma_1, \Gamma_2, s[r]_p{\simeq}t \to \Delta_1, \Delta_2)\sigma_1\sigma_2}$$

where

(i) $\sigma_1 = \mathrm{mgu}(l, l')$, $\sigma_2 = \mathrm{mgu}(\alpha_1^{\simeq}\sigma_1, \alpha_2^{\simeq}\sigma_1)$,
(ii) no literal is selected in the first premise
and $(l{\simeq}r)\sigma_1\sigma_2$ is strictly maximal in $(\Gamma_1 \to \Delta_1, l{\simeq}r)\sigma_1\sigma_2$,
(iii) either $s{\simeq}t$ is selected in the second premise
or no literal is selected and $(s{\simeq}t)\sigma_1\sigma_2$ is maximal in $(\Gamma_2 \to \Delta_2, s{\simeq}t)\sigma_1\sigma_2$,
(iv) $r\sigma_1\sigma_2 \not\succeq l\sigma_1\sigma_2$ and $t\sigma_1\sigma_2 \not\succeq s\sigma_1\sigma_2$, and
(v) l' is not a variable.

Figure 4.1: Rules of the Calculus **SFD** (1)

4.2 First-Order Reasoning in Fixed Domains

Right Superposition:

$$\frac{\alpha_1 \parallel \Gamma_1 \to \Delta_1, l{\simeq}r \quad \alpha_2 \parallel \Gamma_2 \to \Delta_2, s[l']_p{\simeq}t}{(\alpha_1, \alpha_2^{\approx} \parallel \Gamma_1, \Gamma_2 \to \Delta_1, \Delta_2, s[r]_p{\simeq}t)\sigma_1\sigma_2}$$

where

(i) $\sigma_1 = \mathrm{mgu}(l, l')$, $\sigma_2 = \mathrm{mgu}(\alpha_1^{\approx}\sigma_1, \alpha_2^{\approx}\sigma_1)$,
(ii) no literal is selected in any of the premises
and $(l{\simeq}r)\sigma_1\sigma_2$ is strictly maximal in $(\Gamma_1 \to \Delta_1, l{\simeq}r)\sigma_1\sigma_2$
and $(s{\simeq}t)\sigma_1\sigma_2$ is strictly maximal in $(\Gamma_2 \to \Delta_2, s{\simeq}t)\sigma_1\sigma_2$,
(iii) $r\sigma_1\sigma_2 \not\succeq l\sigma_1\sigma_2$ and $t\sigma_1\sigma_2 \not\succeq s\sigma_1\sigma_2$, and
(iv) l' is not a variable.

Constraint Superposition:

$$\frac{\alpha_1 \parallel \Gamma_1 \to \Delta_1, l{\simeq}r \quad \alpha_2[l']_p \parallel \Gamma_2 \to \Delta_2}{(\alpha_2[r]_p, \alpha_1^{\approx} \parallel \alpha_1^{\approx}{\simeq}\alpha_2^{\approx}[r]_p, \Gamma_1, \Gamma_2 \to \Delta_1, \Delta_2)\sigma}$$

where

(i) $\sigma = \mathrm{mgu}(l, l')$,
(ii) no literal is selected in the first premise
and $(l{\simeq}r)\sigma$ is strictly maximal in $(\Gamma_1 \to \Delta_1, l{\simeq}r)\sigma$,
(iii) $r\sigma \not\succeq l\sigma$, and
(iv) l' is not a variable, and
(v) p is a position in the positive part $\alpha_2^{\approx}$ of α_2.

Equality Elimination:

$$\frac{\alpha_1 \parallel \Gamma \to \Delta, l{\simeq}r \quad \alpha_2[r']_p \parallel \Box}{(\alpha_1, \alpha_2^{\approx} \parallel \Gamma \to \Delta)\sigma_1\sigma_2}$$

where

(i) $\sigma_1 = \mathrm{mgu}(r, r')$, $\sigma_2 = \mathrm{mgu}(\alpha_1^{\approx}\sigma_1, \alpha_2^{\approx}[l]_p\sigma_1)$,
(ii) no literal is selected in the first premise
and $(l{\simeq}r)\sigma_1\sigma_2$ is strictly maximal in $(\Gamma \to \Delta, l{\simeq}r)\sigma_1\sigma_2$,
(iii) $r\sigma_1\sigma_2 \not\succeq l\sigma_1\sigma_2$,
(iv) r' is not a variable, and
(v) p is a position in the positive part $\alpha_2^{\approx}$ of α_2.

Figure 4.2: Rules of the Calculus SFD (2)

Chapter 4: A Superposition Calculus for Fixed Domains

I unify $\alpha_1^{\tilde{z}}$ and $\alpha_2^{\tilde{z}}$ in the two-premise rules for efficiency reasons: A natural alternative would be to consider constraints with multiple occurrences of the same existential variable and to take $(\alpha_1, \alpha_2)\sigma_1\sigma_2$ instead of $(\alpha_1, \alpha_2^{\tilde{z}})\sigma_1\sigma_2$ as the constraint of the conclusion. But since constraint equations are syntactic, if $\alpha_1^{\tilde{z}}$ and $\alpha_2^{\tilde{z}}$ are not unifiable then any variable-free instance of α_1, α_2 is unsatisfiable anyway, so this would not add expressiveness to the calculus. Further refinements are of course possible, for example by restricting all inferences to instances where $(\alpha_1^{\tilde{z}}, \alpha_2^{\tilde{z}})\sigma_1\sigma_2$ is satisfiable.

This inference system contains the standard universal superposition calculus as the special case when there are no existential variables at all present, i.e. $\mathcal{V} = \emptyset$ and all constraints are empty: The rules Equality Resolution, Equality Factoring, and Left and Right Superposition reduce to their non-constrained counterparts while the Constraint Superposition and Equality Elimination rules become obsolete.

While the former rules are thus well-known, a few words may be in order to explain the idea behind Constraint Superposition and Equality Elimination. They have been introduced to make the calculus refutationally complete, i.e. to ensure that constrained clause sets that are saturated with respect to the inference system and that do not have a Herbrand model over the given signature always contain "enough" constrained empty clauses (cf. Definition 2.39 and Theorem 4.12).

A notable feature of Constraint Superposition is how the information of both premise constraints is combined in the conclusion. Classically, the existential variables would be Skolemized and the constraint of a constrained clause would be regarded as part of its antecedent. In this setting, superpositions into the constraint part as considered here would not even require a specialized rule but occur naturally in the following form:

$$\frac{\alpha_1, \Gamma_1 \to \Delta_1, l \simeq r \quad \alpha_2[l'], \Gamma_2 \to \Delta_2}{(\alpha_1, \alpha_2[r], \Gamma_1, \Gamma_2 \to \Delta_1, \Delta_2)\sigma}$$

Translated into the language of constrained clauses, the conclusion would, however, not be a well-formed constrained clause. In most inference rules, I circumvent this problem by forcing a unification of the constraints of the premises, so that I can use an equivalent and admissible conclusion. For Constraint Superposition, this approach turns out to be too weak to make the calculus refutationally complete, and in particular to prove Proposition 4.8 below. Therefore, I instead replace α_1 by $\alpha_1 \simeq \alpha_2[r]$ in this inference rule to regain an equivalent and admissible constrained clause.

The resulting Constraint Superposition rule alone is still not sufficient to obtain refutational completeness. Abstractly speaking, it only transfers information about the equality relation from the clausal part into the constraint

4.2 First-Order Reasoning in Fixed Domains

part. For completeness, a transfer must also occur the other way round. Once terms are exhibited that cannot be solutions to the existentially quantified variables, this information must be propagated through the respective equivalence classes in the clausal part. This propagation is performed by the rule Equality Elimination, which deletes equations that are in conflict with the satisfiability of constrained empty clauses.

The rules Constraint Superposition and Equality Elimination are the main reason why SFD can manage theories that are not constructor-based, i.e. where the calculus cannot assume the irreducibility of certain terms.

Example 4.2 (Constraint Superposition and Equality Elimination)
Constraint Superposition and Equality Elimination allow to derive, for example, $v{\simeq}b \,\|\, \square$ from $v{\simeq}b \,\|\, \to a{\simeq}b$ and $v{\simeq}a \,\|\, \square$, although $v{\simeq}a$ and $v{\simeq}b$ are not unifiable:

If $b \succ a$, then $v{\simeq}b \,\|\, \square$ is derived by one step of Equality Elimination:

$$\frac{v{\simeq}b \,\|\, \to b{\simeq}a \quad v{\simeq}a \,\|\, \square}{v{\simeq}b \,\|\, \square} \text{ Equality Elimination}$$

Otherwise, $v{\simeq}b \,\|\, \square$ follows from a step of Constraint Superposition and the subsequent resolution of a trivial equality:

$$\frac{\dfrac{v{\simeq}b \,\|\, \to a{\simeq}b \quad v{\simeq}a \,\|\, \square}{v{\simeq}b \,\|\, b{\simeq}b \to} \text{ Constraint Superposition}}{v{\simeq}b \,\|\, \square} \text{ Equality Resolution}$$

When I work with predicative atoms in the examples, I will not make the translation into the purely equational calculus explicit. If, for example, P is a predicate symbol that is translated into the function symbol f_P, I write a derivation

$$\frac{\alpha_1 \,\|\, \Gamma_1 \to \Delta_1, f_P(s_1, \ldots, s_n){\simeq}c_{\text{true}} \quad \alpha_2 \,\|\, \Gamma_2, f_P(t_1, \ldots, t_n){\simeq}c_{\text{true}} \to \Delta_2}{\dfrac{(\alpha_1, \alpha_2^z \,\|\, \Gamma_1, \Gamma_2, c_{\text{true}}{\simeq}c_{\text{true}} \to \Delta_1, \Delta_2)\sigma_1\sigma_2}{(\alpha_1, \alpha_2^z \,\|\, \Gamma_1, \Gamma_2 \to \Delta_1, \Delta_2)\sigma_1\sigma_2}}$$

consisting of a superposition of predicative atoms and the subsequent resolution of the atom $c_{\text{true}}{\simeq}c_{\text{true}}$ in the following condensed form:

$$\frac{\alpha_1 \,\|\, \Gamma_1 \to \Delta_1, P(s_1, \ldots, s_n) \quad \alpha_2 \,\|\, \Gamma_2, P(t_1, \ldots, t_n) \to \Delta_2}{(\alpha_1, \alpha_2^z \,\|\, \Gamma_1, \Gamma_2 \to \Delta_1, \Delta_2)\sigma_1\sigma_2} \text{ Superposition}$$

Chapter 4: A Superposition Calculus for Fixed Domains

Example 4.3 (The Elevator)
For a simple example involving only superposition on predicative atoms, consider the clause set

$$N_E = \{ \to G(a,p),\ \to G(b,q),\ G(a,x) \to C(a,x),$$
$$C(a,x) \to R(a,x),\ G(b,x) \to R(b,x)\}$$

that describes the elevator example presented in the introduction, and the two constrained clauses $u \simeq x, v \simeq y \,\|\, R(y,x) \to$ and $u \simeq x, v \simeq y \,\|\, \to G(y,x)$. These clauses state that there are a person and an elevator, such that the person can reach the ground floor but not the restaurant floor in this elevator.

Assume a strict term ordering $\succ$ for which $R(y,x) \succ C(y,x) \succ G(y,x)$. With this ordering, the succedent is strictly maximal in each clause of N_E. Because Superposition inferences always work on maximal atoms (condition (ii)), only two inferences between the given constrained clauses are possible:

$$\frac{C(a,x) \to R(a,x) \quad u \simeq x, v \simeq y \,\|\, R(y,x) \to}{u \simeq x, v \simeq a \,\|\, C(a,x) \to}$$

$$\frac{G(b,x) \to R(b,x) \quad u \simeq x, v \simeq y \,\|\, R(y,x) \to}{u \simeq x, v \simeq b \,\|\, G(b,x) \to}$$

The first conclusion can now be superposed with the third clause of N_E:

$$\frac{G(a,x) \to C(a,x) \quad u \simeq x, v \simeq a \,\|\, C(a,x) \to}{u \simeq x, v \simeq a \,\|\, G(a,x) \to}$$

The last two conclusions can in turn be superposed with the constrained clause $u \simeq x, v \simeq y \,\|\, \to G(y,x)$:

$$\frac{u \simeq x, v \simeq y \,\|\, \to G(y,x) \quad u \simeq x, v \simeq a \,\|\, G(a,x) \to}{u \simeq x, v \simeq a \,\|\, \square}$$

$$\frac{u \simeq x, v \simeq y \,\|\, \to G(y,x) \quad u \simeq x, v \simeq b \,\|\, G(b,x) \to}{u \simeq x, v \simeq b \,\|\, \square}$$

Now the only remaining SFD inferences are those between the two constrained clauses $\to G(a,p)$ and $u \simeq x, v \simeq a \,\|\, G(a,x) \to$ and between $\to G(b,q)$ and $u \simeq x, v \simeq b \,\|\, G(b,x) \to$. They are both redundant with respect to the last two conclusions. This means that they do not give any new information on the system and I can ignore them.

In order to present such a series of inferences in a more concise manner, I will write them down as follows, where all constrained clauses are indexed

4.2 First-Order Reasoning in Fixed Domains

and premises to an inference are represented by their indices:

$$
\begin{array}{rrll}
\text{clauses in } N_E\colon 1: & \| & \to G(a,p) \\
2: & \| & \to G(b,q) \\
3: & \| \ G(a,x) & \to C(a,x) \\
4: & \| \ C(a,x) & \to r(a,x) \\
5: & \| \ G(b,x) & \to r(b,x) \\
\text{additional clauses: } 6: & u{\simeq}x, v{\simeq}y \ \| \ R(y,x) & \to \\
7: & u{\simeq}x, v{\simeq}y \ \| & \to G(y,x) \\
\text{Superposition}(4,6) = 8: & u{\simeq}x, v{\simeq}a \ \| \ C(a,x) & \to \\
\text{Superposition}(5,6) = 9: & u{\simeq}x, v{\simeq}b \ \| \ G(b,x) & \to \\
\text{Superposition}(3,7) = 10: & u{\simeq}x, v{\simeq}a \ \| \ G(a,x) & \to \\
\text{Superposition}(7,9) = 11: & u{\simeq}x, v{\simeq}b \ \| & \square \\
\text{Superposition}(7,10) = 12: & u{\simeq}x, v{\simeq}a \ \| & \square \\
\end{array}
$$

4.2.2 Model Construction and Refutational Completeness

By treating each constraint equation as a part of the antecedent and each constraint disequation as a part of the succedent, constrained clauses can be regarded as a special class of unconstrained clauses. Because of this, the construction of a Herbrand interpretation for a set of constrained clauses is strongly connected to the one for universal clause sets (Bachmair and Ganzinger, 1994, c.f. Definition 2.35). The main difference is that I now have to account for existential variables before starting the construction. To define a Herbrand interpretation $\mathcal{I}_N$ of a set N of constrained clauses, I proceed in two steps: First, I identify an instantiation of the existential variables that does not contradict any constrained clauses with empty clausal part, and then I construct the model of a set of unconstrained clause instances.

Although the scope of **SFD** only encompasses positively constrained clauses, the model construction need not be restricted to this setting. Indeed, the construction will later be reused in a context where full constraints occur.

Definition 4.4 (A_N, α_N)
Let $\succ$ be a well-founded strict reduction ordering on atoms over Σ that is total on ground atoms. Given a set N of constrained clauses, let A_N be the set of all constraints of constrained clauses in N with empty clausal part, i.e. $A_N = \{\alpha \mid (\alpha \| \square) \in N\}$.

I distinguish one ground constraint α_N:

- If A_N is not covering (cf. Definition 2.39), then let $\alpha_N = \vec{v}{\simeq}\vec{t}$ be a minimal (with respect to $\succ$) positive ground constraint that is not equal to the positive part of any satisfiable ground instance of a constraint in A_N.

Chapter 4: A Superposition Calculus for Fixed Domains

- If A_N is covering, then let α_N be an arbitrary ground constraint.

For the remainder of this chapter, I will always assume that a well-founded strict reduction ordering $\succ$ on atoms over Σ that is total on ground atoms has been fixed and that this fixed strict ordering is used in both SFD inferences and in the construction of A_N.

Note that even if A_N is not covering, α_N is usually not uniquely defined. E.g. for the constrained clause set $N = \{u{\simeq}0, v{\simeq}0 \,\|\, \Box\}$ over Σ_{nat}, it holds that $A_N = \{(u{\simeq}0, v{\simeq}0)\}$ and both $\alpha_N^1 = \{u{\simeq}0, v{\simeq}s(0)\}$ and $\alpha_N^2 = \{u{\simeq}s(0), v{\simeq}0\}$ are valid choices. When necessary, this ambiguity can be avoided by using an ordering on the existential variables as a tie breaker.

Definition 4.5 ($\mathcal{I}_N$)

Let N be a set of constrained clauses with associated ground constraint α_N. The Herbrand interpretation $\mathcal{I}_N^{\alpha_N}$ is defined as the interpretation $\mathcal{I}_{N|_{\alpha_N}}$ associated with the unconstrained ground clause set

$$N|_{\alpha_N} = \{C\sigma \mid (\alpha \,\|\, C) \in N \text{ and } \sigma : \text{var}(\alpha \,\|\, C) \setminus \mathcal{V} \to \mathcal{T}(\Sigma)$$
$$\text{and } \alpha_N = \alpha^{\simeq}\sigma \text{ and } \alpha\sigma \text{ is satisfiable}$$
$$\text{and } \alpha \,\|\, C \text{ does not contain selected literals}\}$$

as described in Definition 2.35.

It is obvious that the interpretation $\mathcal{I}_N^{\alpha_N}$ is independent of α_N if all clauses in N are unconstrained. Even if that is not the case, the constraint α_N is usually not mentioned explicitly and $\mathcal{I}_N$ abbreviates $\mathcal{I}_N^{\alpha_N}$ if no ambiguities arise from this.

If $(\alpha \,\|\, C) \in N$ contributes an instance $C\sigma$ to $N|_{\alpha_N}$ that produces a rewrite rule $s \to t$ during the construction of $\mathcal{I}_N$, then I will also say that $(\alpha \,\|\, C)\sigma$ is *productive* and *produces* $s \to t$.

Note that, since the same element of $N|_{\alpha_N}$ can correspond to more than one element of N, there may be several constrained clauses producing the same rewrite rule. E.g. both constrained clauses are productive in the set $N = \{\| \to P(0),\ v{\simeq}x \,\| \to P(x)\}$ for $\alpha_N = v{\simeq}0$. However, none of these constrained clauses contains any selected literals.

While it is well known how the construction of $\mathcal{I}_N$ works once α_N is given, it is not that obvious that it is decidable whether A_N is covering and, if it is not, effectively compute α_N. This is, however, possible for finite A_N:

Theorem 4.6 (Decidability of Finite Coverage)

Let N be a set of constrained clauses such that A_N is finite. It is decidable whether A_N is covering, and α_N is computable if A_N is not covering.

4.2 First-Order Reasoning in Fixed Domains

Proof. Consider the formula
$$\phi = \bigwedge_{(v_1 \simeq s_1, \ldots, v_n \simeq s_n, t_1 \not\simeq t'_1, \ldots, t_m \not\simeq t'_m \,\|\, \Box) \in N} v_1 \not\simeq s_1 \vee \ldots \vee v_n \not\simeq s_n \vee t_1 \simeq t'_1 \vee \ldots \vee t_m \simeq t'_m$$
and let $\{x_1, \ldots, x_k\} \subseteq \mathcal{X} \setminus \mathcal{V}$ be the set of universal variables occurring in ϕ. The set A_N is not covering if, and only if, the formula $\forall x_1, \ldots, x_k.\phi$ is satisfiable in $\mathcal{T}(\Sigma)$. In Chapter 3, a terminating algorithm was presented that decides the satisfiability of such a disunification problem and returns an explicit representation of its solutions (cf. in particular Theorem 3.40). ◇

For saturated sets of *positively* constrained clauses, the information contained in the constrained empty clauses is already sufficient to decide whether Herbrand models exist: Specifically, I will now show that a saturated set N of positively constrained clauses has a Herbrand model over Σ (namely $\mathcal{I}_N$) if, and only if, A_N is not covering. In this case, $\mathcal{I}_N$ is a minimal model of the unconstrained clause set used in its construction, and I will also call it the *minimal model of N (with respect to α_N)*. Observe, however, that for other choices of α_N there may be strictly smaller models of N with respect to set inclusion: For $N = \{\|\to P(s(0)),\ v \simeq x \,\|\to P(x)\}$, it holds that $\alpha_N = v \simeq 0$ and $\mathcal{I}_N = \mathcal{I}_N^{\alpha_N} = \{P(0), P(s(0))\}$, and $\mathcal{I}_N$ strictly contains the model $\{P(s(0))\}$ of N that corresponds to the constraint $v \simeq s(0)$.

Since $\mathcal{I}_N$ is defined via a set of unconstrained clauses, it inherits all properties of minimal models of unconstrained clause sets. Above all, I will use the property that the rewrite system R_N constructed in parallel with $\mathcal{I}_N$ is confluent and terminating.

Lemma 4.7 (Irreducibility of α_N)

Let N be a set of positively constrained clauses that is saturated with respect to the calculus SFD. If A_N is not covering then α_N is irreducible by R_N.

Proof. Assume, contrary to the proposition, that A_N is not covering and α_N is reducible. Then there are a position p and a rule $l\sigma \to r\sigma \in R_N$ produced by a ground instance $(\beta \,\|\, \Lambda \to \Pi, l \simeq r)\sigma$ of a positively constrained clause $\beta \,\|\, \Lambda \to \Pi, l \simeq r \in N$, such that $l\sigma = \alpha_N|_p$. By definition of productivity, no literals are selected in this constrained clause.

Because of the minimality of α_N and because $\alpha_N \succ \alpha_N[r\sigma]_p$, there must be a positively constrained clause $\gamma \,\|\, \Box \in N$ and a substitution σ' such that $\gamma\sigma' \simeq \alpha_N[r\sigma]_p$. Since, by definition, α_N is not an instance of γ, the position p is a non-variable position of γ. Since furthermore $\beta\sigma = \alpha_N = \gamma\sigma'[l\sigma]_p$ and σ is a unifier of $\gamma|_p$ and r and $\gamma\sigma'|_p = r\sigma$, there is an Equality Elimination inference as follows:

$$\frac{\beta \,\|\, \Lambda \to \Pi, l \simeq r \quad \gamma \,\|\, \Box}{(\beta \,\|\, \Lambda \to \Pi)\sigma_1\sigma_2} \quad \sigma_1 = \mathrm{mgu}(\gamma|_p, r),\ \sigma_2 = \mathrm{mgu}(\beta\sigma_1, \gamma[l]_p\sigma_1)$$

Because of the saturation of N, the ground instance

$$\frac{(\beta \,\|\, \Lambda \to \Pi, l{\simeq}r)\sigma \quad (\gamma \,\|\, \Box)\sigma'}{(\beta \,\|\, \Lambda \to \Pi)\sigma}$$

of this derivation is redundant. The first premise cannot be redundant because it is productive; the second one cannot be redundant because there are no clauses that are smaller than $\Box$. This means that the constrained clause $(\beta \,\|\, \Lambda \to \Pi)\sigma$ follows from ground instances of constrained clauses in N all of which are smaller than the maximal premise $(\beta \,\|\, \Lambda \to \Pi, l{\simeq}r)\sigma$. But then the same ground instances imply $(\beta \,\|\, \Lambda \to \Pi, l{\simeq}r)\sigma$, which means that this constrained clause cannot be productive. A contradiction. $\Diamond$

Lemma 4.8
Let N be a set of positively constrained clauses that is saturated with respect to SFD and let A_N not be covering. If $\mathcal{I}_N \not\models N$ and if $(\alpha \,\|\, C)\sigma$ is a minimal ground instance of a constrained clause in N such that $\mathcal{I}_N \not\models (\alpha \,\|\, C)\sigma$, then

(i) for every variable $x \in \mathrm{var}(\alpha \,\|\, C)$, it holds that $x\sigma$ is irreducible by R_N, and

(ii) $\alpha\sigma = \alpha_N$.

Proof. To prove the first statement, let $x \in \mathrm{var}(\alpha \,\|\, C)$ and assume that $x\sigma \to_{R_N} t$. Let τ be the substitution that coincides with σ except that $x\tau = t$. Because $\mathcal{I}_N \not\models (\alpha \,\|\, C)\sigma$ and $\mathcal{I}_N \models x\sigma{\simeq}x\tau$, it follows that $\mathcal{I}_N \not\models (\alpha \,\|\, C)\tau$ and hence $(\alpha \,\|\, C)\tau$ contradicts the minimality of $(\alpha \,\|\, C)\sigma$.

For the second statement, let $C = \Gamma \to \Delta$. By definition of entailment, $\mathcal{I}_N \not\models (\alpha \,\|\, C)\sigma$ implies that $\mathcal{I}_N \models \alpha_N{\simeq}\alpha\sigma$, or equivalently $\alpha_N \leftrightarrow^*_{R_N} \alpha\sigma$. I have already shown in Lemma 4.7 that α_N is irreducible. Because of the confluence of R_N, either $\alpha\sigma = \alpha_N$ or $\alpha\sigma$ must be reducible.

Assume the latter, i.e. that $\alpha\sigma|_p = l\sigma'$ for a position p and a rule $l\sigma' \to r\sigma' \in R_N$ that has been produced by the ground instance $(\beta \,\|\, \Lambda \to \Pi, l{\simeq}r)\sigma'$ of a positively constrained clause $\beta \,\|\, \Lambda \to \Pi, l{\simeq}r \in N$. By definition of productivity, no literals are selected in this constrained clause.

If p is a variable position in α or not a position in α at all, then the rule actually reduces σ, which contradicts the minimality of $(\alpha \,\|\, C)\sigma$. By (i), p is a non-variable position in α. So there is a Constraint Superposition inference

$$\frac{\beta \,\|\, \Lambda \to \Pi, l{\simeq}r \quad \alpha \,\|\, \Gamma \to \Delta}{(\alpha[r]_p \,\|\, \beta{\simeq}\alpha[r]_p, \Lambda, \Gamma \to \Pi, \Delta)\tau} \quad \tau = \mathrm{mgu}(\alpha|_p, l)\;.$$

Consider the ground instance $\delta \,\|\, D := (\alpha[r]_p \,\|\, \beta{\simeq}\alpha[r]_p, \Lambda, \Gamma \to \Pi, \Delta)\sigma\sigma'$ of the conclusion. This constrained clause is not modeled by $\mathcal{I}_N$. On the other hand, that N is saturated implies that the above inference and in particular its ground instance

$$\frac{(\beta \,\|\, \Lambda \to \Pi, l{\simeq}r)\sigma' \quad (\alpha \,\|\, \Gamma \to \Delta)\sigma}{(\alpha[r]_p \,\|\, \beta{\simeq}\alpha[r]_p, \Lambda, \Gamma \to \Pi, \Delta)\sigma\sigma'}$$

is redundant. The premises cannot be redundant, because $(\beta \,\|\, \Lambda \to \Pi, l{\simeq}r)\sigma'$ is productive and $(\alpha \,\|\, C)\sigma$ is minimal, so the constrained clause $\delta \,\|\, D$ follows from ground instances of constrained clauses of N all of which are smaller than $\delta \,\|\, D$. Since moreover $\delta \,\|\, D \prec (\alpha \,\|\, C)\sigma$ because $\delta \prec \alpha\sigma$, all these ground instances hold in $\mathcal{I}_N$, hence $\mathcal{I}_N \models \delta \,\|\, D$ by minimality of $(\alpha \,\|\, C)\sigma$. This is a contradiction to $\mathcal{I}_N \not\models \delta \,\|\, D$. ◇

Proposition 4.9 ($\mathcal{I}_N$ is a Model)
Let N be a set of positively constrained clauses such that N is saturated with respect to SFD and A_N is not covering. Then $\mathcal{I}_N \models N$.

Proof. Assume, contrary to the proposition, that N is saturated, A_N is not covering, and $\mathcal{I}_N \not\models N$. Then there is a minimal ground instance $(\alpha \,\|\, C)\sigma$ of a positively constrained clause $\alpha \,\|\, C \in N$ that is not modeled by $\mathcal{I}_N$. In particular it holds that $\mathcal{I}_N \not\models C\sigma$, and Lemma 4.8(ii) shows that $\alpha\sigma = \alpha_N$. I will refute the minimality of $(\alpha \,\|\, C)\sigma$, proceeding by a case analysis of the position of the maximal in $C\sigma$ and whether C contains selected literals. As usual, I assume that the constrained clauses appearing as premises in an inference do not share any universal variables. First consider the case that no literal in C is selected.

(i) $C = \Gamma, s{\simeq}t \to \Delta$ and $s\sigma{\simeq}t\sigma$ is maximal in $C\sigma$ with $s\sigma = t\sigma$. Then s and t are unifiable, and so there is an inference by Equality Resolution as follows:

$$\frac{\alpha \,\|\, \Gamma, s{\simeq}t \to \Delta}{(\alpha \,\|\, \Gamma \to \Delta)\sigma_1} \quad \sigma_1 = \text{mgu}(s,t)$$

Consider the ground instance $(\alpha \,\|\, \Gamma \to \Delta)\sigma$ of the conclusion. From this constrained clause, a contradiction can be obtained as in the proof of Lemma 4.8.

(ii) $C = \Gamma, s{\simeq}t \to \Delta$ and $s\sigma{\simeq}t\sigma$ is maximal in $C\sigma$ with $s\sigma \succ t\sigma$. Since $\mathcal{I}_N \not\models C\sigma$, it follows that $s\sigma{\simeq}t\sigma \in \mathcal{I}_N$, and because R_N only rewrites larger to smaller terms, $s\sigma$ must be reducible by a rule $l\sigma' \to r\sigma' \in R_N$ produced by a ground instance $(\beta \,\|\, \Lambda \to \Pi, l{\simeq}r)\sigma'$ of a positively constrained clause $\beta \,\|\, \Lambda \to \Pi, l{\simeq}r \in N$. So $s\sigma|_p = l\sigma'$ for some position p in $s\sigma$. By Lemma 4.8(i), p is a non-variable position in s. Since $\beta\sigma' =$

$\alpha_N = \alpha\sigma$ and $s\sigma|_p = l\sigma'$, there is an inference by Left Superposition as follows:

$$\frac{\beta \,\|\, \Lambda \to \Pi, l{\simeq}r \quad \alpha \,\|\, \Gamma, s{\simeq}t \to \Delta}{(\beta \,\|\, \Lambda, \Gamma, s[r]_p{\simeq}t \to \Pi, \Delta)\sigma_1\sigma_2} \quad \sigma_1 := \mathrm{mgu}(s|_p, l),\ \sigma_2 = \mathrm{mgu}(\beta\sigma_1, \alpha\sigma_1)$$

As before, a contradiction can be derived from the existence of the ground instance $(\beta \,\|\, \Lambda, \Gamma, s[r]_p{\simeq}t \to \Pi, \Delta)\sigma\sigma'$ of the conclusion.

(iii) $C = \Gamma \to \Delta, s{\simeq}t$ and $s\sigma{\simeq}t\sigma$ is maximal in $C\sigma$ with $s\sigma = t\sigma$. Then $C\sigma$ is a tautology, contradicting $\mathcal{I}_N \not\models C\sigma$.

(iv) $C = \Gamma \to \Delta, s{\simeq}t$ and $s\sigma{\simeq}t\sigma$ is strictly maximal in $C\sigma$ with $s\sigma \neq t\sigma$, i.e. without loss of generality $s\sigma \succ t\sigma$. Since $\mathcal{I}_N \not\models C\sigma$, it follows that $\mathcal{I}_N \models \Gamma\sigma$, $\mathcal{I}_N \not\models \Delta\sigma$, and $\mathcal{I}_N \not\models s\sigma{\simeq}t\sigma$, and thus C did not produce the rule $s\sigma \to t\sigma$. The only possible reason for this is that $s\sigma$ is reducible by a rule $l\sigma' \to r\sigma' \in R_N$ produced by a ground instance $(\beta \,\|\, \Lambda \to \Pi, l{\simeq}r)\sigma'$ of a positively constrained clause $\beta \,\|\, \Lambda \to \Pi, l{\simeq}r \in N$. So $s\sigma|_p = l\sigma'$ for some position p in $s\sigma$. By Lemma 4.8(i), p is a non-variable position in s. Since $\beta\sigma' = \alpha_N = \alpha\sigma$ and $s\sigma|_p = l\sigma'$, there is an inference by Right Superposition as follows:

$$\frac{\beta \,\|\, \Lambda \to \Pi, l{\simeq}r \quad \alpha \,\|\, \Gamma \to \Delta, s{\simeq}t}{(\beta \,\|\, \Lambda, \Gamma \to \Pi, \Delta, s[r]_p{\simeq}t)\sigma_1\sigma_2} \quad \sigma_1 := \mathrm{mgu}(s|_p, l),\ \sigma_2 = \mathrm{mgu}(\beta\sigma_1, \alpha\sigma_1)$$

As before, a contradiction can be derived from the existence of the ground instance $(\beta \,\|\, \Lambda, \Gamma \to \Pi, \Delta, s[r]_p{\simeq}t)\sigma\sigma'$ of the conclusion.

(v) $C = \Gamma \to \Delta, s{\simeq}t$ and $s\sigma{\simeq}t\sigma$ is maximal but not strictly maximal in $C\sigma$ with $s\sigma \succ t\sigma$. Then $\Delta = \Delta', s'{\simeq}t'$ such that $s'\sigma{\simeq}t'\sigma$ is also maximal in $C\sigma$, i.e. without loss of generality $s\sigma = s'\sigma$ and $t\sigma = t'\sigma$. Then there is an inference by Equality Factoring as follows:

$$\frac{\alpha \,\|\, \Gamma \to \Delta', s{\simeq}t, s'{\simeq}t'}{(\alpha \,\|\, \Gamma, t{\simeq}t' \to \Delta', s'{\simeq}t')\sigma_1} \quad \sigma_1 = \mathrm{mgu}(s, s')$$

In analogy to the previous cases, a contradiction can be derived from the existence of the ground instance $(\alpha \,\|\, \Gamma, t{\simeq}t' \to \Delta', s'{\simeq}t')\sigma$ of the conclusion.

(vi) $C\sigma$ does not contain any maximal literal at all, i.e. $C = \Box$. Since $\alpha\sigma = \alpha_N$ by Lemma 4.8(ii) but $\mathcal{I}_N \not\models \alpha\sigma{\simeq}\alpha_N$ by definition of α_N, this cannot happen.

4.2 First-Order Reasoning in Fixed Domains

If $C = \Gamma, s{\simeq}t \to \Delta$, where $s{\simeq}t$ is selected, there are two possibilities: If $s\sigma = t\sigma$, then the same derivation as in case (i) again leads to a contradiction. And if $s\sigma \neq t\sigma$, then the same holds for case (ii). Since a contradiction is obtained in each case, the initial assumption must be false, i.e. the proposition holds. ◊

For the construction of $\mathcal{I}_N$, I require α_N to be minimal. For non-minimal α_N, the proposition does not hold:

Example 4.10 (Non-Minimal Constraints)
If $N_{ab} = \{v{\simeq}a \,\|\, \to a{\simeq}b,\ v{\simeq}b \,\|\, a{\simeq}b \to\}$ and $a \succ b$, then no inference rule from SFD is applicable to N_{ab}, so N_{ab} is saturated. However, N_{ab} implies $v{\simeq}a \,\|\, \Box$. So the Herbrand interpretation constructed with $\alpha_{N_{ab}} = \{v{\simeq}a\}$ is not a model of N_{ab}.

In Section 4.2.3, I will show how to extend SFD in order to ensure that also interpretations constructed from non-minimal constraints are models.

Proposition 4.9 implies that N has a Herbrand model over Σ when A_N is not covering. On the other hand, whenever N has any Herbrand model over Σ, then A_N is not covering:

Proposition 4.11 (Herbrand-Unsatisfiability)
Let N be a set of constrained clauses over Σ for which A_N is covering. Then N does not have any Herbrand model over Σ.

Proof. This follows directly from Lemma 2.43, which states that already the set of constrained empty clauses in N does not have a Herbrand model over Σ. ◊

A constrained clause set N for which A_N is covering may nevertheless have both non-Herbrand models and Herbrand models over an extended signature: If the constant a is the only function symbol and $N = \{v{\simeq}a \,\|\, \Box\}$ then A_N is covering, but any first-order interpretation with a universe of at least two elements is a model of N.

Propositions 4.9 and 4.11 constitute the following theorem:

Theorem 4.12 (Refutational Completeness)
Let N be a set of positively constrained clauses over Σ that is saturated with respect to SFD. Then N has a Herbrand model over Σ if, and only if, A_N is not covering.

Moreover, the classical notions of (first-order) theorem proving derivations and fairness from Bachmair and Ganzinger (1994) carry over to the current setting.

Chapter 4: A Superposition Calculus for Fixed Domains

Definition 4.13 (Theorem Proving Derivations)
A (finite or countably infinite) $\models_\Sigma$ *theorem proving derivation* is a sequence $N_0, N_1, \ldots$ of sets of constrained clauses, such that either

- (Deduction) $N_{i+1} = N_i \cup \{\alpha \,\|\, C\}$ and $N_i \models_\Sigma N_{i+1}$, or

- (Deletion) $N_{i+1} = N_i \setminus \{\alpha \,\|\, C\}$ and $\alpha \,\|\, C$ is redundant with respect to N_i.

If N is a saturated set of positively constrained clauses for which A_N is not covering, a $\models_{Ind}$ *theorem proving derivation for* N is a sequence $N_0, N_1, \ldots$ of constrained clause sets such that $N \subseteq N_0$ and either

- (Deduction) $N_{i+1} = N_i \cup \{\alpha \,\|\, C\}$ and $N \models_{Ind} N_i \implies N \models_{Ind} N_{i+1}$, or

- (Deletion) $N_{i+1} = N_i \setminus \{\alpha \,\|\, C\}$ and $\alpha \,\|\, C$ is redundant with respect to N_i.

Due to the semantics of constrained clauses and specifically the fact that all constrained clauses in a set are connected by common existential quantifiers, it does not suffice to require that $N_i \models_\Sigma \alpha \,\|\, C$ (or $N_i \models_{Ind} \alpha \,\|\, C$, respectively). E.g. for the signature $\Sigma = \{a, b\}$ and $b \succ a$, the constrained clause $\alpha \,\|\, C = v {\simeq} x \,\|\, \to x {\simeq} b$ is modeled by every Herbrand interpretation over Σ, but $\{v {\simeq} x \,\|\, \to x {\simeq} a\} \not\models_{Ind} \{v {\simeq} x \,\|\, \to x {\simeq} a\} \cup \{\alpha \,\|\, C\}$.

The calculus SFD is sound, i.e. I may employ it for deductions in both types of theorem proving derivations:

Lemma 4.14
Let N be a set of constrained clauses over Σ, let $\beta \,\|\, D$ be the conclusion of a SFD inference with premises in N and let $\mathcal{I}$ be a Herbrand interpretation. Then N and $N \cup \{\beta \,\|\, D\}$ have the same solutions in $\mathcal{I}$.

Proof. Surely every solution of $N \cup \{\beta \,\|\, D\}$ in $\mathcal{I}$ is a solution of the subset N.

For the converse implication let $\sigma_0 : \mathcal{V} \to \mathcal{T}(\Sigma)$ be a solution of N and let τ be a substitution that is grounding for $\beta \,\|\, D$ such that $\mathcal{I} \models \beta \sigma_0 \sigma \tau$. It remains to be shown that $\mathcal{I} \models D\tau$.

Note that if $\beta \,\|\, D$ is the conclusion of an inference

$$\frac{\alpha_1 \,\|\, C_1 \quad \alpha_2 \,\|\, C_2}{\beta \,\|\, D}$$

involving the unifier $\sigma = \sigma_1 \sigma_2$, then the premises can be assumed to be renamed such that they do not share any universal variables and τ can hence be

4.2 First-Order Reasoning in Fixed Domains

extended to a grounding substitution with domain $\operatorname{var}(\beta \parallel D) \cup \operatorname{var}(\alpha_1 \parallel C_1\sigma) \cup \operatorname{var}(\alpha_2 \parallel C_2\sigma)$.

Consider the different possible inferences that could produce $\beta \parallel D$:

- Let $\beta \parallel D$ be the conclusion of an Equality Resolution inference:

$$\frac{\alpha \parallel \Gamma, s{\simeq}t \to \Delta}{(\alpha \parallel \Gamma \to \Delta)\sigma}$$

Assume that $\mathcal{I} \models \alpha\sigma_0\sigma\tau$ and $\Gamma\sigma\tau \subseteq \mathcal{I}$ hold. It must be shown that $\Delta\sigma\tau \cap \mathcal{I} \neq \emptyset$. Because σ_0 is a solution of N in $\mathcal{I}$ and $\sigma\tau$ is grounding for the premise, i.e. $\mathcal{I} \models (\Gamma, s{\simeq}t \to \Delta)\sigma\tau$, this implies that either $(s{\simeq}t)\sigma\tau$ does not hold in $\mathcal{I}$ or $\Delta\sigma\tau \cap \mathcal{I} \neq \emptyset$. Because $s\sigma\tau = t\sigma\tau$, the equation $(s{\simeq}t)\sigma\tau$ holds in $\mathcal{I}$, so $\Delta\sigma\tau \cap \mathcal{I} \neq \emptyset$.

- Let $\beta \parallel D$ be the conclusion of an Equality Factoring inference:

$$\frac{\alpha \parallel \Gamma \to \Delta, s{\simeq}t, s'{\simeq}t'}{(\alpha \parallel \Gamma, t{\simeq}t' \to \Delta, s'{\simeq}t')\sigma}$$

Assume that $\mathcal{I} \models \alpha\sigma_0\sigma\tau$ and $(\Gamma, t{\simeq}t')\sigma\tau \subseteq \mathcal{I}$ hold. Because σ_0 is a solution of N in $\mathcal{I}$ and $\sigma\tau$ is grounding for the premise, i.e. $\mathcal{I} \models (\Gamma \to \Delta, s{\simeq}t, s'{\simeq}t')\sigma\tau$, this implies that $(\Delta, s{\simeq}t, s'{\simeq}t')\sigma\tau \cap \mathcal{I} \neq \emptyset$. Because of $s\sigma\tau = s'\sigma\tau$ and the assumption $\mathcal{I} \models (t{\simeq}t')\sigma\tau$, it holds that $\mathcal{I} \models (s{\simeq}t)\sigma\tau$ if, and only if, $\mathcal{I} \models (s'{\simeq}t')\sigma\tau$. Hence $(\Delta, s'{\simeq}t')\sigma\tau \cap \mathcal{I} \neq \emptyset$.

- Let $\beta \parallel D$ be the conclusion of a Left Superposition inference:

$$\frac{\alpha_1 \parallel \Gamma_1 \to \Delta_1, l{\simeq}r \quad \alpha_2 \parallel \Gamma_2, s[l']_p{\simeq}t \to \Delta_2}{(\alpha_1, \alpha_2^{\ddot{z}} \parallel \Gamma_1, \Gamma_2, s[r]_p{\simeq}t \to \Delta_1, \Delta_2)\sigma}$$

Assume that $\mathcal{I} \models (\alpha_1, \alpha_2^{\ddot{z}})\sigma_0\sigma\tau$ and $(\Gamma_1, \Gamma_2, s[r]_p{\simeq}t)\sigma\tau \subseteq \mathcal{I}$ hold. Because $\alpha_1^{\ddot{z}}\sigma\tau = \alpha_2^{\ddot{z}}\sigma\tau$ and σ_0 is a solution of N in $\mathcal{I}$ and $\sigma\tau$ is grounding for the premises, i.e. $\mathcal{I} \models (\Gamma_1 \to \Delta_1, l{\simeq}r)\sigma\tau$ and $\mathcal{I} \models (\Gamma_2, s[l']_p{\simeq}t \to \Delta_2)\sigma\tau$, this implies that

(i) $\Delta_1\sigma\tau \cap \mathcal{I} \neq \emptyset$ or $\mathcal{I} \models (l{\simeq}r)\sigma\tau$, and
(ii) $\mathcal{I} \not\models (s[l']_p{\simeq}t)\sigma\tau$ or $\Delta_2\sigma\tau \cap \mathcal{I} \neq \emptyset$.

If $\Delta_1\sigma\tau \cap \mathcal{I} = \Delta_2\sigma\tau \cap \mathcal{I} = \emptyset$, then $\mathcal{I} \models (l{\simeq}r)\sigma\tau$ and $\mathcal{I} \not\models (s[l']_p{\simeq}t)\sigma\tau$ and the additional identity $l'\sigma\tau = l\sigma\tau$ lead to $\mathcal{I} \not\models (s[r]_p{\simeq}t)\sigma\tau$, which contradicts the assumption. So it holds that $\Delta_1\sigma\tau \cap \mathcal{I} \neq \emptyset$ or $\Delta_2\sigma\tau \cap \mathcal{I} \neq \emptyset$.

Chapter 4: A Superposition Calculus for Fixed Domains

- Let $\beta \| D$ be the conclusion of a Right Superposition inference:

$$\frac{\alpha_1 \| \Gamma_1 \to \Delta_1, l{\simeq}r \quad \alpha_2 \| \Gamma_2 \to \Delta_2, s[l']_p{\simeq}t}{(\alpha_1, \alpha_2^{\not{z}} \| \Gamma_1, \Gamma_2 \to \Delta_1, \Delta_2, s[r]_p{\simeq}t)\sigma_1\sigma_2}$$

Assume that $\mathcal{I} \models (\alpha_1, \alpha_2^{\not{z}})\sigma_0\sigma\tau$ and $(\Gamma_1, \Gamma_2)\sigma\tau \subseteq \mathcal{I}$ hold. Because $\alpha_1^{\simeq}\sigma\tau = \alpha_2^{\simeq}\sigma\tau$ and σ_0 is a solution of N in $\mathcal{I}$ and $\sigma\tau$ is grounding for the premises, i.e. $\mathcal{I} \models (\Gamma_1 \to \Delta_1, l{\simeq}r)\sigma\tau$ and $\mathcal{I} \models (\Gamma_2 \to \Delta_2, s[l']_p{\simeq}t)\sigma\tau$, this implies that

  (i) $\Delta_1\sigma\tau \cap \mathcal{I} \neq \emptyset$ or $\mathcal{I} \models (l{\simeq}r)\sigma\tau$, and
  (ii) $\mathcal{I} \models (s[l']_p{\simeq}t)\sigma\tau$ or $\Delta_2\sigma\tau \cap \mathcal{I} \neq \emptyset$.

If $\Delta_1\sigma\tau \cap \mathcal{I} \neq \emptyset$ or $\Delta_2\sigma\tau \cap \mathcal{I} \neq \emptyset$, then $\mathcal{I} \models D\sigma\tau$. Otherwise $\mathcal{I} \models (l{\simeq}r)\sigma\tau$ and $\mathcal{I} \models (s[l']_p{\simeq}t)\sigma\tau$. The additional identity $l'\sigma\tau = l\sigma\tau$ leads to $\mathcal{I} \models (s[r]_p{\simeq}t)\sigma\tau$, and again $\mathcal{I} \models D\sigma\tau$.

- Let $\beta \| D$ be the conclusion of a Constraint Superposition inference:

$$\frac{\alpha_1 \| \Gamma_1 \to \Delta_1, l{\simeq}r \quad \alpha_2[l']_p \| \Gamma_2 \to \Delta_2}{(\alpha_2[r]_p, \alpha_1^{\not{z}} \| \alpha_1^{\simeq}{\simeq}\alpha_2^{\simeq}[r]_p, \Gamma_1, \Gamma_2 \to \Delta_1, \Delta_2)\sigma}$$

Assume that $\mathcal{I} \models (\alpha_2[r]_p, \alpha_1^{\not{z}})\sigma_0\sigma\tau$ and $(\alpha_1^{\simeq}{\simeq}\alpha_2^{\simeq}[r]_p, \Gamma_1, \Gamma_2)\sigma\tau \subseteq \mathcal{I}$ hold. Because σ_0 is a solution of N in $\mathcal{I}$ and $\sigma\tau$ is grounding for the premises, this implies that

  (i) $\mathcal{I} \models \alpha_1\sigma_0\sigma\tau$ implies $\Delta_1\sigma\tau \cap \mathcal{I} \neq \emptyset$ or $\mathcal{I} \models (l{\simeq}r)\sigma\tau$, and
  (ii) $\mathcal{I} \models \alpha_2[l']_p\sigma_0\sigma\tau$ implies $\Delta_2\sigma\tau \cap \mathcal{I} \neq \emptyset$.

Assume that $\Delta_1\sigma\tau \cap \mathcal{I} = \Delta_2\sigma\tau \cap \mathcal{I} = \emptyset$. Then $\mathcal{I} \not\models \alpha_2[l']_p\sigma_0\sigma\tau$. Because of $\mathcal{I} \models \alpha_2[r]_p\sigma_0\sigma\tau$ and $l'\sigma\tau = l\sigma\tau$, this directly implies $\mathcal{I} \not\models (l{\simeq}r)\sigma\tau$. So (i) yields $\mathcal{I} \not\models \alpha_1\sigma_0\sigma\tau$, which in combination with $\mathcal{I} \models \alpha_1^{\simeq}{\simeq}\alpha_2^{\simeq}[r]_p$ contradicts $\mathcal{I} \models (\alpha_2[r]_p, \alpha_1^{\not{z}})\sigma_0\sigma\tau$. So it holds that $\Delta_1\sigma\tau \cap \mathcal{I} \neq \emptyset$ or $\Delta_2\sigma\tau \cap \mathcal{I} \neq \emptyset$.

- Let $\beta \| D$ be the conclusion of a Equality Elimination inference:

$$\frac{\alpha_1 \| \Gamma \to \Delta, l{\simeq}r \quad \alpha_2[r']_p \| \Box}{(\alpha_1, \alpha_2^{\not{z}} \| \Gamma \to \Delta)\sigma}$$

Assume that $\mathcal{I} \models (\alpha_1, \alpha_2^{\not{z}})\sigma_0\sigma\tau$ and $\Gamma\sigma\tau \subseteq \mathcal{I}$ hold. Because σ_0 is a solution of N in $\mathcal{I}$ and $\sigma\tau$ is grounding for the premises, i.e. $\mathcal{I} \models (\Gamma \to \Delta, l{\simeq}r)\sigma\tau$ and $\mathcal{I} \not\models \alpha_2[r']_p\sigma_0\sigma\tau$, this implies that

  (i) $\Delta\sigma\tau \cap \mathcal{I} \neq \emptyset$ or $\mathcal{I} \models (l{\simeq}r)\sigma\tau$, and

(ii) $\mathcal{I} \not\models \alpha_{\tilde{2}}[r']_p \sigma_0 \sigma \tau$.

Assume $\mathcal{I} \models (l \simeq r)\sigma \tau$. The additional identity $r'\sigma\tau = r\sigma\tau$ leads to $\mathcal{I} \not\models \alpha_{\tilde{2}}[l]_p \sigma_0 \sigma \tau$, which contradicts $\mathcal{I} \models \alpha_{\tilde{1}} \sigma_0 \sigma \tau$ because $\alpha_{\tilde{1}}\sigma = \alpha_{\tilde{2}}[l]_p\sigma$.
So $\Delta \sigma \tau \cap \mathcal{I} \neq \emptyset$, an hence $\mathcal{I} \models D\sigma\tau$. $\diamond$

Proposition 4.15 (Soundness)
The calculus SFD is sound for $\models_\Sigma$ and $\models_{Ind}$ theorem proving derivations:

(i) Let $\alpha \parallel C$ be the conclusion of a SFD inference with premises in N. Then $N \models_\Sigma N \cup \{\alpha \parallel C\}$.

(ii) Let N be saturated with respect to SFD, let A_N not be covering, and let $\alpha \parallel C$ be the conclusion of a SFD inference with premises in $N \cup N'$. Then $N \models_{Ind} N'$ if, and only if, $N \models_{Ind} N' \cup \{\alpha \parallel C\}$.

Proof. This follows directly from Lemma 4.14. $\diamond$

As usual, fairness can be ensured by systematically adding conclusions of non-redundant inferences, making these inferences redundant.

Because it relies on redundancy and fairness rather than on a concrete inference calculus (as long as this calculus is sound), the proof of the next theorem is exactly as in the unconstrained case (Bachmair and Ganzinger, 1994, Theorem 5.12):

Theorem 4.16 (Saturation)
Let $N_0, N_1, N_2, \ldots$ be a fair $\models_\Sigma$ theorem proving derivation. Then the set $N_\infty = \bigcup_j \bigcap_{k \geq j} N_k$ is saturated. Moreover, N_0 has a Herbrand model over Σ if, and only if, N_∞ does.

Let $N_0, N_1, \ldots$ be a fair $\models_{Ind}$ theorem proving derivation for N. Then the set $N \cup N_\infty$ is saturated. Moreover, $N \models_{Ind} N_0$ if, and only if, $N \models_{Ind} N_\infty$.

Example 4.17 (The Elevator, Revisited)
Consider again the example of the elevator presented in Examples 1.1 and 4.3. I will now prove that $\forall y, x. G(y, x) \to R(y, x)$ is valid in all Herbrand models of N_E over the signature Σ_E containing two constants a, b of sort S_{Person} and two constants e, f of sort S_{Elevator}, i.e. that $N_E \cup \{\neg \forall y, x. G(y, x) \to R(y, x)\}$ does not have any Herbrand models over Σ_E. Following the line of thought presented above, the negated query is transformed into the constrained clause set

$$\{ u \simeq x, v \simeq y \parallel R(y, x) \to, \quad u \simeq x, v \simeq y \parallel \to G(y, x) \},$$

where $x : S_{\text{Person}}$ and $y : S_{\text{Elevator}}$, and then saturated together with N_E. This saturation is exactly what happened in Example 4.3. The derived constrained empty clauses are $u{\simeq}x, v{\simeq}a \,\|\, \Box$ and $u{\simeq}x, v{\simeq}b \,\|\, \Box$. Their constraints are covering for Σ_E, which means that the inital constrained clause set does not have any Herbrand models over Σ_E, i.e. that $N_E \models_{\Sigma_E} \forall y, x.G(y,x) \rightarrow R(y,x)$.

4.2.3 Other Herbrand Models of Constrained Clause Sets

A so far open question in the definition of the minimal model $\mathcal{I}_N$ is whether there is the alternative of choosing a non-minimal constraint α_N. Example 4.10 shows that this is in general not possible for sets N that are saturated with respect to the present calculus, but I have also shown after Theorem 4.6 that models corresponding to non-minimal constraints may well be of interest. Such a situation will occur again in Example 4.28 and in Chapter 5, where knowledge about all models will allow me to find a complete set of counterexamples to a query.

To include also Herbrand models arising from non-minimal constraints, I now change the calculus. The trade-off is that I introduce a new and prolific inference rule that may introduce constrained clauses that are larger than the premises. This makes even the saturation of simple constrained clause sets non-terminating. E.g. a derivation starting from

$$\{\,\| \rightarrow f(a){\simeq}a,\ v{\simeq}a \,\| \rightarrow P(a)\}$$

will successively produce all of the increasingly large constrained clauses $v{\simeq}f(a) \,\| \rightarrow P(a),\ v{\simeq}f(f(a)) \,\| \rightarrow P(a)$ and so on.

Definition 4.18 (SFD$^+$)
The *Extended Superposition Calculus for Fixed Domains SFD$^+$* arises from SFD by replacing the Equality Elimination inference rule by the more general rule from Figure 4.3.

Example 4.19 (Treatment of Non-Minimal Constraints)
Reconsider the constrained clause set $N_{ab} = \{v{\simeq}a \,\| \rightarrow a{\simeq}b,\ v{\simeq}b \,\| \, a{\simeq}b \rightarrow\}$ from Example 4.10. The only witness of the Herbrand satisfiability of this set is the instantiation $v \mapsto b$.

For $b \succ a$, the alternative $v \mapsto a$ can be excluded using SFD by applying Constraint Superposition:

$$\begin{array}{rrll}
\text{clauses in } N_{ab}: & 1: & v{\simeq}a \,\| & \rightarrow b{\simeq}a \\
& 2: & v{\simeq}b \,\| & b{\simeq}a \rightarrow \\
\text{Constraint Superposition}(1,2) = & 3: & v{\simeq}a \,\| & a{\simeq}a, a{\simeq}a \rightarrow \\
\text{Equality Resolution}(3) = & 4: & v{\simeq}a \,\| & a{\simeq}a \rightarrow \\
\text{Equality Resolution}(4) = & 5: & v{\simeq}a \,\| & \Box
\end{array}$$

4.2 First-Order Reasoning in Fixed Domains

Generalized Equality Elimination:

$$\frac{\alpha_1 \parallel \Gamma_1 \to \Delta_1, l{\simeq}r \quad \alpha_2[r']_p \parallel \Gamma_2 \to \Delta_2}{(\alpha_2[l]_p, \alpha_1^{\not\approx} \parallel \alpha_1^{\approx}{\simeq}\alpha_2^{\approx}[l], \Gamma_1, \Gamma_2 \to \Delta_1, \Delta_2)\sigma}$$

where

(i) $\sigma = \mathrm{mgu}(r, r')$,
(ii) no literal is selected in the first premise and $l\sigma{\simeq}r\sigma$ is strictly maximal in $(\Gamma_1 \to \Delta_1, l{\simeq}r)\sigma$,
(iii) $r\sigma \not\succeq l\sigma$,
(iv) r' is not a variable, and
(v) p is a position in the positive part $\alpha_2^{\approx}$ of α_2.

Figure 4.3: The Additional Rule of the Calculus SFD$^+$

For $a \succ b$, the set N_{ab} is saturated with respect to SFD and $v \mapsto a$ is only implicitly by the minimality requirement. However, additional inferences are possible using SFD$^+$, resulting in a derivation similar to the one above:

clauses in N_{ab}:
$\quad 1:\ v{\simeq}a \parallel \qquad\qquad \to a{\simeq}b$
$\quad 2:\ v{\simeq}b \parallel \qquad a{\simeq}b \to$
Generalized Equality Elimination(1,2) $= 3:\ v{\simeq}a \parallel a{\simeq}a, a{\simeq}a \to$
Equality Resolution(3) $= 4:\ v{\simeq}a \parallel \qquad a{\simeq}a \to$
Equality Resolution(4) $= 5:\ v{\simeq}a \parallel \qquad\qquad\qquad\quad \square$

So all non-covered constraints of the SFD$^+$-saturated set provide models of N_{ab}.

The extended calculus is also sound:

Lemma 4.20
Let N be a set of constrained clauses over Σ, let $\beta \parallel D$ be the conclusion of a SFD$^+$ inference with premises in N and let $\mathcal{I}$ be a Herbrand interpretation. Then N and $N \cup \{\beta \parallel D\}$ have the same solutions in $\mathcal{I}$.

Proof. Surely every solution of $N \cup \{\beta \parallel D\}$ in $\mathcal{I}$ is a solution of the subset N.

For the converse implication let $\sigma_0 : \mathcal{V} \to \mathcal{T}(\Sigma)$ be a solution of N and let τ be a substitution that is grounding for $\beta \parallel D$ such that $\mathcal{I} \models \beta\sigma_0\sigma\tau$. It remains to be shown that $\mathcal{I} \models D\tau$.

Chapter 4: A Superposition Calculus for Fixed Domains

The only new case compared to Lemma 4.14 is the one where $\beta \parallel D$ is the conclusion of a Generalized Equality Elimination inference:

$$\frac{\alpha_1 \parallel \Gamma_1 \to \Delta_1, l{\simeq}r \quad \alpha_2[r']_p \parallel \Gamma_2 \to \Delta_2}{(\alpha_2[l]_p, \alpha_1^{\neq} \parallel \alpha_1^{\simeq}{\simeq}\alpha_2^{\simeq}[l], \Gamma_1, \Gamma_2 \to \Delta_1, \Delta_2)\sigma}$$

Again, τ can without loss of generality be considered as extended to a substitution that is also grounding for the premises.

Assume that $\mathcal{I} \models (\alpha_2[l]_p, \alpha_1^{\neq})\sigma_0\sigma\tau$ and $(\alpha_1^{\simeq}{\simeq}\alpha_2^{\simeq}[l], \Gamma_1, \Gamma_2)\sigma\tau \subseteq \mathcal{I}$ hold. Because σ_0 is a solution of N in $\mathcal{I}$ and $\sigma\tau$ is grounding for the premises, this implies that

(i) $\mathcal{I} \models \alpha_1\sigma_0\sigma\tau$ implies $\Delta_1\sigma\tau \cap \mathcal{I} \neq \emptyset$ or $\mathcal{I} \models (l{\simeq}r)\sigma\tau$, and

(ii) $\mathcal{I} \models \alpha_2[r']_p\sigma_0\sigma\tau$ implies $\Delta_2\sigma\tau \cap \mathcal{I} \neq \emptyset$.

Assume that $\Delta_1\sigma\tau \cap \mathcal{I} = \Delta_2\sigma\tau \cap \mathcal{I} = \emptyset$. Then $\mathcal{I} \not\models \alpha_2[r']_p\sigma_0\sigma\tau$. Because of $\mathcal{I} \models \alpha_2[l]_p\sigma_0\sigma\tau$ and $r'\sigma\tau = r\sigma\tau$, this directly implies $\mathcal{I} \not\models (l{\simeq}r)\sigma\tau$. So (i) yields $\mathcal{I} \not\models \alpha_1\sigma_0\sigma\tau$, which in combination with $\mathcal{I} \models \alpha_1^{\simeq}{\simeq}\alpha_2^{\simeq}[l]_p$ contradicts $\mathcal{I} \models \alpha_2[l]_p\sigma_0\sigma\tau$.

So the assumption was false and $\Delta_1\sigma\tau \cap \mathcal{I} \neq \emptyset$ or $\Delta_2\sigma\tau \cap \mathcal{I} \neq \emptyset$ holds, and hence $\mathcal{I} \models D\sigma\tau$. ◇

Note that in a purely predicative setting, i.e. when all equations outside constraints are of the form $t{\simeq}c_{\text{true}}$, the separation of the predicative sort from all other sorts prevents the application of both the original and the new Equality Elimination rule. So the calculi SFD and SFD$^+$ coincide in this case.

Definition 4.21 (α_N)
Let N be a set of constrained clauses. If A_N is not covering, then let α_N be *any* ground constraint that is not an instance of any constraint in A_N (note that α_N does not have to be minimal). Otherwise let α_N be arbitrary.

Since the proof of Lemma 4.7 depends strongly on the minimality of α_N, I have to change the proof strategy and cannot rely on previous results.

Lemma 4.22
Let N be a set of positively constrained clauses that is saturated with respect to SFD$^+$. Assume that A_N is not covering and fix some α_N. If $\mathcal{I}_N \not\models N$, then there is a ground instance $(\alpha \parallel C)\sigma$ of a constrained clause in N such that $\mathcal{I}_N \not\models (\alpha \parallel C)\sigma$ and $\alpha\sigma = \alpha_N$.

Proof. Let $(\alpha \parallel C)\sigma$ be the minimal ground instance of a constrained clause in N such that $\mathcal{I}_N \not\models (\alpha \parallel C)\sigma$. I first show that it suffices to examine the case where α_N rewrites to $\alpha\sigma$ using R_N and then solve this case.

4.2 First-Order Reasoning in Fixed Domains

$\mathcal{I}_N \not\models (\alpha \,\|\, C)\sigma$ implies $\mathcal{I}_N \models \alpha\sigma {\simeq} \alpha_N$, thus by confluence of R_N, it holds that

$$\alpha\sigma \to^*_{R_N} \alpha_0 \quad \text{and} \quad \alpha_N \to^*_{R_N} \alpha_0 \,,$$

where α_0 is the normal form of α_N under R_N. I show that $\alpha\sigma = \alpha_0$.

If $\alpha\sigma \neq \alpha_0$, then there is a rule $l\sigma' \to r\sigma' \in R_N$ that was produced by the ground instance $(\beta \,\|\, \Lambda \to \Pi, l{\simeq}r)\sigma'$ of a positively constrained clause $\beta \,\|\, \Lambda \to \Pi, l{\simeq}r \in N$ such that $\alpha\sigma[l\sigma']_p$ reduces via R_N to $\alpha\sigma[r\sigma']_p$. By definition of productivity, no literals are selected in this constrained clause.

If p is a variable position in α or not a position in α at all, then the rule actually reduces σ, which contradicts the minimality of $(\alpha \,\|\, C)\sigma$. So p must be a non-variable position of α. Let $C = \Gamma \to \Delta$. Then there is a Constraint Superposition inference as follows:

$$\frac{\beta \,\|\, \Lambda \to \Pi, l{\simeq}r \quad \alpha \,\|\, \Gamma \to \Delta}{(\alpha[r]_p \,\|\, \beta{\simeq}\alpha[r]_p, \Lambda, \Gamma \to \Pi, \Delta)\tau} \quad \tau = \mathrm{mgu}(\alpha|_p, l)$$

The ground instance $\delta \,\|\, D := (\alpha[r]_p \,\|\, \beta{\simeq}\alpha[r]_p, \Lambda, \Gamma \to \Pi, \Delta)\sigma\sigma'$ of the conclusion is not modeled by $\mathcal{I}_N$. On the other hand, because N is saturated, the ground instance

$$\frac{(\beta \,\|\, \Lambda \to \Pi, l{\simeq}r)\sigma' \quad (\alpha \,\|\, \Gamma \to \Delta)\sigma}{(\alpha[r]_p \,\|\, \beta{\simeq}\alpha[r]_p, \Lambda, \Gamma \to \Pi, \Delta)\sigma\sigma'}$$

of the above inference is redundant. The first premise cannot be redundant because it is productive; the second one cannot be redundant because of the minimality of $(\alpha \,\|\, \Gamma \to \Delta)\sigma$. This means that the conclusion follows from ground instances of constrained clauses in N all of which are smaller than the maximal premise $(\alpha \,\|\, \Gamma \to \Delta)\sigma$. All these ground instances are modeled by $\mathcal{I}_N$, and so $\mathcal{I}_N \models \delta \,\|\, D$.

So whenever $\mathcal{I}_N \not\models N$, there is a ground instance $(\alpha \,\|\, C)\sigma$ of a constrained clause in N such that $\mathcal{I}_N \not\models (\alpha \,\|\, C)\sigma$ and $\alpha\sigma = \alpha_0$. In particular $\alpha_N \xrightarrow{*}_{R_N} \alpha\sigma$. Let $n \in \mathbb{N}$ be the minimal number for which there is a ground instance $(\alpha \,\|\, C)\sigma$ of a constrained clause $\alpha \,\|\, C = \alpha \,\|\, \Gamma \to \Delta$ in N such that $\mathcal{I}_N \not\models (\alpha \,\|\, C)\sigma$ and α_N rewrites to $\alpha\sigma$ via R_N in n steps, written $\alpha_N \to^n_{R_N} \alpha\sigma$. I have to show that $n = 0$.

Assume $n > 0$. Then the last step of the derivation $\alpha_N \to^n_{R_N} \alpha\sigma$ is of the form $\alpha\sigma[l\sigma']_p \to_{R_N} \alpha\sigma[r\sigma']_p = \alpha\sigma$, where the rule $l\sigma' \to r\sigma' \in R_N$ has been produced by a constrained clause $\beta \,\|\, \Lambda \to \Pi, l{\simeq}r \in N$ with $\beta\sigma' = \alpha_N$. By definition of productivity, no literals are selected in this constrained clause. There are two cases to consider:

- If p is a variable position in α or not a position in α at all, let $p = p'p''$ such that $\alpha|_{p'} = x$ is a variable. Let τ be the substitution that coincides with σ except that $x\tau = x\sigma[l\sigma']_{p''}$. Then $\mathcal{I}_N \not\models (\alpha \,\|\, C)\tau$ and $\alpha_N \to_{R_N}^{n-1} \alpha\tau$ contradicts the minimality of n.

- Otherwise there is an Equality Elimination inference as follows:

$$\frac{\beta \,\|\, \Lambda \to \Pi, l{\simeq}r \quad \alpha \,\|\, \Gamma \to \Delta}{(\alpha[l]_p \,\|\, \beta{\simeq}\alpha[l]_p, \Lambda, \Gamma \to \Pi, \Delta)\tau} \quad \tau = \mathrm{mgu}(\alpha|_p, r)$$

The ground instance $\delta \,\|\, D := (\alpha[l]_p \,\|\, \beta{\simeq}\alpha[l]_p, \Lambda, \Gamma \to \Pi, \Delta)\sigma\sigma'$ of the conclusion is not modeled by $\mathcal{I}_N$. In particular, $\mathcal{I}_N \models \delta$ and $\mathcal{I}_N \not\models D$.

Since the inference, and hence also the constrained clause $\delta \,\|\, D$ is redundant, there are constrained clauses $\delta_1 \,\|\, D_1, \ldots, \delta_m \,\|\, D_m \in N$ together with substitutions $\sigma_1, \ldots, \sigma_m$, such that all $\delta_i\sigma_i$ are satisfiable and $\delta^{\simeq} = \delta_i^{\simeq}\sigma_i$ for all i and $D_1\sigma_1, \ldots, D_m\sigma_m \models D$. This implies that $\mathcal{I}_N \not\models (\delta_i \,\|\, D_i)\sigma_i$ for at least one of the constrained clause instances $(\delta_i \,\|\, D_i)\sigma_i$. Since $\alpha_N \to_{R_N}^{n-1} \delta_i^{\simeq}\sigma_i = \delta^{\simeq} = \alpha\sigma[l\sigma']_p$, this contradicts the minimality of n.

So $n = 0$ follows, which proves $\alpha\sigma = \alpha_N$. ◇

With this preparatory work done, Proposition 4.11 and Theorem 4.12 can be reproved in this new setting:

Proposition 4.23 ($\mathcal{I}_N$ is a Model)
Let N be a set of positively constrained clauses that is saturated with respect to SFD$^+$. Then $\mathcal{I}_N^{\alpha_N} \models N$ for any ground constraint α_N that is not covered by $\mathcal{A}_N$.

Proof. The proof is almost identical to the proof of Proposition 4.9. The only difference is that, instead of reasoning about the minimal ground instance $(\alpha \,\|\, C)\sigma$ of a positively constrained clause $\alpha \,\|\, C \in N$ that is not modeled by $\mathcal{I}_N$, the minimal such instance that additionally satisfies $\alpha\sigma = \alpha_N$ can be considered. Lemma 4.22 states that this is sufficient. ◇

Theorem 4.24 (Refutational Completeness)
Let N be a set of positively constrained clauses over Σ that is saturated with respect to SFD$^+$. Then N has a Herbrand model over Σ if, and only if, $\mathcal{A}_N$ is not covering.

4.3 Minimal Model Reasoning

Given a constrained or unconstrained clause set N, it is often not only of interest whether N is (un)satisfiable (with or without respect to a fixed domain), but which properties specific Herbrand models of a N over Σ have, especially $\mathcal{I}_N$. These are not always disjoint problems: I will show in Proposition 4.25 that, for some N and queries of the form $\exists \vec{x}.A_1 \wedge \ldots \wedge A_n$, first-order validity and validity in $\mathcal{I}_N$ coincide, so that the latter can be explored with first-order techniques.

The result can be extended further: I will use the superposition calculus SFD to demonstrate classes of constrained clause sets N and H for which $N \models_\Sigma H$ and $N \models_{Ind} H$ coincide (Proposition 4.26). Finally, I will present a way to improve the termination of the approach for proving properties of $\mathcal{I}_N$ (Theorem 4.34).

In this context, it is important to carefully observe the semantics of an expression $N \models_{Ind} H$ when N is constrained. Consider for example a signature containing two constants a, b with $a \succ b$, $N_P = \{v \simeq x \,\|\, \to P(x)\}$ and $H_P = \{v \simeq x \,\|\, P(x) \to\}$. Then $N_P \cup H_P$ is unsatisfiable, but nevertheless H_P is valid in the model $\mathcal{I}_{N_P} = \{P(b)\}$, i.e. $N_P \models_{Ind} H_P$. These difficulties vanish when the existential variables in N_P and H_P are renamed apart.

4.3.1 Relations between First-order, Fixed Domain, and Minimal Model Validity

Even with standard first-order superposition, it is possible to prove that first-order validity and validity in $\mathcal{I}_N$ coincide for some N and properties Γ:

Proposition 4.25 (Minimal Model and First-order Validity)
If N is a saturated set of unconstrained Horn clauses over Σ and Γ is a conjunction of positive literals over Σ with existential closure $\exists \vec{x}.\Gamma$, then

$$N \models_{Ind} \exists \vec{x}.\Gamma \iff N \models \exists \vec{x}.\Gamma .$$

Proof. $N \models \exists \vec{x}.\Gamma$ holds if, and only if, the set $N \cup \{\forall \vec{x}.\neg\Gamma\}$ is unsatisfiable. N is Horn, so during saturation of $N \cup \{\neg\Gamma\}$, where inferences between clauses in N need not be performed, only purely negative, hence non-productive, clauses can appear. That means that the Herbrand interpretation $\mathcal{I}_{N'}$ is the same for every clause set N' in the derivation. So $N \cup \{\neg\Gamma\}$ is unsatisfiable if, and only if, $N \not\models_{Ind} \forall \vec{x}.\neg\Gamma$, which is in turn equivalent to $N \models_{Ind} \exists \vec{x}.\Gamma$. ◊

If N and Γ additionally belong to the Horn fragment of a first-order logic (clause) class decidable by unconstrained superposition, such as for example

Chapter 4: A Superposition Calculus for Fixed Domains

the monadic class with equality (Bachmair et al., 1993) or the guarded fragment with equality (Ganzinger and Nivelle, 1999), it is thus decidable whether $N \models_{Ind} \exists \vec{x}.\Gamma$.

Given the superposition calculus for fixed domains SFD, it is also possible to show that a result similar to Proposition 4.25 holds for universally quantified queries.

Proposition 4.26 (Minimal Model and Fixed Domain Validity)
If N is a saturated set of Horn clauses over Σ and Γ is a conjunction of positive literals over Σ with universal closure $\forall \vec{v}.\Gamma$, then

$$N \models_{Ind} \forall \vec{v}.\Gamma \iff N \models_\Sigma \forall \vec{v}.\Gamma .$$

Proof. $N \models_\Sigma \forall \vec{v}.\Gamma$ holds if, and only if, $N \cup \{\exists \vec{v}.\neg \Gamma\}$ does not have a Herbrand model over Σ.

If $N \cup \{\exists \vec{v}.\neg \Gamma\}$ does not have a Herbrand model over Σ, then obviously $N \not\models_{Ind} \exists \vec{v}.\neg \Gamma$.

Otherwise, consider the positively constrained clause $\alpha \,\|\, \Delta \to$ corresponding to the formula $\exists \vec{v}.\neg \Gamma$ and assume without loss of generality that the existential variables in N and α are renamed apart. The minimal models of the two sets N and $N \cup \{\alpha \,\|\, \Delta \to\}$ are identical, since during the saturation of $N \cup \{\alpha \,\|\, \Delta \to\}$ inferences between clauses in N need not be performed and so only purely negative, hence non-productive, constrained clauses can be derived. This in turn just means that $N \models_{Ind} \exists \vec{v}.\neg \Gamma$. ◇

These propositions can also be proved using arguments from model theory. The shown proofs using standard superposition or SFD, respectively, notably the argument about the lack of new productive clauses, illustrate recurring crucial concepts of superposition-based theorem proving in minimal models. Example 4.28 will show that other superposition-based algorithms often fail because they cannot obviate the derivation of productive clauses.

Example 4.27
Consider the partial definition of the usual ordering on the naturals given by the clause set $N_{GT} = \{\to GT(s(0), 0),\ GT(x, y) \to GT(s(x), s(y))\}$ over the signature $\Sigma_{GT} = (\{GT\}, \{s, 0\})$, as shown in the introduction. I will use Proposition 4.26 to check whether or not $N_{GT} \models_{\Sigma_{GT}} \forall x. GT(s(x), x)$. The first

112

4.3 Minimal Model Reasoning

steps of a possible derivation are as follows:

clauses in N:	1:		$\to GT(s(0),0)$
	2:		$GT(x,y) \to GT(s(x),s(y))$
negated conjecture:	3:	$v{\simeq}x$	$\| GT(s(x),x) \to$
Superposition(1,3) =	4:	$v{\simeq}0$	$\|$ $\square$
Superposition(2,3) =	5:	$v{\simeq}s(y)$	$\| GT(s(y),y) \to$
Superposition(1,5) =	6:	$v{\simeq}s(0)$	$\|$ $\square$
Superposition(2,5) =	7:	$v{\simeq}s(s(z))$	$\| GT(s(z),z) \to$

In the sequel, the constrained clauses 1 and 2 are repeatedly superposed into (descendants of) the constrained clause 5. This way, all constrained clauses of the forms $v{\simeq}s^n(x) \,\|\, GT(s(x),x) \to$ and $v{\simeq}s^n(0) \,\|\, \square$ are successively derived, where the expression $s^n(0)$ denotes the n-fold application $s(\ldots s(s(0))\ldots)$ of s to 0, and analogously for $s^n(x)$. Since the constraints of the derived constrained empty clauses are covering in the limit, it follows that $N_{GT} \models_{\Sigma_{GT}} \forall x.\,GT(s(x),x)$.

Because saturation does not terminate on the previous example, an *automated* proof of $N_{GT} \models_{\Sigma_{GT}} \forall x.\,GT(s(x),x)$ using SFD alone is not possible. I will later present two extensions of the calculus for which saturation does terminate and the proof thus becomes completely automated (cf. Examples 4.36 and 6.52).

Using Proposition 4.26, the calculus SFD can be employed for fixed domain reasoning to also decide properties of minimal models. This is even possible in cases for which neither the approach of Ganzinger and Stuber (1992, cf. Section 1.3.3) nor the one of Comon and Nieuwenhuis (2000, cf. Section 1.3.4) works.

Example 4.28
Consider yet another partial definition of the usual ordering on the naturals given by the saturated set $N'_{GT} = \{\to GT(s(x),0),\ GT(x,s(y)) \to GT(x,0)\}$ over the signature Σ_{GT}. I will compare different approaches to proving that $N'_{GT} \not\models_{Ind} \forall x,y.\,GT(x,y)$.

- I start with the constrained clause $u{\simeq}x, v{\simeq}y \,\|\, GT(x,y) \to$ and do the following one step derivation:

clauses in N:	1:		$\to GT(s(x),0)$
	2:		$\| GT(x,s(y)) \to GT(x,0)$
negated conjecture:	3:	$u{\simeq}x, v{\simeq}y$	$\| GT(x,y) \to$
Superposition(1,3) =	4:	$u{\simeq}s(x), v{\simeq}0$	$\|$ $\square$

Chapter 4: A Superposition Calculus for Fixed Domains

All further inferences are redundant (even for the extended calculus SFD$^+$ from Section 4.2.3), thus the counter examples to the query are exactly those for which no constrained empty clause was derived, i.e. instantiations of u and v which are not an instance of $\{u \mapsto s(x), v \mapsto 0\}$. Hence, these counter examples take on exactly the form $\{u \mapsto 0, v \mapsto t_2\}$ or $\{u \mapsto t_1, v \mapsto s(t_2)\}$ for any $t_1, t_2 \in \mathcal{T}(\Sigma_{GT})$.

Thus $N'_{GT} \not\models_{\Sigma_{GT}} \forall x,y. GT(x,y)$, and since the query is positive, it also follows that $N'_{GT} \not\models_{Ind} \forall x,y. GT(x,y)$.

- In comparison, the algorithm by Ganzinger and Stuber starts a derivation with the clause $\rightarrow GT(x,y)$, derives in one step the potentially productive clause $\rightarrow GT(x,0)$ and terminates with the answer "don't know".

  Ganzinger and Stuber also developed an extended approach that uses a predicate Gnd defined by $\{\rightarrow Gnd(0), Gnd(x) \rightarrow Gnd(s(x))\}$. In this context, they guard each free variable x in a clause of N and the conjecture by a literal $Gnd(x)$ in the antecedent. These literals mimic the effect of restricting the instantiation of variables to ground terms over Σ_{GT}. The derivation then starts with the following clause set:

  clauses defining Gnd: $\rightarrow Gnd(0)$
  $Gnd(x) \rightarrow Gnd(s(x))$
  modified N: $Gnd(x) \rightarrow GT(s(x), 0)$
  $Gnd(x), Gnd(y), GT(x, s(y)) \rightarrow GT(x,0)$
  conjecture: $Gnd(x), Gnd(y) \rightarrow GT(x,y)$

  Whenever the conjecture or a derived clause contains negative Gnd literals, one of these is selected, e.g. always the leftmost one. This allows a series of superposition inferences with the clause $Gnd(x) \rightarrow Gnd(s(x))$, deriving the following infinite series of clauses:

  $Gnd(x), Gnd(y) \rightarrow GT(x,y)$
  $Gnd(x_1), Gnd(y) \rightarrow GT(s(x_1), y)$
  $Gnd(x_2), Gnd(y) \rightarrow GT(s(s(x_2)), y)$
  $\ldots$

  The extended algorithm diverges without producing an answer to the query. For other selection strategies, the concrete derivation will change, but the algorithm still diverges.

- The approach by Comon and Nieuwenhuis fails as well. Before starting the actual derivation, a completion of GT has to be computed. As

4.3 Minimal Model Reasoning

presented in Chapter 3, this involves a quantifier elimination procedure, that fails since the succedent of the clause $GT(x, s(y)) \rightarrow GT(x, 0)$ does not contain all variables of the clause: GT is defined in the minimal model $\mathcal{I}_{N'_{GT}}$ by

$$GT(x, y) \iff (y = 0 \land \exists z.x = s(z)) \lor (y = 0 \land \exists z.GT(x, s(z))) \,,$$

so its negation is defined by

$$\neg GT(x, y) \iff (y \neq 0 \lor \forall z.x \neq s(z)) \land (y \neq 0 \lor \forall z.\neg GT(x, s(z))) \,.$$

Quantifier elimination simplifies this to

$$\neg GT(x, y) \iff (y \neq 0 \lor x = 0) \land (y \neq 0 \lor \forall z.\neg GT(x, s(z))) \,,$$

but cannot get rid of the remaining universal quantifier:

$$\begin{aligned}
\neg GT(x, y) &\iff (y \neq 0 \lor \forall z.x \neq s(z)) \\
&\quad \land (y \neq 0 \lor \forall z.\neg GT(x, s(z))) \\
&\iff (y \neq 0 \lor (\forall z.x \neq s(z) \land x = 0) \\
&\quad \lor (\exists w.\forall z.x \neq s(z) \land x = s(w))) \\
&\quad \land (y \neq 0 \lor \forall z.\neg GT(x, s(z))) \qquad \text{by Explosion on } x \\
&\iff (y \neq 0 \lor x = 0 \\
&\quad \lor (\exists w.\forall z.x \neq s(z) \land x = s(w))) \\
&\quad \land (y \neq 0 \lor \forall z.\neg GT(x, s(z))) \\
&\iff (y \neq 0 \lor x = 0) \\
&\quad \land (y \neq 0 \lor \forall z.\neg GT(x, s(z)))
\end{aligned}$$

Almost all rules are reduction or simplification rules. The only exception is the Explosion rule which, as shown in Chapter 3, performs a signature-based case distinction on the possible instantiations for the variable x: either $x = 0$ or $x = s(t)$ for some term t.

No rule is applicable to the last formula, but there is still a universal quantifier left. Hence the completion is not successful.

The previous example can, alternatively, be solved using test sets (Bouhoula and Rusinowitch, 1995; Bouhoula and Jouannaud, 1997). Test set approaches describe the minimal model of the specification by a set of rewrite rules in such a way that the query holds if, and only if, it can be reduced to a tautology (or a set thereof) by the rewrite rules. Such approaches rely on the decidability of ground reducibility (Plaisted, 1985; Kapur et al., 1991; Kounalis, 1992; Comon and Jacquemard, 1997).

Chapter 4: A Superposition Calculus for Fixed Domains

Following Bouhoula and Jouannaud, N'_{GT} corresponds to the following term rewrite system:

$$GT(s(x), 0) \to true$$
$$GT(x, 0) \to GT(x, s(y))$$
$$GT(0, y) \to false$$

To prove $N'_{GT} \not\models_{Ind} \forall x, y. GT(x, y)$, the algorithm maintains a set of currently regarded formulas with side conditions, which are reducible to tautologies if, and only if, $N'_{GT} \models_{Ind} \forall x, y. GT(x, y)$. It starts with the query $\{GT(x, y) \simeq true\}$. Using the *Rewrite Splitting* rule, a case distinction based on the possible applications of rewrite rules to $GT(x, y) \simeq true$ is performed. The result is the formula set

$$\left\{ \begin{array}{ll} true \simeq true & \text{if } x = s(x') \wedge y = 0 \\ GT(x, y') \simeq true & \text{if } y = 0 \wedge y' = s(y'') \\ false \simeq true & \text{if } x \simeq 0 \end{array} \right\}.$$

Since the last formula is not reducible to a tautology, $N \not\models_{Ind} \forall x, y. GT(x, y)$ follows.

Here is a second example where all previously mentioned methods fail:

Example 4.29
The formula $\forall x. \exists y. x \not\simeq 0 \to GT(x, y)$ is obviously valid in each Herbrand model of the theory $N'_{GT} = \{\to GT(s(x), 0),\ GT(x, s(y)) \to GT(x, 0)\}$ from Example 4.28 over the signature Σ_{GT}, i.e. it holds that $N'_{GT} \models_{\Sigma_{GT}} \forall x. \exists y. x \not\simeq 0 \to GT(x, y)$. Using SFD, this can again be proved in a two step derivation:

clauses in N:	1:	$\|$	$\to GT(s(x), 0)$
	2:	$\| GT(x, s(y))$	$\to GT(x, 0)$
negated conjecture:	3:	$v \simeq x\ \|$	$x \simeq 0 \to$
	4:	$v \simeq x\ \|$	$GT(x, y) \to$
Equality Resolution(3) =	5:	$v \simeq 0\ \|$	$\square$
Superposition(1,4) =	6:	$v \simeq s(x)\ \|$	$\square$

The constraints $v \simeq 0$ and $v \simeq s(x)$ of the constrained empty clauses are covering, which proves that $N'_{GT} \models_{\Sigma_{GT}} \forall x. \exists y. x \not\simeq 0 \to GT(x, y)$.

However, all previously mentioned approaches fail to prove even the weaker proposition $N'_{GT} \models_{Ind} \forall x. \exists y. x \not\simeq 0 \to GT(x, y)$, because they cannot cope with the quantifier alternation.

4.3.2 The Inductive Superposition Calculus IS(H)

As Example 4.27 shows, a proof of fixed domain validity using SFD may require the computation of infinitely many constrained empty clauses. This is not surprising, because the task is to show that an existentially quantified formula cannot be satisfied in a term-generated infinite domain. In the context of the concrete model $\mathcal{I}_N$ of a saturated and Σ-satisfiable constrained clause set N, additional structure provided by this model can be exploited. To do so, I introduce a further inference that enables the termination of derivations in additional cases. The given version of this rule is in general not sound for the general fixed domain semantics but glued to the currently considered model $\mathcal{I}_N$; however, analogous results hold for every Herbrand model of N over Σ and even for arbitrary sets of such models, in particular for the set of all Herbrand models of N over Σ.

Over any domain where an induction theorem is applicable, i.e. a domain on which a (non-trivial) well-founded partial ordering can be defined, this structure can be exploited to concentrate on finding minimal solutions. I do this by adding a form of induction hypothesis to the constrained clause set. If, e.g., P is a unary predicate over the natural numbers and n is the minimal number such that $P(n)$ holds, then it is trivial that at the same time $P(n-1), P(n-2), \ldots$ do not hold. This idea will now be cast into an inference rule (Definition 4.32) that can be used during a SFD-based $\models_{Ind}$ theorem proving derivation (Theorem 4.34).

Definition 4.30 (Ordering on $\mathcal{I}_N$)
Let $>$ be a well-founded strict partial ordering on on the elements of $\mathcal{I}_N$, i.e. on $\mathcal{T}(\Sigma)/_{R_N}$. If s, t are non-ground terms with equivalence classes $[s]$ and $[t]$, then define $[s] > [t]$ if, and only if, $[s\sigma] > [t\sigma]$ for all grounding substitutions $\sigma\colon \mathcal{X}' \to \mathcal{T}(\Sigma)$, where $\mathcal{X}' \subseteq \mathcal{X}$. The definition lifts to equivalence classes $[\sigma], [\rho]\colon \mathcal{X}' \to \mathcal{T}(\Sigma, \mathcal{X})/_{R_N}$ of substitutions, where the ordering $>$ is extended by defining $[\rho] > [\sigma]$ if, and only if, $[x\rho] > [x\sigma]$ for all $x \in \mathcal{X}'$.

Lemma 4.31
Let N be a saturated constrained clause set over Σ and $\mathcal{V}$ and let A_N be not covering. Let $\mathcal{V} = \{v_1, \ldots, v_k\}$, let $\alpha = v_1 \simeq x_1, \ldots, v_k \simeq x_k$ be a positive constraint that contains only variables and let $\mathcal{X}_\alpha = \{x_1, \ldots, x_k\}$ be the set of non-existential variables in α. Let $H = \{\alpha \,\|\, C_1, \ldots, \alpha \,\|\, C_n\}$ be a set of constrained clauses containing only variables in $\mathcal{V} \cup \mathcal{X}_\alpha$. Furthermore, let $\rho_1, \rho_2\colon \mathcal{X}_\alpha \to \mathcal{T}(\Sigma, \mathcal{X} \setminus \mathcal{V})$ be substitutions with $[\rho_2] > [\rho_1]$.

If $\mathcal{I}_N \models H$ and if $[\sigma_{\min}]\colon \mathcal{V} \to \mathcal{T}(\Sigma)/_{R_N}$ is a minimal (with respect to $>$) solution of H in $\mathcal{I}_N$, then $\mathcal{I}_N \models \alpha\sigma_{\min}\tau$ implies $\mathcal{I}_N \models \neg C_1\rho_1\tau \vee \ldots \vee \neg C_n\rho_1\tau$ for every grounding substitution τ.

Chapter 4: A Superposition Calculus for Fixed Domains

Proof. Let $\mathcal{X}_{\rho_2}$ be the set of variables in the codomain of ρ_2 and let $\tau\colon \mathcal{X}_{\rho_2} \to \mathcal{T}(\Sigma)$ be a substitution such that $\mathcal{I}_N \models \alpha\sigma_{\min}\rho_2\tau$. Note that these ground equations take the form $v_1\sigma_{\min}\simeq x_1\rho_2\tau, \ldots, v_k\sigma_{\min}\simeq x_k\rho_2\tau$ because the domains of $\rho_2\tau$ and $\sigma_{\min}$ are disjoint.

To achieve a more concise representation of the proof of $\mathcal{I}_N \models \neg C_1\rho_1\tau \vee \ldots \vee \neg C_n\rho_1\tau$, I employ the symbols $\forall$ and $\exists$ on the meta level, where they are also used for higher-order quantification. The restriction of a substitution σ to the set $\mathcal{V}$ of existential variables is denoted by $\sigma|_\mathcal{V}$, and $\sigma_\alpha\colon \mathcal{V} \to \mathcal{T}(\Sigma, \mathcal{X})$ is the substitution induced by α, i.e. σ_α maps v_i to x_i.

$\quad [\rho_2] > [\rho_1]$
$\iff [\sigma_\alpha\rho_2] > [\sigma_\alpha\rho_1]$
$\quad$ because $\mathcal{X}_\alpha \cap \mathcal{V} = \emptyset$
$\implies [(\sigma_\alpha\rho_2\tau)|_\mathcal{V}] > [(\sigma_\alpha\rho_1\tau)|_\mathcal{V}]$
$\quad$ Since $\mathcal{I}_N \models \alpha\sigma_{\min}\rho_2\tau$, the former class equals $[\sigma_{\min}]$.
$\implies (\sigma_\alpha\rho_1\tau)|_\mathcal{V}$ is not a solution of H in $\mathcal{I}_N$
$\quad$ because of the minimality of $[\sigma_{\min}]$
$\implies \exists\tau'. \mathcal{T}(\Sigma) \models \alpha(\sigma_\alpha\rho_1\tau)|_\mathcal{V}\tau'$ and $\mathcal{I}_N \not\models C_1\tau' \wedge \ldots \wedge C_n\tau'$
$\implies \exists\tau'. \forall i.\, v_i\sigma_\alpha\rho_1\tau = x_i\tau'$ and $\mathcal{I}_N \not\models C_1\tau' \wedge \ldots \wedge C_n\tau'$
$\quad$ because τ' and $(\sigma_\alpha\rho_1\tau)|_\mathcal{V}$ affect different sides of each equation in α
$\implies \exists\tau'. \forall i.\, x_i\rho_1\tau = x_i\tau'$ and $\mathcal{I}_N \not\models C_1\tau' \wedge \ldots \wedge C_n\tau'$
$\implies \exists\tau'. \forall x \in \mathcal{X}_\alpha.\, x\rho_1\tau = x\tau'$ and $\mathcal{I}_N \models \neg C_1\tau' \vee \ldots \vee \neg C_n\tau'$
$\quad$ because $C_1\tau' \wedge \ldots \wedge C_n\tau'$ is ground
$\implies \mathcal{I}_N \models \neg C_1\rho_1\tau \vee \ldots \vee \neg C_n\rho_1\tau$
$\quad$ because $\text{var}(C_i) \subseteq \mathcal{X}_\alpha$

for $i \in \{1, \ldots, k\}$ and $\tau'\colon \mathcal{X}_\alpha \to \mathcal{T}(\Sigma)$. This completes the proof. $\Diamond$

Usually when sets of constrained clauses are considered, all constrained clauses are supposed to have been renamed in advance so that they do not have any universal variables in common. I deviate from this habit here by forcing the common constraint $\alpha = v_1\simeq x_1, \ldots, v_k\simeq x_k$ upon all constrained clauses in H. Note that this does not affect the semantics because of the order of existential and universal quantifiers. For example, the constrained clause set $\{v\simeq x \parallel P(x) \to,\ v\simeq y \parallel \to P(y)\}$ has the semantics

$$\exists v. \forall x, y. (v\not\simeq x \vee \neg P(x)) \wedge (v\not\simeq y \vee P(y)),$$

which is equivalent to the semantics

$$\exists v. \forall x. (v\not\simeq x \vee \neg P(x)) \wedge (v\not\simeq x \vee P(x))$$

118

4.3 Minimal Model Reasoning

Induction with respect to H:

$$\frac{\alpha \,\|\, C_1 \quad \ldots \quad \alpha \,\|\, C_n}{\alpha\rho_2 \,\|\, D\rho_1}$$

where

(i) $H = \{\alpha \,\|\, C_1, \ldots, \alpha \,\|\, C_n\}$
(ii) $\alpha = v_1 {\simeq} x_1, \ldots, v_m {\simeq} x_m$ is a positive constraint containing only equations between variables (and $\mathcal{V} = \{v_1, \ldots, v_m\}$),
(iii) all variables of the premises occur in α,
(iv) $\rho_1, \rho_2 : \{x_1, \ldots, x_m\} \to \mathcal{T}(\Sigma, \mathcal{X} \setminus \mathcal{V})$ and $[\rho_1] < [\rho_2]$, and
(v) D is an element of the conjunctive normal form of $\neg C_1 \vee \ldots \vee \neg C_n$.

Figure 4.4: The Induction Rule

of the constrained clause set $\{v {\simeq} x \,\|\, P(x) \to, \ v {\simeq} x \,\|\, \to P(x)\}$.

The formula $\neg C_1 \rho_1 \vee \ldots \vee \neg C_n \rho_1$ can usually not be written as a single equivalent clause if some C_i contains more than one literal. However, if $D_1 \wedge \ldots \wedge D_m$ is a conjunctive normal form of $\neg C_1 \vee \ldots \vee \neg C_n$, then each D_j is a disjunction of literals and so $\alpha\rho_2 \,\|\, D_j\rho_1$ is a constrained clause. Then the previous lemma can be restated as $[\sigma_{\min}]$ also being a solution of these constrained clauses.

These ideas will now be cast into an inference rule.

Definition 4.32 (IS(H))
The *Inductive Superposition Calculus IS(H)* with respect to a finite constrained clause set H is the union of SFD and the inference rule from Figure 4.4.

Lemma 4.31 ensures that all constrained clauses derived by the Induction inference rule with respect to H will have a common solution with the initial query H, because the preserved solution $[\sigma_{\min}]$ is independent of the choices of ρ_1 and ρ_2.

Example 4.33
Let $\Sigma_P = (\{P\}, \{0, s\})$ and $N_P = \{\to P(s(s(x)))\}$. All clauses that are derivable by the Induction inference rule with respect to $H_P = \{v{\simeq}x \,\|\, \to P(x)\}$ are of one of the forms

$$v{\simeq}s^{n+m}(0) \,\|\, P(s^n(0)) \to$$
$$\text{or } v{\simeq}s^{n+m}(0) \,\|\, P(s^n(x)) \to$$
$$\text{or } v{\simeq}s^{n+m}(x) \,\|\, P(s^n(x)) \to$$

Chapter 4: A Superposition Calculus for Fixed Domains

for natural numbers n, m with $m > 0$. All these formulas and the initial constrained clause set H_P have in $\mathcal{I}_{N_P}$ the common solution $\{v \mapsto s(s(0))\}$.

To decide the validity of H in $\mathcal{I}_N$, the Induction inference rule for H can thus be used in a theorem proving derivation:

Theorem 4.34 (Soundness of the Induction Rule)
Let N be a positively constrained clause set that is saturated with respect to SFD and let A_N be not covering. Let $\mathcal{V} = \{v_1, \ldots, v_k\}$ be a set of existential variables, let $\alpha = v_1 \simeq x_1, \ldots, v_k \simeq x_k$ be a constraint that contains only variables and let $\mathcal{X}_\alpha = \{x_1, \ldots, x_k\}$ be the set of non-existential variables in α. Let H be a finite set of constrained clauses containing only variables in $\mathcal{V} \cup \mathcal{X}_\alpha$.
If $N \cup H'$ is derived from $N \cup H$ using $\text{IS}(H)$, then $\mathcal{I}_N \models H$ if, and only if, $\mathcal{I}_N \models H'$.

Proof. This follows directly from Proposition 4.15, which implies that the solutions of H are not changed by the rules in SFD, and Lemma 4.31, which states that minimal solutions are invariant under the Induction inference rule for H. ◇

This theorem basically states that the addition of constrained clauses of the presented form is a valid step in a $\models_{Ind}$ theorem proving derivation that starts from N and H and uses the calculus SFD. Before I come to applications of the Induction rule, I want to shortly investigate the side conditions to this rule. Conditions (iv) and (v) are direct consequences of the ideas developed at the beginning of this section. Conditions (i)–(iii) are needed to guarantee soundness.

Example 4.35 (Conditions on the Applicability of the Induction Rule)
I present some examples to show how a violation of one of the conditions (i)–(iii) makes the Induction rule unsound.

(i) It is important to use the Induction rule on the whole query set only (condition (i)), because the minimal solution of a subset of the query may not be equal to the minimal solution of the whole query. Consider for example the constrained clause set $N_{(i)} = \{\rightarrow P(x), Q(a) \rightarrow, \rightarrow Q(b)\}$ over the signature $(\{P, Q\}, \{a, b\})$ where $[b] < [a]$, and the query $H_{(i)} = \{v \simeq x \,\|\, \rightarrow P(x), v \simeq x \,\|\, \rightarrow Q(x)\}$. The set $N_{(i)} \cup H_{(i)}$ is satisfiable over $\{a, b\}$: just set $v \mapsto b$. Using the Induction rule for $H_{(i)}$, only the redundant constrained clause $v \simeq b \,\|\, P(a), Q(a) \rightarrow$ is derivable, namely for $\rho_1(x) = b$ and $\rho_2(x) = a$. If the Induction rule is applied for $\{v \simeq x \,\|\, \rightarrow P(x)\}$ instead of $H_{(i)}$, ignoring condition (i), the

120

4.3 Minimal Model Reasoning

constrained clause $v{\simeq}b \,\|\, P(a) \to$ can be derived. The combined set $N_{(\mathrm{i})} \cup H_{(\mathrm{i})} \cup \{v{\simeq}b \,\|\, P(a) \to\}$ is unsatisfiable over $\{a,b\}$.

(ii) For an example illustrating the need for condition (ii), consider the constrained clause set $N_{(\mathrm{ii})} = \{s(0){\simeq}0 \to, \ \to s(s(x)){\simeq}x\}$ over the signature $\Sigma_{\mathrm{nat}} = (\{\}, \{s, 0\})$. In the minimal model of $N_{(\mathrm{ii})}$, all ground terms representing even numbers are equivalent, as are all ground terms representing odd numbers, i.e. there are exactly two equivalence classes, $[0]$ and $[s(0)]$. Let $[0] < [s(0)]$ and consider the query $H_{(\mathrm{ii})} = \{v{\simeq}s(x) \,\|\, \to x{\simeq}0\}$. The instantiation $v \mapsto 0$ is a witness of the validity of $H_{(\mathrm{ii})}$ in the minimal model of $N_{(\mathrm{ii})}$. However, applying the Induction rule on $H_{(\mathrm{ii})}$ in violation of condition (ii) with $\rho_1(x) = 0$ and $\rho_2(x) = s(0)$, the constrained clause $v{\simeq}s(s(0)) \,\|\, 0{\simeq}0 \to$ can be derived. The only instantiation validating this constrained clause in the minimal model of $N_{(\mathrm{ii})}$ is $v \mapsto 0$, i.e. the combined set $H_{(\mathrm{ii})} \cup \{v{\simeq}s(s(0)) \,\|\, 0{\simeq}0 \to\}$ is not valid in this model.

(iii) Now consider the empty theory $N_{(\mathrm{iii})} = \{\}$ over the signature Σ_{nat} with $[0] < [s(0)] < [s(s(0))] < \ldots$ and query $H_{(\mathrm{iii})} = \{v{\simeq}x \,\|\, y{\simeq}x \to y{\simeq}s(0)\}$. The instantiation $v \mapsto s(0)$ shows that $H_{(\mathrm{iii})}$ is valid in the minimal model $\mathcal{T}(\Sigma_{\mathrm{nat}})$ of $N_{(\mathrm{iii})}$. Note that no other instantiation of v can show this. By ignoring condition (iii) and applying the Induction rule to $H_{(\mathrm{iii})}$ with $\rho_1(x) = x$ and $\rho_2(x) = s(x)$, the constrained clause $v{\simeq}s(x) \,\|\, y{\simeq}s(0) \to$ can be derived. This constrained clause can only be satisfied in the minimal model of $N_{(\mathrm{iii})}$ by the instantiation $v \mapsto 0$. Since this instantiation is not suited for $H_{(\mathrm{iii})}$, the set $H_{(\mathrm{iii})} \cup \{v{\simeq}s(x) \,\|\, y{\simeq}s(0) \to\}$ is not valid in the minimal model of $N_{(\mathrm{iii})}$.

Some further examples will demonstrate the power of the extended calculus $\mathrm{IS}(H)$. In these examples, there will always be a unique (non-empty) set H satisfying the side conditions of the Induction rule, and I will write IS instead of $\mathrm{IS}(H)$.

In contrast to the other inference rules, which have a finite number of possible conclusions for each given set of premises, the Induction rule will often enable the derivation of an unbounded number of conclusions. So the exhaustive application of this rule in all possible ways is clearly unfeasible. It seems appropriate to employ it only when a conclusion can directly be used for a Superposition inference simplifying another constrained clause. I will use this heuristic in the examples below.

Example 4.36

Reconsider the partial definition of the usual ordering on the naturals given by the set $N_{GT} = \{\to GT(s(0), 0), \ GT(x, y) \to GT(s(x), s(y))\}$, as shown in

Chapter 4: A Superposition Calculus for Fixed Domains

the introduction and in Example 4.27. Again, I want to check whether or not $N_{GT} \models_{\Sigma_{GT}} \forall x.GT(s(x), x)$. While the derivation in Example 4.27 diverges, a derivation using IS terminates after only a few steps:

clauses in N_{GT}:	1:	$\parallel$		$\to GT(s(0), 0)$
	2:	$\parallel$	$GT(x,y) \to$	$GT(s(x), s(y))$
negated conjecture:	3:	$v{\simeq}x \parallel$	$GT(s(x), x) \to$	
Superposition(1,3) =	4:	$v{\simeq}0 \parallel$	$\square$	
Superposition(2,3) =	5:	$v{\simeq}s(y) \parallel$	$GT(s(y), y) \to$	
Induction(3) =	6:	$v{\simeq}s(z) \parallel$		$\to GT(s(z), z)$
Superposition(6,5) =	7:	$v{\simeq}s(z) \parallel$	$\square$	

The Induction rule was applied using $H = \{v{\simeq}x \parallel GT(s(x), x) \to\}$, $\rho_1(x) = z$ and $\rho_2(x) = s(z)$. At this point, the constrained clauses $v{\simeq}0 \parallel \square$ and $v{\simeq}s(z) \parallel \square$ have been derived. Their constraints are covering for $\{s, 0\}$, which means that $N_{GT} \models_{Ind} \forall x.GT(s(x), x)$. Because of Proposition 4.26, this implies $N_{GT} \models_{\Sigma_{GT}} \forall x.GT(s(x), x)$.

Example 4.37

A standard equational example that can be solved by various approaches (e.g. Ganzinger and Stuber, 1992; Comon and Nieuwenhuis, 2000) is the theory of addition on the natural numbers: $N_+ = \{\to 0 + y{\simeq}y, \to s(x) + y{\simeq}s(x+y)\}$ over $\Sigma_+ = (\{\}, \{0, s, +\})$. A proof of $N_+ \models_{Ind} \forall x.x + 0{\simeq}x$ with IS terminates quickly:

clauses in N_+:	1:	$\parallel$		$\to 0 + y{\simeq}y$
	2:	$\parallel$		$\to s(x) + y{\simeq}s(x+y)$
negated conjecture:	3:	$v{\simeq}x \parallel$	$x + 0{\simeq}x \to$	
Superposition(1,3) =	4:	$v{\simeq}0 \parallel$	$0{\simeq}0 \to$	
Equality Resolution(4) =	5:	$v{\simeq}0 \parallel$	$\square$	
Superposition(2,3) =	6:	$v{\simeq}s(y) \parallel$	$s(y + 0){\simeq}s(y) \to$	
Induction(3) =	7:	$v{\simeq}s(z) \parallel$		$\to z + 0{\simeq}z$
Superposition(7,6) =	8:	$v{\simeq}s(z) \parallel$	$s(z){\simeq}s(z) \to$	
Equality Resolution(8) =	9:	$v{\simeq}s(z) \parallel$	$\square$	

The Induction rule was applied using $H = \{v{\simeq}x \parallel x + 0{\simeq}x \to\}$, $\rho_1(x) = z$ and $\rho_2(x) = s(z)$. At this point, the constrained clauses $v{\simeq}0 \parallel \square$ and $v{\simeq}s(z) \parallel \square$ have been derived. Their constraints cover all constraints of the form $v{\simeq}t$, $t \in \mathcal{T}(\Sigma_+, \mathcal{X} \setminus \mathcal{V})$, which means that $N_+ \not\models_{Ind} v{\simeq}x \parallel x + 0{\simeq}x \to$, or in other words $N_+ \models_{Ind} \forall x.x + 0{\simeq}x$.

Without the Induction rule, the derivation in this example would resemble the one in Example 4.27 and diverge. It would thus not even reveal information about the $\models_{\Sigma_+}$ validity of the query. Here, however, Proposition 4.26 can be applied to show additionally that $N_+ \models_{\Sigma_+} \forall x.x + 0{\simeq}x$.

Along the same lines, one can also prove that addition is symmetric, i.e. that $N_+ \models_{Ind} \forall x, y. x + y \simeq y + x$. In this case, the Induction rule must be applied twice to obtain the additional clauses

$$u \simeq x, v \simeq s(y') \,\|\, \to x + y' \simeq y' + x$$

and

$$u \simeq s(x'), v \simeq y \,\|\, \to x' + y \simeq y + x' \ .$$

Example 4.38
Given the theory $N_{\text{Even}} = \{\to \text{Even}(0), \text{Even}(x) \to \text{Even}(s(s(x)))\}$ of the natural numbers together with a predicate Even describing the even numbers, I show that $N_E \not\models_{Ind} \forall x.\text{Even}(x)$. A possible derivation runs as follows:

clauses in N_{Even}:	1 :	$\|$	$\to$ Even(0)
	2 :	$\|$ Even(x)	$\to$ Even(s(s(x)))
negated conjecture:	3 : $v \simeq x$	$\|$ Even(x)	$\to$
Superposition(1,3) =	4 : $v \simeq 0$	$\|$	$\square$
Superposition(2,3) =	5 : $v \simeq s(s(y))$	$\|$ Even(y)	$\to$
Induction(3) =	6 : $v \simeq s(s(z))$	$\|$	$\to$ Even$z$)
Superposition(6,5) =	7 : $v \simeq s(s(z))$	$\|$	$\square$

The Induction rule was applied using $H = \{v \simeq x \,\|\, \text{Even}(x) \to\}$, $\rho_1(x) = z$ and $\rho_2(x) = s(s(z))$. The set $\{(1) - (7)\}$ is saturated with respect to SFD. One could, of course, use the Induction rule to derive one more non-redundant constrained clause, namely $v \simeq s(z) \,\|\, \to \text{Even}(z)$. However, this constrained clause cannot be used in any further inference. All other constrained clauses derivable by the Induction rule are redundant.

The derived constrained empty clauses are $v \simeq 0 \,\|\, \square$ and $v \simeq s(s(z)) \,\|\, \square$. Their constraints are not covering: They miss exactly the constraint $v \simeq s(0)$, and in fact it holds that $N_E \models_{Ind} \text{Even}(s(0)) \to$.

Note that, although it also holds that $N_E \models_{Ind} \text{Even}(s(s(s(0)))) \to$, this cannot be derived, nor can any other additional counterexample. This is due to the fact that the application of the Induction rule preserves only the minimal solution.

4.4 Conclusion

I have presented the superposition calculi SFD and SFD$^+$, which are sound and refutationally complete for a fixed domain semantics for first-order logic. Compared to other approaches to reasoning over fixed domains, my approach is applicable to a larger class of clause sets. I have shown that standard

Chapter 4: A Superposition Calculus for Fixed Domains

first-order and fixed domain superposition-based reasoning, respectively, delivers minimal model results for some cases. Moreover, I presented a way to prove the validity of minimal model properties by use of the calculus $\text{IS}(H)$, combining SFD and a specific Induction rule.

The most general theorem proving methods for minimal models based on saturation so far are those by Ganzinger and Stuber (1992) and Comon and Nieuwenhuis (2000). Both approaches work only on sets of purely universal and universally reductive (Horn) clauses. Given such a clause set N and a query $\forall \vec{x}.C$, Comon and Nieuwenhuis compute a so-called I-axiomatization A such that $N \models_{Ind} A$ and $N \cup A$ has only one Herbrand model, and then check the first-order satisfiability of $N \cup A \cup \{C\}$. Like mine, this method is refutationally complete but not terminating. In fact, the clause set A does in general not inherit properties of N like universal reductiveness or being Horn, so that the saturation of $N \cup A \cup \{C\}$ does not necessarily terminate even if $N \cup \{C\}$ belongs to a finitely saturating fragment. Ganzinger and Stuber, on the other hand, basically saturate $N \cup \{C\}$. Even if $N \cup \{C\}$ saturates finitely, this results in a non-complete procedure because productive clauses may be derived. They also present a way to guarantee completeness by forcing all potentially productive atoms to the ground level. This effectively results in an enumeration of ground instances, at the cost that the resulting algorithm almost never terminates.

I gave an example of a purely universal minimal model theorem proving problem that can be solved using SFD while neither of the above approaches works (Example 4.28). Additionally, I showed how one can also prove formulas with a $\forall \exists$ quantifier alternation, i.e. check the validity of $\forall^* \exists^*$-quantified formulas. The opposite $\exists \forall$ quantifier alternation or subsequent alternations can currently not be tackled by the calculus and are one potential subject for future work.

Another intensely studied approach to theorem proving in minimal models is via test sets (Bouhoula and Rusinowitch, 1995; Bouhoula and Jouannaud, 1997). Test sets rely on the existence of a set of constructor symbols that are either free or specified by unconditional equations only. Such properties are not needed for the applicability of the calculus SFD. However, in order to effectively apply the induction rule, the strict ordering $>$ on $\mathcal{I}_N$, i.e. on the R_N equivalence classes, must be decidable. The existence of constructor symbols is often useful to establish this property. Examples 4.27 and 4.29 are not solvable via test sets, whereas Example 4.28 is.

Finally, works in the tradition of Caferra and Zabel (1992) or Kapur (Kapur et al., 1991; Kapur and Subramaniam, 2000; Giesl and Kapur, 2003; Falke and Kapur, 2006) consider only restricted forms of equality literals and related

124

4.4 Conclusion

publications by Peltier (2003) pose strong restrictions on the clause sets (for example that they have a unique Herbrand model).

In summary, my approach does not need many of the prerequisites required by previous approaches, like solely universally reductive clauses in N, solely Horn clauses, solely purely universal clauses, solely non-equational clauses, the existence and computability of a completion making the minimal model the unique Herbrand model, or the existence of explicit constructor symbols.

For universally reductive clause sets N, it is possible to make the calculus $\text{IS}(H)$ refutationally complete for a minimal model semantics, following the approach of Ganzinger and Stuber (1992) as depicted in Section 1.3. As in their context, the particular required superposition strategy carries the disadvantage of enumerating all ground instances of all clauses over to the current setting. So it can hardly be turned into a decision procedure for clause classes having infinite Herbrand models. In some cases, the induction rule might constitute a remedy: In case a clause set N can be finitely saturated, the ordering $<$ on its minimal model $\mathcal{I}_N$ may become effective and hence the induction rule may be effectively usable to finitely saturate clause sets that otherwise have an infinite saturation.

The hope connected to SFD is of course that the success of the superposition-based saturation approach on identifying decidable classes with respect to the classical first-order semantics can be extended to new classes for the fixed domain and minimal model semantics. Decidability results for the fixed domain semantics are hard to obtain for infinite Herbrand domains but the problem can now be attacked using the sound and refutationally complete calculus SFD. In the next chapters, I will present classes of models where this is indeed possible.

5 A Superposition-Based Decision Procedure for Minimal Model Validity

5.1 Introduction

In general, SFD derivations do not necessarily terminate. When they do, however, they can be used to decide fixed domain validity. I will now explore a framework in which SFD is indeed guaranteed to terminate and even decides not only fixed domain but also minimal model validity.

Given a model representation formalism, according to Fermüller and Leitsch (1996) and Caferra et al. (2004), each model representation should ideally

(i) represent a *unique* single interpretation,

(ii) provide an *atom test* deciding ground atoms,

(iii) support a *formula evaluation* procedure deciding arbitrary formulas, and

(iv) support an algorithm deciding *equivalence* of two model representations.

By definition, the model generation procedure by Bachmair and Ganzinger (1994, cf. Definition 2.35) produces a unique minimal model $\mathcal{I}_{N^*}$ out of the saturation N^* of a clause set N according to a term ordering $\succ$. This satisfies the above uniqueness postulate. As first-order logic is only semi-decidable, the saturated set N^* may be infinite and hence decision procedures for properties of $\mathcal{I}_{N^*}$ are in general hard to find. Even if N^* is finite, any other properties like the ground atom test, formula evaluation, and equivalence of models are still undecidable in general. This shows the expressiveness of the saturation concept. For particular cases, however, more is known. The ground atom test is decidable if N^* is finite and all clauses $\Gamma \to \Delta, s{\simeq}t \in N^*$ are universally reductive, i.e. $\text{var}(\Gamma \to \Delta, s{\simeq}t) \subseteq \text{var}(s)$ and s is the strictly maximal term in $\Gamma \to \Delta, s{\simeq}t$ (Ganzinger and Stuber, 1992). This basically generalizes the well-known decidability result of the word problem for convergent rewrite systems to full clause representations. Even for a finite universally reductive clause set N^*, clause evaluation (and therefore formula evaluation) and the equivalence of the minimal models of two such clause sets remain undecidable.

More specific resolution strategies produce forms of universally reductive saturated clause sets with better decidability properties. An eager selection strategy results in a hyper-resolution style saturation process where, starting with a Horn clause set N, eventually all clauses contributing to the model $\mathcal{I}_{N^*}$ are positive units. Such strategies decide, e.g., minimal model validity for the clause classes $\mathcal{VED}$ and $\mathcal{PVD}$ (Fermüller and Leitsch, 1996; Caferra et al., 2004). The positive unit clauses in N^* represent so-called ARMs (Atomic Representations of term Models). Saturations of resolution calculi with constraints (Nieuwenhuis and Rubio, 2001; Caferra et al., 2004) produce in a similar setting positive unit clauses with constraints. Restricted to syntactic disequality constraints, the minimal model of the saturated clause set can be represented by a DIG (a Disjunction of Implicit Generalizations). DIGs generalize ARMs in that positive units may be further restricted by syntactic disequations. They were first studied by Lassez and Marriott (1987). Fermüller and Pichler (2005; 2007) showed that the expressive power of DIGs corresponds to the one of so-called *contexts* used in the model evolution calculus (Baumgartner and Tinelli, 2003) and that the ground atom test as well as the clause evaluation test and the equivalence test are decidable.

I will now extend the results of Fermüller and Pichler for DIGs and ARMs to more expressive formulas with quantifier alternations using saturation-based techniques. I do so in three steps:

(i) First a DIG D is transformed into a set $N_0(D)$ of constrained predicative clauses the minimal model of which is the interpretation described by the DIG.

(ii) This set is then completed using the predicate completion algorithm PC from Chapter 3. The resulting completion $N(D)$ has a unique Herbrand model over its signature, which means that fixed domain and minimal model semantics coincide for $N(D)$.

(iii) Finally, the *Ordered Resolution Calculus for Fixed Domains* ORFD, a restriction of SFD to this setting, will be employed as a decision procedure for model equivalence and minimal model validity for DIGs.

I will first restrict the superposition calculus for fixed domains SFD to predicative clauses in Section 5.2, which results in the sound and complete calculus ORFD (Theorem 5.5). The translation of ARMs and DIGs into suitable representations by saturated sets of constrained clauses will be explained in Section 5.3. In Section 5.4, I will present the new ORFD-based decidability

results. In particular, I will, given an ARM representation N, show that
$$\mathcal{I}_N \models \forall \vec{x}.\exists \vec{y}.\phi \text{ and } \mathcal{I}_N \models \exists \vec{x}.\forall \vec{y}.\phi$$
are both decidable, where ϕ is an arbitrary quantifier-free formula (Theorem 5.25). For more expressive DIG representations N, I show among other results that
$$\mathcal{I}_N \models \forall \vec{x}.\exists \vec{y}.C \text{ and } \mathcal{I}_N \models \exists \vec{x}.\forall \vec{y}.C'$$
are decidable for any clause C, and for any clause C' in which no predicate occurs both positively and negatively (Theorem 5.24).

The main results in this chapter have been published as (Horbach and Weidenbach, 2009a,d).

5.2 The Constrained Ordered Resolution Calculus ORFD

In Chapter 4, I introduced the superposition-based calculus SFD to address the problem whether a query $\forall \vec{x}.\exists \vec{y}.\phi$ holds in every Herbrand model of N over the signature Σ, written $N \models_\Sigma \forall \vec{x}.\exists \vec{y}.\phi$, where N is a set of unconstrained clauses and ϕ is a quantifier-free formula over Σ. There, both N and ϕ may contain equational atoms.

As examples like 4.27 demonstrate, derivations with respect to SFD do in general not terminate. This is especially due to the two rules Constraint Superposition and Equality Elimination, that will often produce clauses with ever increasing constraints.

The calculus SFD works on clauses of general equational atoms. As explained in the preliminaries, predicates are encoded as equations as usual, i.e. $P(\vec{t})$ is encoded as $f_P(\vec{t}) \simeq c_{\text{true}}$, where c_{true} is a new and minimal constant symbol. Because of the focus on predicative clauses, signatures in this chapter will always be given in the form $\Sigma = (\mathcal{P}, \mathcal{F})$ (cf. Section 2.2.5). When only predicative atoms are present, several of the rules of SFD are not applicable, among them the two just mentioned. The resulting calculus ORFD is presented in this section, along with proofs of its soundness and refutational completeness with respect to Herbrand satisfiability. As in the case of SFD, the inference rules in ORFD are defined with respect to a well-founded strict reduction ordering $\succ$ on atoms over Σ that is total on ground atoms and with respect to a selection function that assigns to every clause a (possibly empty) set of antecedent atoms.

Definition 5.1 (ORFD)
Let $\succ$ be a well-founded strict reduction ordering on atoms over Σ that is

Chapter 5: A Superposition-Based Decision Procedure for Minimal Models

---

Ordered Resolution:

$$\frac{\alpha_1 \,\|\, \Gamma_1 \to \Delta_1, A_1 \quad \alpha_2 \,\|\, \Gamma_2, A_2 \to \Delta_2}{(\alpha_1, \alpha_2^{\not\approx} \,\|\, \Gamma_1, \Gamma_2 \to \Delta_1, \Delta_2)\sigma_1\sigma_2}$$

where

(i) $\sigma_1 = \mathrm{mgu}(A_1, A_2)$ and $\sigma_2 = \mathrm{mgu}(\alpha_1^{\widetilde{}}\sigma_1, \alpha_2^{\widetilde{}}\sigma_1)$,

(ii) no atom is selected in the first premise and $A_1\sigma_1\sigma_2$ strictly maximal in $(\Gamma_1 \to \Delta_1, A_1)\sigma_1\sigma_2$, and

(iii) either A_2 is selected in the second premise, or no atom is selected and $A_2\sigma_1\sigma_2$ is maximal in the clause $(\Gamma_2, A_2 \to \Delta_2)\sigma_1\sigma_2$.

Ordered Factoring:

$$\frac{\alpha \,\|\, \Gamma \to \Delta, A, A'}{(\alpha \,\|\, \Gamma \to \Delta, A)\sigma}$$

where

(i) $\sigma = \mathrm{mgu}(A, A')$ and

(ii) no atom is selected in the premise and $A\sigma$ is maximal in the clause $(\Gamma \to \Delta, A, A')\sigma$.

Figure 5.1: Rules of the Calculus ORFD

total on ground atoms. The *Ordered Resolution Calculus for Fixed Domains* ORFD consists of the two inference rules from Figure 5.1, where all (strict) maximality constraints have to be considered with respect to $\succ$.

As in Chapter 4, I will always implicitly assume that a well-founded strict reduction ordering $\succ$ on atoms over Σ that is total on ground atoms is fixed for all following considerations.

When all clauses are predicative, the calculi SFD and SFD$^+$ coincide. Hence the choice of α_N need not be restricted to minimal constraints:

Definition 5.2 (α_N)
Let N be a set of constrained clauses. If A_N is not covering, then let α_N, as in Section 4.2.3, be *any* ground constraint that is not an instance of any constraint in A_N. Otherwise let α_N be arbitrary.

Example 5.3
As an example consider the signature $\Sigma_{\mathrm{Nat}} = (\emptyset, \{0, s\})$, where 0 is a constant

5.2 The Constrained Ordered Resolution Calculus ORFD

and s is unary, a single existential variable v and the two constrained clause sets

$$M = \{v{\simeq}0 \,\|\, \square,\ v{\simeq}s(0) \,\|\, \square,\ v{\simeq}s(s(0)) \,\|\, \square,\ \ldots\} \text{ and}$$
$$N = \{v{\simeq}s(x), x{\not\simeq}0 \,\|\, \square\} \ .$$

Then A_M is covering but A_N is not, and either $\{v{\simeq}0\}$ or $\{v{\simeq}s(0)\}$ may be chosen for α_N.

In contrast to Chapter 4 (in particular Proposition 4.9), this calculus is also refutationally complete for constrained clauses with constraints that contain disequations:

Proposition 5.4 (Σ-Completeness for Saturated Clause Sets)
Let N be set of constrained clauses over Σ such that N is saturated with respect to ORFD and A_N is not covering for Σ. Then $\mathcal{I}_N \models N$ for any admissible choice of α_N.

Proof. Let $\alpha_N = v_1{\simeq}t_1, \ldots, v_n{\simeq}t_n$ and assume, contrary to the proposition, that $\mathcal{I}_N \not\models N$. Then there are a constrained clause $\alpha \,\|\, C \in N$ and a substitution $\sigma : \mathrm{var}(\alpha \,\|\, C) \to \mathcal{T}(\mathcal{F})$ such that $\mathcal{I}_N \not\models (\alpha \,\|\, C)\sigma$. Because $\mathcal{I}_N$ contains only predicative atoms, this implies that $\sigma(v_i) = t_i$ for all i, $\alpha\sigma$ is satisfiable, and $\mathcal{I}_N \not\models C\sigma$. Let $C\sigma$ be minimal with these properties.

I will refute this minimality. I proceed by a case analysis of the position of selected or maximal literal occurrences in $C\sigma$.

- $C\sigma$ does not contain any literal at all, i.e. $C = \square$. Then the satisfiability of $\alpha\sigma$ contradicts the choice of α_N.

- $C = \Gamma, A \to \Delta$ and $A\sigma$ is selected or $A\sigma$ is maximal and no literal is selected in $C\sigma$. Since $\mathcal{I}_N \not\models C\sigma$, it holds that $A\sigma \in \mathcal{I}_N$. The literal A must be produced by a ground instance $(\beta \,\|\, \Lambda \to \Pi, B)\sigma'$ of a constrained clause in N in which no literal is selected. Note that both ground constrained clauses $(\alpha \,\|\, C)\sigma$ and $(\beta \,\|\, \Lambda \to \Pi, B)\sigma'$ are not redundant with respect to N.

  Because $\alpha{\simeq}\sigma = \beta{\simeq}\sigma' = \alpha_N\sigma$ and because σ is a unifier of A and B, i.e. an instance of $\sigma_1 := \mathrm{mgu}(A, B)$, there is an inference by ordered resolution as follows:

$$\frac{\beta \,\|\, \Lambda \to \Pi, B \quad \alpha \,\|\, \Gamma, A \to \Delta}{(\alpha, \beta^{\not=} \,\|\, \Lambda, \Gamma \to \Pi, \Delta)\sigma_1\sigma_2} \quad \sigma_2 = \mathrm{mgu}(\beta{\simeq}\sigma_1, \alpha{\simeq}\sigma_1)$$

The ground instance $\delta \,\|\, D = (\alpha, \beta^{\not=} \,\|\, \Lambda, \Gamma \to \Pi, \Delta)\sigma$ of the conclusion shows that δ is satisfiable and $\mathcal{I}_N \not\models D$.

On the other hand, as the inference is redundant, so is the constrained clause $\delta \,\|\, D$, i.e. D follows from ground instances $\delta \,\|\, C_i$ of constrained clauses of N all of which are smaller than $(\alpha \,\|\, C)\sigma$. Because of the minimality of $C\sigma$, all C_i hold in $\mathcal{I}_N$. So $\mathcal{I}_N \models D$, which contradicts $\mathcal{I}_N \not\models D$.

- $C = \Gamma \to \Delta, A$ and $A\sigma$ is strictly maximal in $C\sigma$. This is not possible, since then either $C\sigma$ or a smaller clause must have produced $A\sigma$, and hence $\mathcal{I}_N \models C\sigma$, which contradicts the choice of $C\sigma$.

- No literal in $C = \Gamma \to \Delta, A$ is selected and $A\sigma$ is maximal but not strictly maximal in $C\sigma$. Then $\Delta = \Delta', A'$ such that $A'\sigma = A\sigma$. So there is an inference by ordered factoring as follows:

$$\frac{\alpha \,\|\, \Gamma \to \Delta', A, A'}{(\alpha \,\|\, \Gamma \to \Delta', A')\sigma_1} \quad \sigma_1 = \mathrm{mgu}(s, s')$$

As above, $\alpha\sigma$ is satisfiable and both $\mathcal{I}_N \models (\Gamma \to \Delta', A')\sigma$ and $N \not\models (\Gamma \to \Delta', A')\sigma$ can be derived, which is a contradiction. ◊

As a reduct of SFD and SFD$^+$, ORFD hence satisfies the following theorem:

Theorem 5.5 (Saturation)
If $N_0, N_1, \ldots$ is a fair ORFD derivation, then the constrained clause set $N_\infty = \bigcup_j \bigcap_{k \geq j} N_k$ is saturated with respect to ORFD. Moreover, N_0 has a Herbrand model over Σ if, and only if, A_{N^*} is not covering.

Proof. This is a direct consequence of Theorem 4.16 and Proposition 5.4. ◊

5.3 Clausal Representations of Disjunctions of Implicit Generalizations

5.3.1 Disjunctions of Implicit Generalizations

In Chapter 4 and the previous section, I showed how saturated sets of constrained clauses can be regarded as (implicitly) representing certain Herbrand models. Other representations of Herbrand interpretations include sets of non-ground atoms or the more flexible so-called disjunctions of implicit generalizations of Lassez and Marriott (1987). I will now show how both types of representation can be regarded as special cases of the representation by saturated constrained clause sets.

Based on this view, I reprove that the equivalence of any given pair of representations by disjunctions of implicit generalizations is decidable, and

5.3 Clausal Representations of Disjunctions of Implicit Generalizations

extend the known results on the decidability of clause and formula entailment (cf. Fermüller and Pichler, 2007). To do so, I translate a query $\mathcal{I} \models \phi$ over a signature Σ, where $\mathcal{I}$ is represented by a disjunction of implicit generalizations, into a constrained clause set that is Herbrand-unsatisfiable over Σ if, and only if, $\mathcal{I} \models \phi$ holds. The Herbrand-unsatisfiability can then be decided using the calculus ORFD.

Definition 5.6 (Disjunctions of Implicit Generalizations)
An *implicit generalization* G over Σ is an expression of the form

$$G = A/\{A_1, \ldots, A_n\},$$

where $A, A_1, \ldots, A_n$ are predicative atoms over Σ. A finite set D of implicit generalizations over Σ is called a *disjunction of implicit generalizations* or *DIG*. A DIG D is an *atomic representation of a term model (ARM)*, if all implicit generalizations in D are of the form $A/\{\}$.

The Herbrand interpretation $\mathcal{I}(\{A/\{A_1, \ldots, A_n\}\})$ represented by a DIG consisting of a single implicit generalization $A/\{A_1, \ldots, A_n\}$ is exactly the set of all atoms that are instances of the atom A but not of any A_i. The interpretation $\mathcal{I}(D)$ represented by a general DIG $D = \{G_1, \ldots, G_m\}$ is the union $\mathcal{I}(\{G_1\}) \cup \ldots \cup \mathcal{I}(\{G_m\})$ of the interpretations represented by the implicit generalizations in D.

Example 5.7
Let $\Sigma = (\{P\}, \{s, 0\})$, where 0 is a constant, s is a unary function symbol and P is a binary predicate. Let $D = \{G_1, G_2\}$ be a DIG over Σ, where the two implicit generalizations in D are given by $G_1 = P(s(x), s(y))/\{P(x, x)\}$ and $G_2 = P(0, y)/\{P(x, 0)\}$. The interpretation represented by D is

$$\mathcal{I}(D) = \{P(t, t') \mid t, t' \in \mathcal{T}(\{s, 0\}) \text{ and } t \neq t' \text{ and } t' \neq 0\}.$$

If an implicit generalization $G = A/\{A_1, \ldots, A_n\}$ contains an atom A_i that cannot be unified with A, then eliminating A_i from G does not change the Herbrand interpretation represented by $\{G\}$. If A_i and A can be unified by a most general unifier σ, then replacing A_i by $A_i\sigma$ in G does not change the Herbrand interpretation represented by $\{G\}$ either.

Without loss of generality, it may thus be assumed for each implicit generalization $G = A/\{A_1, \ldots, A_n\}$ that all atoms $A_1, \ldots, A_n$ are instances of A.

Definition 5.8 (DIG over $\{P_1, \ldots, P_n\}$)
If A is of the form $A = P(\vec{t})$, then $G = A/\{A_1, \ldots, A_n\}$ is an implicit generalization *over P*. If $G_1, \ldots, G_n$ are implicit generalizations over $P_1, \ldots, P_n$, respectively, then $\{G_1, \ldots, G_n\}$ is a DIG *over* $\{P_1, \ldots, P_n\}$.

5.3.2 Clausal Representations

I will now translate each DIG D into a set of constrained clauses whose minimal model is $\mathcal{I}(D)$. My first approach to this translation will result in a set $N_0(D)$ that has the desired minimal model but may also have other Herbrand models. This means that in general $\models_{Ind}$ and $\models_\Sigma$ do not agree for $N_0(D)$. Hence the calculus ORFD is not complete for $\mathcal{I}(D)$ based on $N_0(D)$ alone. In Section 5.3.3, I will use the predicate completion procedure from Section 3.3 to enrich $N_0(D)$ by additional constrained clauses, such that the resulting clause set $N(D)$ has exactly one Herbrand model over the given signature.

Definition 5.9 ($N_0(D)$)

For each DIG D, define a constrained clause set $N_0(D)$ as follows: If $D = \{G_1, \ldots, G_n\}$ is a DIG over $\{P\}$, let $\dot{P}_1, \check{P}_1, \ldots \dot{P}_n, \check{P}_n$ be fresh predicates.

For $G_i = P(\vec{s}_i)/\{P(\vec{s}_{i1}), \ldots, P(\vec{s}_{in})\}$, the predicate $\dot{P}_i$ will be used to describe the atom $P(\vec{s}_i)$ and serve as an over-approximation of P, and $\check{P}_i$ will be used to describe the atoms $P(\vec{s}_{ij})$. Define auxiliary clause sets

$$N_0(G_i) = \{\to \dot{P}_i(\vec{s}_i),\ \to \check{P}_i(\vec{s}_{i1}),\ \ldots,\ \to \check{P}_i(\vec{s}_{in})\}.$$

Then

$$N_0(D) = \bigcup_{1 \leq i \leq n} N_0(G_i) \cup \{\dot{P}_i(\vec{x}) \to \check{P}_i(\vec{x}), P(\vec{x})\}\ .$$

If $D = D_1 \cup \ldots \cup D_m$ such that each D_i is a DIG over a single predicate and D_i and D_j are DIGs over different predicates whenever $i \neq j$, let

$$N_0(D) = N_0(D_1) \cup \ldots \cup N_0(D_m)\ .$$

Let fresh predicates be smaller with respect to $\prec$ than all predicates from the original signature and let $\dot{P}_i \prec \check{P}_j$ for all fresh predicates $\dot{P}_i$ and $\check{P}_j$.

Example 5.10

Consider the DIG D from Example 5.7. The sets $N_0(G_1)$ and $N_0(G_2)$ consist of the following unconstrained clauses:

$$N_0(G_1) = \{\to \dot{P}_1(s(x), s(y)),\quad \to \check{P}_1(x, x)\}$$
$$N_0(G_2) = \{\to \dot{P}_2(0, y),\quad \to \check{P}_2(x, 0)\}$$

$N_0(D)$ additionally contains the unconstrained clauses

$$\dot{P}_1(x, y) \to \check{P}_1(x, y), P(x, y)\text{ and}$$
$$\dot{P}_2(x, y) \to \check{P}_2(x, y), P(x, y)\ .$$

5.3 Clausal Representations of Disjunctions of Implicit Generalizations

Note that each clause in $N_0(D)$ has a unique strictly maximal literal occurrence and that this occurrence is in the succedent. Hence $N_0(D)$ is saturated with respect to ORFD (with a selection function selecting no literals at all) and $\mathcal{I}_{N_0(D)}$ is a minimal Herbrand model of $N_0(D)$ over the extended signature.

Proposition 5.11 (Equivalence of D and $N_0(D)$)
Let D be a DIG. Then $\mathcal{I}(D) = \mathcal{I}_{N_0(D)}$.

Proof. Let $D = \{G_1, \ldots, G_m\}$ and let $P(\vec{t})$ be a ground atom. Then $\mathcal{I}(D) \models P(\vec{t})$ holds if, and only if, there is an implicit generalization G_i such that $\mathcal{I}(\{G_i\}) \models P(\vec{t})$. For $G_i = P(\vec{s})/\{P(\vec{s}_1), \ldots, P(\vec{s}_n)\}$, this is equivalent to $P(\vec{t})$ being an instance of $P(\vec{s})$ but not of any $P(\vec{s}_j)$. This in turn is equivalent to $N_0(\{G_i\}) \models_{Ind} \dot{P}_i(\vec{t})$ and $N_0(\{G_i\}) \not\models_{Ind} \check{P}_i(\vec{t})$. That this holds for some i is equivalent to $N_0(D) \models_{Ind} P(\vec{t})$. ◇

In general, the set $N_0(D)$ will have more than one Herbrand model over the given extended signature:

Example 5.12
The set $N_0(D)$ from Example 5.10 has several Herbrand models over the extended signature $(\{P, \dot{P}_1, \dot{P}_2, \check{P}_1, \check{P}_2\}, \{s, 0\})$. One of them is $\mathcal{I}(D)$, another one is the interpretation in which all of $\dot{P}_1(t, t')$, $\dot{P}_2(t, t')$, $\check{P}_1(t, t')$, $\check{P}_2(t, t')$, and $P(t, t')$ are valid for all ground terms t, t'.

In the next section, I will remedy this ambiguity by completing the set $N_0(D)$.

5.3.3 Completed Clausal Representations

Using the predicate completion algorithm PDU from Section 3.3, it is possible to extend the clause set $N_0(D)$ in order to exclude non-minimal models.

Definition 5.13 ($N(D)$)
Let D be a DIG. If $N_0'(D)$ is the completion of $N_0(D)$, as defined in Section 3.3, then define the set $N(D)$ as arising from $N_0'(D)$ by moving all succedent equations into the constraint:

$$N(D) = \big\{\, (\alpha^{\not\simeq} \,\|\, \Gamma \to \Delta) \mid \Gamma \to \Delta, E \in N_0'(D),$$
$$\Delta \text{ is predicative and } E \text{ is equational,}$$
$$\alpha^{\not\simeq} = \{t_1 \not\simeq t_2 \mid t_1 \simeq t_2 \in E\} \,\big\}$$

The set $N_0(D)$ is obviously universally reductive:

Chapter 5: A Superposition-Based Decision Procedure for Minimal Models

Lemma 5.14 (Universal Reductiveness of $N_0(D)$)
Let D be a DIG. Then all clauses in $N_0(D)$ are universally reductive.

Proof. All clauses of $N_0(D)$ are either positive units or of the form

$$\dot{P}_i(\vec{x}) \to \check{P}_i(\vec{x}), P(\vec{x}) ,$$

where the literal $P(\vec{x})$ is strictly maximal and contains all variables of the clause. Both types of clauses are universally reductive. ◇

Hence Theorem 3.38 states that minimal model validity of predicative queries for $N_0(D)$ coincides with fixed domain validity for $N(D)$:

Lemma 5.15 ($N_0(D)$ and $N(D)$)
Let D be a DIG over $\Sigma = (\mathcal{P}, \mathcal{F})$ and let $\mathcal{P}'$ be the set of fresh predicates in $N_0(D)$. Then for every predicative formula ϕ over $\Sigma' = (\mathcal{P} \cup \mathcal{P}', \mathcal{F})$, it holds that $N_0(D) \models_{Ind} \phi$ if, and only if, $N(D) \models_\Sigma \phi$ if, and only if, the set $N(D) \cup \{\neg\phi\}$ is Herbrand-unsatisfiable over Σ'.

Together with Proposition 5.11, this implies that validity in $\mathcal{I}(D)$ is equivalent to validity in all Herbrand models of $N(D)$:

Corollary 5.16 (Equivalence of D and $N(D)$)
Let D be a DIG and let ϕ be a formula over Σ. Then $\mathcal{I}(D) \models \phi$ if, and only if, $N(D) \models_\Sigma \phi$.

Example 5.17
Consider the DIG D and the set $N_0(D)$ from Examples 5.7 and 5.10. To compute $N(D)$, inspect the sets of clauses defining the predicates $\dot{P}_1, \dot{P}_2, \check{P}_1, \check{P}_2$, and P:

$$N_{\dot{P}_1} = \{\to \dot{P}_1(s(x), s(y))\} \qquad N_{\check{P}_1} = \{\to \check{P}_1(x, x)\}$$
$$N_{\dot{P}_2} = \{\to \dot{P}_2(0, y)\} \qquad N_{\check{P}_2} = \{\to \check{P}_2(x, 0)\}$$
$$N_P = \{\dot{P}_1(x, y) \to \check{P}_1(x, y), P(x, y) , \quad \dot{P}_2(x, y) \to \check{P}_2(x, y), P(x, y)\} .$$

The negation of $\dot{P}_1$ in the minimal model of $N_0(D)$ is obviously defined by the equivalence $\neg\dot{P}_1(x, y) \iff \neg\exists x', y'. x \simeq s(x') \land y \simeq s(y')$. Disunification simplifies the right hand side $\neg\exists x', y'. x \simeq s(x') \land y \simeq s(y')$ of this equivalence to $x \simeq 0 \lor y \simeq 0$. This results in the unconstrained completion

$$N'_{\dot{P}_1} = \{\dot{P}_1(0, y) \to, \ \dot{P}_1(x, 0) \to\} .$$

5.3 Clausal Representations of Disjunctions of Implicit Generalizations

Analogously, the negation of $\check{P}_1$ in the minimal model of $N_0(D)$ is defined by the equivalence $\neg \check{P}_1(x,y) \iff x \not\approx y$. The corresponding completion is not unconstrained:

$$N'_{\check{P}_1} = \{x \not\approx y \,\|\, \check{P}_1(x,y) \to\}$$

The completions of $\dot{P}_2$ and $\check{P}_2$ are computed analogously as

$$N'_{\dot{P}_2} = \{\dot{P}_2(s(x),y) \to\} \text{ and}$$
$$N'_{\check{P}_2} = \{\check{P}_2(x,s(y)) \to\} \ .$$

For P, note that the clauses in N_P could equivalently be written as

$$\dot{P}_1(x,y) \wedge \neg \check{P}_1(x,y) \to P(x,y) \text{ and}$$
$$\dot{P}_2(x,y) \wedge \neg \check{P}_2(x,y) \to P(x,y) \ ,$$

and $P(x,y)$ is maximal in both cases. Hence $\neg P(x,y) \iff (\neg \dot{P}_1(x,y) \vee \check{P}_1(x,y)) \wedge (\neg \dot{P}_2(x,y) \vee \check{P}_2(x,y))$. Rewriting the right hand side of this equivalence to its disjunctive normal form

$$(\check{P}_1(x,y) \wedge \check{P}_2(x,y))$$
$$\vee (\check{P}_1(x,y) \wedge \neg \dot{P}_2(x,y))$$
$$\vee (\check{P}_2(x,y) \wedge \neg \dot{P}_1(x,y))$$
$$\vee (\neg \dot{P}_1(x,y) \wedge \neg \dot{P}_2(x,y))$$

forms the basis to translate this definition into the following clause set:

$$\begin{aligned} N'_P = \{ & P(x,y), \check{P}_1(x,y), \check{P}_2(x,y) \to, \\ & P(x,y), \check{P}_1(x,y) \to \dot{P}_2(x,y) \ , \\ & P(x,y), \check{P}_2(x,y) \to \dot{P}_1(x,y) \ , \\ & P(x,y) \to \dot{P}_1(x,y), \dot{P}_2(x,y) \} \end{aligned}$$

The set $N(D)$ is then the union of the starting set $N_0(D)$ and all partial completions N'_Q for $Q \in \{\dot{P}_1, \dot{P}_2, \check{P}_1, \check{P}_2, P\}$.

In this example, constraints consisting of disequations appear exactly in the completion of $N_{\check{P}_1} = \{\to \check{P}_1(x,x)\}$, because the completion has to capture the fact that $P_1(x,y)$ can only be false if x and y are different. In general, such constraints always arise from clauses in which the maximal literal is non-linear, i.e. whenever a variable appears twice in this literal. E.g. the completion of $\{\to Q(x,x,x)\}$ adds the clauses $x \not\approx y \,\|\, Q(x,y,z) \to$, $x \not\approx z \,\|\, Q(x,y,z) \to$, and $y \not\approx z \parallel Q(x, y, z) \rightarrow$. Such non-linearities are also the only reason for the appearance of constraint disequations.

Because SFD and SFD$^+$ are sound and refutationally complete for the semantics $\models_\Sigma$, the same of course also holds for their restriction ORFD in a purely predicative setting. Hence Corollary 5.16 implies that the calculus ORFD can be used to reason about validity in $\mathcal{I}(D)$. In the next section, I will explore when this approach results in a decision procedure.

5.4 Decidability Results

Representing DIGs as sets of constrained clauses allows for the deduction of various superposition-based decidability results. Because of the simple shape of the clauses in N_0, a lemma by Ganzinger and Stuber (1992) guarantees that the validity of ground queries in DIG-represented interpretations is decidable (Corollary 5.19). More general queries can be decided using ORFD: For interpretations represented by ARMs, the validity of formulas of the form $\forall \vec{x}.\exists \vec{y}.\phi$ and $\exists \vec{x}.\forall \vec{y}.\phi$ with quantifier-free ϕ is decidable (Theorem 5.25). For DIGs, the validity of several subclasses is decidable (Theorem 5.24). This extends results by Fermüller and Pichler, who proved the validity of unconstrained clauses to be decidable (Fermüller and Pichler, 2005, 2007).

5.4.1 Decidability of Ground Queries

The question whether a ground query holds in $\mathcal{I}(D)$ is decidable even without completion, using an approach by Ganzinger and Stuber (1992). This approach relies only on the saturation of $N_0(D)$ and its universal reductiveness (cf. Definition 2.22).

Lemma 5.18 (Ganzinger and Stuber, 1992, Lemma 4)
Let N be a saturated, finite and universally reductive set of clauses. Then it is decidable whether a ground atom A is valid in $\mathcal{I}_N$.

Proof. If $\mathcal{I}_N \models A$, then there must be a ground instance $(\Gamma \rightarrow \Delta, B)\sigma$ of a clause $\Gamma \rightarrow \Delta, B \in N$ producing A. This is the case if, and only if,

(i) $A = B\sigma$ is an instance of B (assuming without loss of generality that $B\sigma$ is maximal in $(\Gamma \rightarrow \Delta, B)\sigma$),

(ii) every atom of $\Gamma\sigma$ is true in $\mathcal{I}_N$, and

(iii) every atom of $\Delta\sigma$ is false in $\mathcal{I}_N$.

5.4 Decidability Results

Because $\Gamma \to \Delta, B$ is universally reductive and $B\sigma$ is ground, every atom of $\Gamma\sigma$ and $\Delta\sigma$ is ground. Moreover, every such atom is strictly smaller than A, so deciding their validity is strictly simpler than deciding the validity of the original query A. ◇

Because $N_0(D)$ is indeed saturated and universally reductive (Lemma 5.14), it directly follows that ground queries are decidable for DIGs.

Corollary 5.19 (Decidability of Ground Queries)
Let D be a DIG and let A be a ground atom. Then it is decidable whether $\mathcal{I}(D) \models A$.

5.4.2 Decidability of DIG Equivalence

Let me investigate in more detail what the constrained clauses in the completion $N(D)$ of $N_0(D)$ look like.

Consider first a single implicit generalization $G = P(\vec{t})/\{P(\vec{s}_1), \ldots, P(\vec{s}_n)\}$. All constrained clauses in $N_0(G)$ are unconstrained units. The only clause in $N_0(G)$ defining $\dot{P}$ is $\to \dot{P}(\vec{t})$, i.e. $\vec{x} \simeq \vec{t} \Longrightarrow \dot{P}(\vec{x})$ is valid in every model of $N_0(G)$. In the minimal model, both implications $\vec{x} \simeq \vec{t} \Longrightarrow \dot{P}(\vec{x})$ and $\vec{x} \simeq \vec{t} \Longleftarrow \dot{P}(\vec{x})$ hold. So the complement of $\dot{P}$ in the minimal model of $N_0(G)$ is defined by $\neg \dot{P}(\vec{x}) \iff \neg(\vec{x} \simeq \vec{t})$, or (in addition to the clause $\to \dot{P}(\vec{t})$) by the constrained clauses

$$x_i \not\simeq t_i \parallel \dot{P}(\vec{x}) \to .$$

In the case of $\check{P}$, there are several defining clauses, and the completion consists of the constrained clauses of the form

$$x_{i_1} \not\simeq s_{1,i_1}, \ldots, x_{i_n} \not\simeq s_{n,i_n} \parallel \check{P}(\vec{t}) \to .$$

For a DIG D, $N_0(D)$ contains, in addition to the clauses presented above, only clauses of the form $\dot{P}_i(\vec{x}) \to \check{P}_i(\vec{x}), P(\vec{x})$, where $P(\vec{x})$ is the maximal literal occurrence. So P is defined in the minimal model of $N_0(D)$ by $P(\vec{x}) \iff \bigvee_{1 \in \{1\ldots n\}} \dot{P}_i(\vec{x}) \wedge \neg \check{P}_i(\vec{x})$. Its complement is hence defined by $\neg P(\vec{x}) \iff \bigwedge_{1 \in \{1\ldots n\}} \neg \dot{P}_i(\vec{x}) \vee \check{P}_i(\vec{x})$, or, bringing the right hand side into disjunctive normal form, by

$$\neg P(\vec{x}) \iff \bigvee_{i_1, \ldots, i_n \in \{1\ldots n\}} \check{P}_{j_1}(\vec{x}) \wedge \ldots \wedge \check{P}_{j_m}(\vec{x}) \wedge \dot{P}_{j_{m+1}}(\vec{x}) \wedge \ldots \wedge \dot{P}_{j_n}(\vec{x}) ,$$

where $\dot{P}_{j_1}, \check{P}_{j_1}, \ldots, \dot{P}_{j_n}, \check{P}_{j_n}$ are the fresh predicates introduced for P. The disjuncts correspond to the unconstrained clauses

$$P(\vec{x}), \check{P}_{j_1}(\vec{x}), \ldots, \check{P}_{j_m}(\vec{x}) \to \dot{P}_{j_{m+1}}(\vec{x}), \ldots, \dot{P}_{j_n}(\vec{x}) .$$

Chapter 5: A Superposition-Based Decision Procedure for Minimal Models

Note that all constrained non-unit clauses contain a unique literal that is maximal for all instances of the constrained clause, namely $P(\vec{x})$.

The calculus ORFD does not terminate on every input. If, however, the input is a set $N(D) \cup N$ where N contains only constrained unit clauses, then only constrained clauses belonging to a very restricted class can be derived:

Lemma 5.20
Let D be a DIG over $\Sigma = (\mathcal{P}, \mathcal{F})$ and let $\mathcal{P}'$ be the set of fresh predicates in $N(D)$. Then the set of predicative constrained clauses over $(\mathcal{P} \cup \mathcal{P}', \mathcal{F})$ of the following forms is closed under the inference rules of ORFD:

(i) $\alpha \,\|\, \to A$ or $\alpha \,\|\, A \to$ or $\alpha \,\|\, \square$

(ii) $\alpha \,\|\, \dot{P}_i(\vec{t}) \to \check{P}_i(\vec{t})$

(iii) $\alpha \,\|\, \check{P}_{i_1}(\vec{t}), \ldots, \check{P}_{i_k}(\vec{t}), \dot{P}_{i_{k+1}}(\vec{t}), \ldots, \dot{P}_{i_l}(\vec{t}) \to \dot{P}_{i_{l+1}}(\vec{t}), \ldots, \dot{P}_{i_m}(\vec{t})$
where each part of the constrained clause may be empty and all predicates have identical term arguments.

Moreover, the saturation of a finite set of such constrained clauses with ORFD and an empty selection function terminates.

Proof. Ordered Factoring inferences can only take constrained clauses of type (iii) as premise and obviously yield a constrained clause of type (iii) again. Because of the fact that $\dot{P}_i \prec \check{P}_j$ for all $\dot{P}_i, \check{P}_j \in \mathcal{P}'$ and thus Ordered Resolution primarily works on predicates $\check{P}_j$, one easily checks closure under Ordered Resolution.

To show termination, extend the partial ordering $\prec$ to a complete ordering on the set $\mathcal{P} \cup \mathcal{P}'$ of all predicates and write $\mathcal{P} \cup \mathcal{P}' = \{Q_1, \ldots, Q_n\}$ such that $Q_{i+1} \prec Q_i$ for all $1 \leq i < n$. Given a constrained clause $\alpha \,\|\, C$, let p_i be the number of positive and q_i the number of negative occurrences of the predicate Q_i in C. In each inference between constrained clauses of the given form, the tuple $(p_1, q_1, \ldots, p_n, q_n)$ is lexicographically strictly smaller for the conclusion than for each premise: This is obvious for factoring inferences. An Ordered Resolution inference always has the form

$$\frac{\alpha_1 \,\|\, \Gamma_1 \to \Delta_1, Q_k(\vec{t}_1) \quad \alpha_2 \,\|\, \Gamma_2, Q_k(\vec{t}_2) \to}{(\alpha_1, \alpha_2^{\neq} \,\|\, \Gamma_1, \Gamma_2 \to \Delta_1, \Delta_2)\sigma_1\sigma_2}.$$

Note that for constrained clauses of form (i)–(iii), all literals in the first (or second, respectively) premise are of the form $Q_i(\vec{t}_1)$ (or $Q_i(\vec{t}_2)$) with identical argument terms, $Q_k(\vec{t}_1)\sigma_1\sigma_2$ is strictly maximal in the first premise and

5.4 Decidability Results

$Q_k(\vec{t}_2)\sigma_1\sigma_2$ is maximal in the second premise with respect to $\prec$. Hence Q_k is the maximal predicate appearing in both premises and it occurs only once in the first premise and only negatively in the second premise. So for the first premise, the first non-zero component of $(p_1, q_1, \ldots, p_n, q_n)$ is $p_k = 1$; for the second premise, it is q_k. For the conclusion, the first possibly non-zero component is q_k, and this component is one smaller for the conclusion than for the second premise.

So the conclusion of every inference is smaller (in a well-founded way) than all premises. Hence only finitely many clauses (up to renaming of universal variables) can be derived using ORFD from a finite set of such constrained clauses.

Note that, while redundancy is undecidable in general, the very restricted notion of redundancy that suffices here, where an inference is redundant if its conclusion or a variant thereof has already been derived, is obviously decidable. ◇

Lemma 5.21 (Decidability of Unit Queries)
Let D be a DIG over $\Sigma = (\mathcal{P}, \mathcal{F})$ and let $\mathcal{P}'$ be the set of fresh predicates in $N(D)$. If N is a set of predicative constrained clauses over Σ containing at most one literal each, then it is decidable whether $N(D) \cup N$ is Herbrand-satisfiable over $\Sigma' = (\mathcal{P} \cup \mathcal{P}', \mathcal{F})$.

Proof. Let M^* be a saturation of $M = N(D) \cup N$ by the calculus ORFD with a selection function that does not select any literals. By Theorem 5.5, Herbrand-unsatisfiability of M over Σ' is equivalent to the coverage of A_{M^*}, which by Theorem 4.6 is decidable if M^* is finite.

To prove that M^* is finite, I show that any derivation starting from M is finite. I first show that only finitely many constrained clauses containing predicates from $\mathcal{P}$ can be derived. The only constrained clauses containing at least two literals and a predicate symbol of $\mathcal{P}$ are of the form $\dot{P}_i(\vec{x}) \to P(\vec{x}), \check{P}_i(\vec{x})$ or of the form $P(\vec{x}), \check{P}_{j_1}(\vec{x}), \ldots, \check{P}_{j_m}(\vec{x}) \to \dot{P}_{j_{m+1}}(\vec{x}), \ldots, \dot{P}_{j_n}(\vec{x})$, where $P \in \mathcal{P}$, and where $\dot{P}_{j_1}, \ldots, \dot{P}_{j_n}, \check{P}_{j_1}, \ldots, \check{P}_{j_n} \in \mathcal{P}'$ are the fresh predicates introduced for P. Note that for each i, either $\dot{P}_{j_i}(\vec{x})$ or $\check{P}_{j_i}(\vec{x})$ occurs in each constrained clause of the latter type, and $P(\vec{x})$ is the maximal literal occurrence in both types of constrained clauses (cf. the initial remarks in this Section). Since each inference between constrained clauses containing a predicate symbol of $\mathcal{P}$ eliminates this predicate, there are only finitely many such inferences.

The conclusion of an inference

$$\frac{\parallel \dot{P}_i(\vec{x}) \to P(\vec{x}), \check{P}_i(\vec{x}) \quad \parallel P(\vec{x}), \check{P}_{j_1}(\vec{x}), \ldots, \check{P}_{j_m}(\vec{x}) \to \dot{P}_{j_{m+1}}(\vec{x}), \ldots, \dot{P}_{j_n}(\vec{x})}{\parallel \Gamma \to \Delta}$$

between two constrained clauses in $N(D)$ using $P \in \mathcal{P}$ is a tautology (and thus redundant), because either $\dot{P}_i(\vec{x})$ or $\check{P}_i(\vec{x})$ appears in both Γ and Δ. The remaining derivable constrained clauses over $(\mathcal{P}', \Sigma)$ obey the restrictions of Lemma 5.20, hence the saturation terminates. ◇

With this preliminary work done, it can be decided whether two DIGs represent the same model:

Theorem 5.22 (DIG Equivalence)
Equivalence of DIGs is decidable by ORFD.

Proof. Let D, D' be two DIGs. Because $\mathcal{I}(D) = \bigcup_{G \in D} \mathcal{I}(\{G\})$, and because $\mathcal{I}(D) = \mathcal{I}(D')$ if, and only if, $\mathcal{I}(D) \subseteq \mathcal{I}(D')$ and $\mathcal{I}(D') \subseteq \mathcal{I}(D)$, it suffices to show the decidability of $\mathcal{I}(D) \subseteq \mathcal{I}(D')$ in the case where $D = \{G\}$ consists of a single implicit generalization $G = P(\vec{s})/\{P(\vec{s}\sigma_1), \ldots, P(\vec{s}\sigma_n)\}$.

Without loss of generality, assume that $P(\vec{s})$ and $P(\vec{s}\sigma_1), \ldots, P(\vec{s}\sigma_n)$ do not share any variables. Let $\vec{x}$ be the variables in $P(\vec{s})$ and let $\vec{y}$ be the variables in $P(\vec{s}\sigma_1), \ldots, P(\vec{s}\sigma_n)$. The implicit generalization G states that the formula $\forall \vec{x}.(\forall \vec{y}.\vec{x} \not\simeq \vec{x}\sigma_1 \wedge \ldots \wedge \vec{x} \not\simeq \vec{x}\sigma_n) \implies P(\vec{s})$ holds in $\mathcal{I}(D)$.

By Proposition 5.16, $\mathcal{I}(D) \subseteq \mathcal{I}(D')$ holds if, and only if, $N(D') \models_\Sigma P(\vec{t})$ for every atom $P(\vec{t}) \in \mathcal{I}(D)$. Equivalently, the set

$$N(D') \cup \{\exists \vec{x}.\forall \vec{y}.\vec{x} \not\simeq \vec{x}\sigma_1 \wedge \ldots \wedge \vec{x} \not\simeq \vec{x}\sigma_n \wedge \neg P(\vec{s})\}$$

does not have a Herbrand model over Σ.

The latter formula corresponds to the set

$$\{\vec{v} \simeq \vec{x}\sigma_1 \parallel \square, \ldots, \vec{v} \simeq \vec{x}\sigma_n \parallel \square, \vec{v} \simeq \vec{x} \parallel P(s) \to\}$$

of constrained clauses, and so

$$N(D') \cup \{\vec{v} \simeq \vec{x}\sigma_1 \parallel \square, \ldots, \vec{v} \simeq \vec{x}\sigma_n \parallel \square, \vec{v} \simeq \vec{x} \parallel P(s) \to\}$$

also does not have a Herbrand model over Σ. By Lemma 5.21, whether this constrained clause set has a Herbrand model over Σ is decidable by means of the calculus ORFD. ◇

Example 5.23
The DIG $D' = \{P(x, s(y))/\{P(s(x'), s(x'))\}\}$ and the DIG D from Examples 5.7, 5.10 and 5.17 describe the same model. I only show that $\mathcal{I}(D) \supseteq \mathcal{I}(D')$.

Expressing this as a satisfiability problem of constrained clauses, amounts to checking whether $N(D) \cup \{v_1 \simeq x, v_2 \simeq y \parallel P(x, s(y)) \to, v_1 \simeq s(x'), v_2 \simeq x' \parallel \square\}$

5.4 Decidability Results

is Herbrand-satisfiable over Σ. To do so, I saturate this set with respect to ORFD.

Since $N(D) \cup \{v_1 \simeq s(x'), v_2 \simeq x' \,\|\, \Box\}$ is saturated, all non-redundant inferences use at least one descendant of $v_1 \simeq x, v_2 \simeq y \,\|\, P(x, s(y)) \to$. The following constrained clauses can be derived. The new constrained clauses are indexed by (0)...(9). Each of these constrained clauses is derived from one clause in $N(D)$ (which is not repeated here) and another clause that is indicated by its index:

index	constrained clause	derived from
(0)	$v_1 \simeq s(x'), v_2 \simeq x' \,\|\, \qquad\qquad\qquad \Box$	
(1)	$v_1 \simeq x, v_2 \simeq y \,\|\, P(x, s(y)) \to$	
(2)	$v_1 \simeq x, v_2 \simeq y \,\|\, \dot{P}_1(x, s(y)) \to \check{P}_1(x, s(y))$	(1)
(3)	$v_1 \simeq x, v_2 \simeq y \,\|\, \dot{P}_2(x, s(y)) \to \check{P}_2(x, s(y))$	(1)
(4)	$v_1 \simeq s(x), v_2 \simeq y \,\|\, \qquad\qquad \to \check{P}_1(s(x), s(y))$	(2)
(5)	$v_1 \simeq s(x), v_2 \simeq y, x \not\simeq s(y) \,\|\, \dot{P}_1(x, s(y)) \to$	(2)
(6)	$v_1 \simeq s(x), v_2 \simeq y, s(x) \not\simeq s(y) \,\|\, \qquad\qquad\qquad \Box$	(4) or (5)
(7)	$v_1 \simeq 0, v_2 \simeq y \,\|\, \qquad\qquad \to \check{P}_2(0, s(y))$	(3)
(8)	$v_1 \simeq x, v_2 \simeq y \,\|\, \dot{P}_2(x, s(y)) \to$	(3)
(9)	$v_1 \simeq 0, v_2 \simeq y \,\|\, \qquad\qquad\qquad \Box$	(7) or (8)

No further non-redundant constrained clauses can be derived. The constraint set

$$\{(v_1 \simeq s(x'), v_2 \simeq x'), (v_1 \simeq s(x), v_2 \simeq y, s(x) \not\simeq s(y)), (v_1 \simeq 0, v_2 \simeq y)\}$$

consisting of the constraints of the constrained clauses (0), (6), and (9) is covering, which means that the whole constrained clause set is Herbrand-unsatisfiable over the extended signature Σ', i.e. that $\mathcal{I}(D) \supseteq \mathcal{I}(D')$.

5.4.3 Decidability of Formula Entailment

Going beyond deciding equivalence of DIG representations, it can be decided for formulas from a number of classes whether they are true in interpretations represented by DIGs.

Theorem 5.24 (Decidability of DIG Formula Entailment)
Let D be a DIG and let ϕ be a quantifier-free predicative formula over Σ with variables $\vec{x}, \vec{y}$. The following problems are decidable:

(i) $\mathcal{I}(D) \models \forall \vec{x}.\exists \vec{y}.\phi$ is decidable if one of the following holds:

    a) ϕ is a clause

    b) ϕ is a conjunction of clauses of the form $\to \Delta$

Chapter 5: A Superposition-Based Decision Procedure for Minimal Models

      c) ϕ is a conjunction of clauses of the form $\Gamma \to$

      d) ϕ is a conjunction of unit clauses where no predicate appears in both a positive and a negative literal

(ii) $\mathcal{I}(D) \models \exists \vec{x}. \forall \vec{y}. \phi$ is decidable if one of the following holds:

      a) ϕ is a conjunction of literals

      b) ϕ is a conjunction of clauses of the form $\Gamma \to$

      c) ϕ is a conjunction of clauses of the form $\to \Delta$

      d) ϕ is a clause where no predicate appears in both a positive and a negative literal

Proof. First consider the case (i,a). Let $\Sigma = (\mathcal{P}, \mathcal{F})$ and let $\mathcal{P}'$ be the set of fresh predicates in $N(D)$. Let $\phi = C = A_1, \ldots, A_n \to B_1, \ldots, B_m$ and let

$$N = \{\vec{v} \simeq \vec{x} \,\|\, \to A_1, \ \ldots, \ \vec{v} \simeq \vec{x} \,\|\, \to A_n, \vec{v} \simeq \vec{x} \,\|\, B_1 \to, \ \ldots, \ \vec{v} \simeq \vec{x} \,\|\, B_n \to\} \ .$$

By Proposition 5.16, that $\mathcal{I}(D) \models \forall \vec{x}. \exists \vec{y}. \phi$ is equivalent to the relation $N(D) \models_\Sigma \forall \vec{x}. \exists \vec{y}. \phi$. This in turn is equivalent to the Herbrand-unsatisfiability of $N(D) \cup \{\exists \vec{x}. \forall \vec{y}. \neg \phi\}$, or equivalently of $N(D) \cup N$, over the signature $\Sigma' = (\mathcal{P} \cup \mathcal{P}', \mathcal{F})$. By Lemma 5.21, the Herbrand-unsatisfiability of $N(D) \cup N$ over Σ' is decidable.

The proofs for (i,b)–(i,d) are exactly analogous, using slight variations of Lemma 5.21. The decidability of the problems (ii,a)–(ii,d) reduces to the cases (i,a)–(i,d), respectively, because $\mathcal{I}(D) \models \exists \vec{x}. \forall \vec{y}. \phi$ holds if, and only if, $\mathcal{I}(D) \not\models \forall \vec{x}. \exists \vec{y}. \neg \phi$.   ◇

The simple nature of atomic representations makes it possible to go one step further:

Theorem 5.25 (Decidability of ARM Formula Entailment)
Let D be an ARM over Σ and let ϕ be a quantifier-free predicative formula over Σ with variables $\vec{x}, \vec{y}$. It is decidable whether $\mathcal{I}(D) \models \forall \vec{x}. \exists \vec{y}. \phi$ and whether $\mathcal{I}(D) \models \exists \vec{x}. \forall \vec{y}. \phi$.

Proof. I first show the decidability of $\mathcal{I}(D) \models \forall \vec{x}. \exists \vec{y}. \phi$. Let $\Sigma = (\mathcal{P}, \mathcal{F})$ and let $\mathcal{P}'$ be the set of fresh predicates in $N(D)$. Write the formula $\neg \phi$ as an equivalent finite set $N_{\neg \phi}$ of unconstrained clauses and set N to be the set $N = \{(\vec{v} \simeq \vec{x} \,\|\, C) \,|\, C \in N_{\neg \phi}\}$.

Consider first some unconstrained clause $C = A_1, \ldots, A_m \to B_1, \ldots, B_n$ and assume that constrained clauses in $N(D)$ and C do not share any universal variables. Because all elements of $N(D)$ are constrained unit clauses, it holds that $\mathcal{I}(D) \not\models C$ if, and only if, there are constrained clauses $\alpha_i \,\|\, \to A'_i$ and $\beta_j \,\|\, B'_j \to$ in $N(D)$ and a substitution $\tau : \mathcal{X} \to \mathcal{T}(\Sigma)$ such that

(i) $A_i\tau = A'_i\tau$,
(ii) $B_j\tau = B'_j\tau$,
(iii) and $\alpha_i\tau$ and $\beta_j\tau$ are satisfiable for all i,j (note that all β_j are purely negative and so none of them contains any existential variables).

By definition of $N(D)$, all positive clauses in $N(D)$ are unconstrained, so this is equivalent to the formula $\bigvee \beta\tau$ being satisfiable, where the disjunction ranges over all $\beta = \beta_1, \ldots, \beta_k$ and τ such that there are constrained clauses $\| \to A'_i$ and $\beta_j \| B'_j \to$ in $N(D)$ and τ is a most general simultaneous unifier of all (A_i, A'_i) and (B_j, B'_j).

Coming back to the validity of N, $\mathcal{I}(D) \not\models N$ holds if, and only if, for every substitution $\sigma : V \to \mathcal{T}(\Sigma)$ there is a substitution $\tau : \text{var}(\alpha \| C) \setminus V \to \mathcal{T}(\Sigma)$ and a constrained clause $\alpha \| C \in N$, such that $\alpha\sigma\tau$ is satisfiable and $\mathcal{I} \not\models C\tau$. By the considerations above, this is equivalent to the satisfiability of the formula $\bigwedge_{\alpha \| C \in N} \bigvee \alpha\tau \wedge \beta\tau$, which can be decided by disunification, e.g. with the algorithm PDU.

$\mathcal{I}(D) \models \exists \vec{x}.\forall \vec{y}.\phi$ is decided analogously, without negating ϕ. ◇

5.5 Implementation

I have implemented a the algorithm ORFD on top of the automated theorem prover SPASS (Weidenbach et al., 2009), using the implementation of PDU and PC presented in Section 3.5. SPASS is superposition-based and provides a powerful saturation machinery, which makes this prover well-suited as a basis for the calculus.

Because the current version of SPASS does not support constraints, a constrained clause $\vec{v} \simeq \vec{t}, s_1 \not\simeq s'_1, \ldots, s_n \not\simeq s'_n \| \Gamma \to \Delta$ is modeled internally by a regular clause of the form

$$\text{Ex}(\vec{t}), \text{CDis}(s_1, s'_1), \ldots, \text{CDis}(s_n, s'_n), \Gamma \to \Delta ,$$

where Ex and CDis are new predicates that remember the current instantiation of the existential variables and the constraint disequations, respectively. An unconstrained clause $\| \Gamma \to \Delta$ is not equipped with a Ex literal, i.e. the abbreviation used in this chapter carries over to the code.

The inference rules in ORFD (Figure 5.1) are defined in such a way that only the clausal part is considered for all maximality conditions, but due to the modeling of constraints as part of the antecedent, SPASS will also consider the constraint literals. To deter literals with the predicates Ex and CDis from interfering with the saturation process, they are artificially kept minimal in the superposition ordering. To avoid the accumulation of multiple Ex literals,

Chapter 5: A Superposition-Based Decision Procedure for Minimal Models

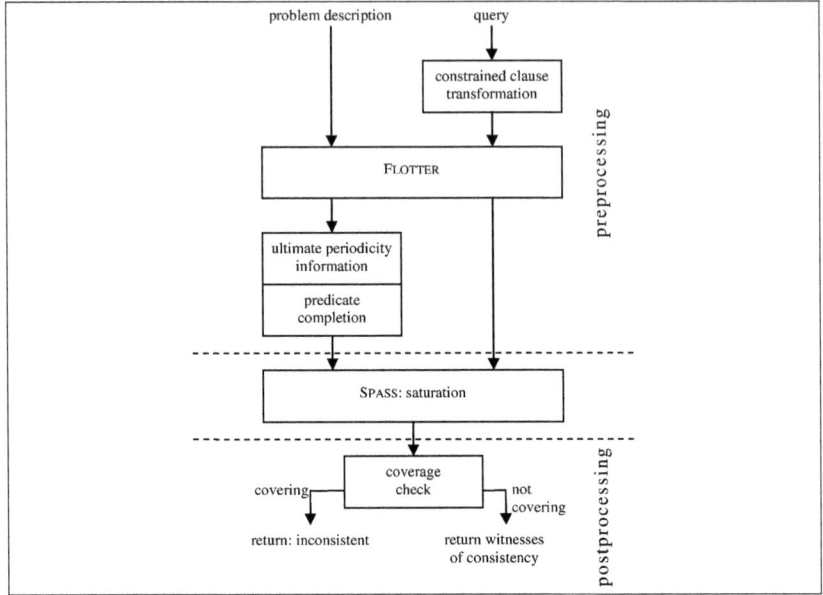

Figure 5.2: Structure of the Implementation

the code of Resolution inferences in SPASS has been changed such that Ex literals are additionally unified during each inference step. This is the only change to the actual saturation machinery of SPASS: The whole saturation process for ORFD can then be performed with the built-in mechanisms.

To use ORFD as a decision procedure for DIGs, the implementations of the single algorithms are combined as follows: First the input, which consists of the clauses in $N_0(D)$, is completed using the implementation of PC and equations in the completion are transferred into the constraint as in Definition 5.13. The query formula of the form $\exists \vec{x}.\forall \vec{y}.\phi$ is changed to $\forall \vec{x}, \vec{y}.\mathrm{Ex}(\vec{x}) \to \phi$ to eliminate the existential variables and then transformed into a set of clauses using FLOTTER, the clause normal form generator of SPASS. The resulting clauses are automatically guarded by the antecedent atom $\mathrm{Ex}(\vec{x})$. The input clauses, their completion and the transformed query are then saturated together. Finally, coverage of the constrained empty clauses is checked by means of the implementation of PDU. This implementation constitutes a decision procedure for all decidability problems presented in Theorem 5.24. Figure 5.2 gives an overview over the information flow in the implementation.

146

5.5 Implementation

So far, only simple optimizations have been implemented, like the addition of a clause $CDis(x, x) \rightarrow$ that directly makes all clauses with unsatisfiable constraints redundant and hence, for example, excludes inferences between clauses in $N(D)$. On the other hand, two strong optimizations in SPASS must be deactivated for the work with constrained clauses: *Splitting* changes the minimal model and is hence unsound and the especially efficient algorithms for reasoning about *sort theories* interferes with the semantics of constrained clauses because they select Ex and CDis literals. While splitting is inherently unsuited for minimal model reasoning, the latter could be remedied by an explicit integration of constraints into the clause language of SPASS.

Because there are no libraries of theorem proving problems for DIGs, the implementation has been tested on hand-crafted problems. It is available from the SPASS homepage (www.spass-prover.org/prototypes/).

Example 5.26
To show that the formula $\exists x.P(s(x), x)$ holds in the model of the DIG D' from Example 5.23, the following input is given to SPASS:

```
begin_problem(X).
list_of_descriptions.
name({*DIG Example*}).
author({*Matthias Horbach*}).
status(satisfiable).
description({*Proves a DIG Property*}).
end_of_list.

list_of_symbols.
functions[(s,1),(0,0)].
predicates[(P,2), (Pp,2), (Pn,2)].
end_of_list.

list_of_formulae(axioms).
formula(forall([x,y],Pp(x,s(y)))).
formula(forall([x],Pn(s(x),s(x)))).
formula(forall([x,y],implies(Pp(x,y),or(Pn(x,y),P(x,y))))).
end_of_list.

list_of_formulae(conjectures).
formula(exists([x],P(s(x),x))).
end_of_list.

list_of_settings(SPASS).
{*
set_flag(PComp,1).
```

Chapter 5: A Superposition-Based Decision Procedure for Minimal Models

```
set_flag(Select,0).
set_flag(Sorts,0).
set_precedence(P,Pp,Pn).
set_DomPred(P,Pn,Pp).
*}
end_of_list.
end_problem.
```

The `list_of_descriptions` contains some information on the problem. In the following `list_of_symbols`, the signature is fixed (Pp denotes $\dot{P}$ and Pn denotes $\check{P}$), and the clauses of $N_0(D')$ are given in the `list_of_formulae`. Finally, SPASS is told in the `list_of_settings` to apply the predicate completion algorithm to the input, disable selection and the special handling of sorts and choose the precedence P $\succ$ Pn $\succ$ Pp. The last setting causes constraint literals to be minimal. The output of SPASS when run on this input begins with the following lines:

```
Perfect SPASS: Conjecture prepared.
Perfect SPASS: Input completed.
-------------------------SPASS-START-------------------------
```

This signals that the conjecture has been transformed into a constrained clause and the input has been completed. Then the completion is output:

```
Input Problem:
1[0:Inp]  ||    -> Pp(U,s(V))*.
2[0:Inp]  ||    -> Pn(s(U),s(U))*.
3[0:Inp]  || ExVars(U) -> P(s(U),U)*.
4[0:Inp]  || Pp(U,V) -> P(U,V)* Pn(U,V).
5[0:Inp]  || P(U,V)* -> Pp(U,V).
6[0:Inp]  || P(U,V)* Pn(U,V) -> .
7[0:Inp]  || Pn(s(U),V)* CDis(V,s(U)) -> .
8[0:Inp]  || Pn(0,U)* -> .
9[0:Inp]  || Pp(U,0)* -> .
10[0:Inp] || CDis(U,U)* -> .
```

Clause 3 is the conjecture, the clauses 1,2 and 4–9 form the completed set $N(D')$ and clause 10 is the additional clause $x \not\approx x \,\|\, \square$. SPASS then analyses and saturates the input using the adapted inference rules:

```
This is a first-order Non-Horn problem without equality.
Axiom clauses: 9 Conjecture clauses: 1
Inferences: IORe=1 IOFc=1
Reductions: RFMRR=1 RBMRR=1 RObv=1 RUnC=1 RTaut=1 RFSub=1
            RBSub=1 RCon=1
```

148

5.5 Implementation

```
Extras     : Input Saturation, No Selection, Full Splitting,
             Full Reduction, Ratio: 5, FuncWeight: 1, VarWeight: 1
Precedence: s > nequal > div > id > CDis > P > Pp > Pn > ExVars > 0
Ordering   : KBO
Processed Problem:

Worked Off Clauses:

Usable Clauses:
8[0:Inp]  ||  Pn(0,U)* -> .
9[0:Inp]  ||  Pp(U,0)* -> .
10[0:Inp] ||  CDis(U,U)* -> .
1[0:Inp]  ||   -> Pp(U,s(V))*.
2[0:Inp]  ||   -> Pn(s(U),s(U))*.
3[0:Inp]  ||  ExVars(U) -> P(s(U),U)*.
5[0:Inp]  ||  P(U,V)* -> Pp(U,V).
6[0:Inp]  ||  Pn(U,V) P(U,V)* -> .
4[0:Inp]  ||  Pp(U,V) -> Pn(U,V) P(U,V)*.
7[0:Inp]  ||  CDis(U,s(V)) Pn(s(V),U)* -> .
        Given clause: 8[0:Inp]  ||  Pn(0,U)* -> .
        Given clause: 9[0:Inp]  ||  Pp(U,0)* -> .
        Given clause: 10[0:Inp] ||  CDis(U,U)* -> .
        Given clause: 1[0:Inp]  ||   -> Pp(U,s(V))*.
        Given clause: 2[0:Inp]  ||   -> Pn(s(U),s(U))*.
        Given clause: 3[0:Inp]  ||  ExVars(U) -> P(s(U),U)*.
        Given clause: 5[0:Inp]  ||  P(U,V)* -> Pp(U,V).
        Given clause: 11[0:Res:3.1,5.0] || ExVars(U) -> Pp(s(U),U)*.
        Given clause: 12[0:Res:11.1,9.0] || ExVars(0)* -> .
        Given clause: 6[0:Inp]  ||  Pn(U,V) P(U,V)* -> .
        Given clause: 13[0:Res:3.1,6.1] || ExVars(U) Pn(s(U),U)* -> .
        Given clause: 7[0:Inp]  ||  CDis(U,s(V)) Pn(s(V),U)* -> .
        Given clause: 4[0:Inp]  ||  Pp(U,V) -> Pn(U,V) P(U,V)*.
SPASS V 3.5c
SPASS beiseite: Completion found.
```

The only derived constrained empty clause is clause 12: $u \simeq 0 \,\|\, \Box$. Consequently, the final coverage check yields that the conjecture holds for all other instantiations of the existential variable:

```
Conjecture holds in the minimal model of the axioms
     for the following instances: (not (equal U (0)))
Problem: dig.dfg
SPASS derived 6 clauses, backtracked 0 clauses, performed 0 splits
     and kept 13 clauses.
SPASS allocated 25242 KBytes.
```

```
SPASS spent      0:00:00.16 on the problem.
                 0:00:00.02 for the input.
                 0:00:00.02 for the FLOTTER CNF translation.
                 0:00:00.00 for the input completion.
                 0:00:00.00 for inferences.
                 0:00:00.00 for the backtracking.
                 0:00:00.00 for the reduction.
                 0:00:00.00 for the coverage check.
------------------------SPASS-STOP----------------------------
```

A description of the implementation of the decision procedures has been published as (Horbach, 2011b).

5.6 Conclusion

I have extended the decidability results of Fermüller and Pichler (2005, 2007) for ARMs to arbitrary formulas with one quantifier alternation and for DIGs to several more restrictive formula structures with one quantifier alternation. This provides a first concrete application where the calculi SFD/SFD$^+$ result in decision procedures.

The approach has potential for further research. I restricted my attention to a non-equational setting, whereas the initial fixed domain calculus considers equations as well. It is an open problem to what extend the presented results also hold in an equational setting. In Fermüller and Pichler (2005, 2007), the finite and infinite signature semantics for DIGs were considered. My results refer to the finite signature semantics where actually only the signature symbols of a finite saturated set are considered in the minimal model. It is not known what an infinite signature semantics means to this approach, or if the employed predicate completion procedure can be extended to infinite signatures. Finally, in Fermüller and Pichler (2007) the question was raised what happens if one considers more restrictive, e.g. linear, DIGs. Linear DIGs require less effort in predicate completion than general DIGs but it is an open question whether this has further effects on decidability or complexity results.

6 Generic Superposition-based Decidability of Minimal Model Validity

6.1 Introduction

As I have shown in the previous chapter, the special shape of the interpretation-describing clauses in the case of disjunctions of implicit generalizations makes the validity of a variety of queries decidable. The main reason for this is that the description does not exhibit a recursive behaviour. For minimal models of more general clauses, decidability quickly fails. The following example shows that even if all signature symbols are at most unary and all positive literals in N are linear, unsatisfiability in the minimal model is already undecidable:

Example 6.1 (Post Correspondence Problem)
Consider a *Post correspondence problem* over the alphabet $\{a, b\}$ with given word pairs (u_i, v_i). Words are modeled by monadic terms over the unary function symbols a and b with empty word 0. Then the Post correspondence problem has a solution if, and only if, the following Horn clause set is unsatisfiable:

$$\to \text{PCP}(0,0)$$
$$\text{PCP}(x,y) \to \text{PCP}(u_i(x), v_i(y))$$
$$\text{PCP}(a(x), a(x)) \to$$
$$\text{PCP}(b(x), b(x)) \to$$

Equivalently, it has a solution if, and only if,

$$\{\to \text{PCP}(0,0),\ \text{PCP}(x,y) \to \text{PCP}(u_i(x), v_i(y))\}$$
$$\models_{Ind} \exists x.\text{PCP}(a(x), a(x)) \vee \text{PCP}(b(x), b(x)) \ .$$

Note that describing the goal by $\text{PCP}(x,x)$ is too simplistic, because it would yield a contradiction by resolution with the first clause.

In this chapter, I identify a range of classes of clause sets and of query formulas for which validity in the minimal model is decidable. The main result is as follows:

Chapter 6: Generic Superposition-based Decidability of Minimal Model Validity

Let N be a satisfiable set of predicative Horn clauses over a signature Σ and let A_{ij} be predicative atoms over Σ with empty succedent, where

(1) all function symbols in Σ are at most unary,

(2) all positive literals in N are linear, i.e. every variable occurs at most once, and

(3) $N \cup \{A_{11}, \ldots, A_{1m_1} \to, \ldots, A_{n1}, \ldots, A_{nm_n} \to\}$ can be finitely saturated by Ordered Resolution, where deletion steps are restricted to the deletion of variants and tautologies.

Then the problem

$$N \models_{Ind} \forall x. \exists y_1, \ldots, y_m . \phi$$

is decidable, where $\phi = \bigvee_i \bigwedge_j A_{ij}$ and $x, y_1, \ldots, y_m$ are the variables in ϕ. There are no restrictions on purely negative clauses as well as no restrictions on the structure of the terms appearing in negative literals.

The unsatisfiability problem for Horn classes satisfying conditions (1)–(2) is still undecidable, as the above encoding of the Post correspondence problem shows. Therefore, the basis of the presented decidability result is finite first-order saturation (3). The side conditions (1)–(2) as well as the restriction to variant subsumption and tautology deletion for the saturation process are needed for the current proof. The latter is not an essential restriction, since most decidability results based on saturation show termination by restricting the depth of the occurring terms and the number of variables in each clause, which corresponds exactly to a saturation modulo variants and tautologies (cf. e.g. Ganzinger and Nivelle, 1999).

The proof of this result is constructive. I will demonstrate it on the example clause set

$$N_{GT} = \{ \begin{array}{rl} & \to GT(s(s(0)), s(0)) \;, \\ GT(x, y) & \to GT(s(x), s(y)) \quad, \\ GT(s(x), s(y)) & \to GT(x, y) \end{array} \}$$

with query $\forall x. \exists y. GT(y, x)$. In the minimal model of N_{GT}, the relation GT is again the "one greater than" relation on the naturals. The clause set N satisfies conditions (1)–(2) and can be finitely saturated by Ordered Resolution, generating one additional clause $\to GT(s(0), 0)$. It can also be finitely saturated after adding $GT(y, x) \to$.

To use the calculus **SFD** of Chapter 4 for the current example, the query is negated and transformed into the constrained clause $v \simeq x \parallel G(y, x) \to$. In general, the application of **SFD** does not terminate, i.e. it does not decide

6.1 Introduction

(and not even semi-decide) whether a given query holds in a minimal model. This even holds on a set N and a constrained query clause that satisfy conditions (1)–(3). In the example, infinitely many non-redundant constrained clauses

$$v \simeq x \parallel G(y,x) \to, \quad v \simeq s(x) \parallel G(y,x) \to, \quad v \simeq s(s(x)) \parallel G(y,x) \to, \quad \ldots \quad \text{and}$$
$$v \simeq 0 \parallel \Box, \quad v \simeq s(0) \parallel \Box, \quad v \simeq s(s(0)) \parallel \Box, \quad \ldots$$

are generated.

The contribution of this chapter is to generalize the previously developed constraint language to "regular" *substitution expressions* for the existentially quantified variables (Section 6.2). For example a constraint $v \simeq x\sigma^*$ represents all possible constraints of the form $v \simeq x\sigma^n$. Together with conditions (1)–(3), this enables the termination of the saturation process (Proposition 6.32). For the above example, the derived constrained clauses can be represented as

$$v \simeq x \parallel G(y,x) \to, \quad v \simeq x\sigma \parallel G(y,x) \to, \quad v \simeq x\sigma^2 \parallel G(y,x) \to, \quad \ldots \quad \text{and}$$
$$v \simeq x\tau \parallel \Box, \quad v \simeq x\sigma\tau \parallel \Box, \quad v \simeq x\sigma^2\tau \parallel \Box, \quad \ldots$$

for $\sigma = \{x \mapsto s(x)\}$, $\tau = \{x \mapsto 0\}$. When these constrained clauses are melted, the two additional constrained clauses

$$v \simeq x\sigma^* \parallel G(y,x) \to \quad \text{and}$$
$$v \simeq x\sigma^*\tau \parallel \Box$$

are obtained.

What remains to be shown is that the substitutions in the constraints of all derived constrained empty clauses are covering, i.e. represent all possible instantiations for the variables $\vec{x}$: If this is the case, then the clause set does not have a Herbrand model over the given signature. The conjunction of all regular substitution expressions for the constrained empty clauses can be transformed into a monadic Horn clause set containing only linear clauses whose head literal contains all variables of the clause (Section 6.4.1). The initial substitution expressions are covering if, and only if, a certain predicate P introduced in the translation is interpreted as the total relation in the minimal model of the generated Horn clause set. For the example above, this translation results in the following Horn clauses:

$$\to P_1(0)$$
$$P(x) \to P_2(s(x))$$
$$P_1(x) \to P(x)$$
$$P_2(x) \to P(x)$$

Deciding totality for such clause sets is usually difficult. However, several results are known about the decidability of emptiness. Applying a variant of the predicate completion algorithm PC from Chapter 3, I will generate a Horn clause set for the complement of P, named $\check{P}$, for any Horn clause set generated from a substitution expression, such that P is total if, and only if, $\check{P}$ is empty in the minimal models of the respective Horn clause sets (Section 6.4.2). The clause set for $\check{P}$ is simpler than the one for P: It does not contain function symbols in negative literals anymore. Moreover, because of the restriction of the signature to unary function symbols, the translation causes the clause set to contain monadic predicates only. These properties enable the final decidability of the emptiness of $\check{P}$ by ordered resolution (Theorem 6.49). The complement $\check{P}$ of P for the example is defined by the clauses

$$\to \check{P}_1(s(x))$$
$$\to \check{P}_2(0)$$
$$\check{P}(x) \to \check{P}_2(s(x))$$
$$\check{P}_1(x), \check{P}_2(x) \to \check{P}(x)$$

that belong to a class where emptiness is decidable by ordered resolution (Weidenbach, 1999; Seidl and Verma, 2004). For the above clause set, the theory of the relation $\check{P}$ is empty in the minimal model, hence $N \models_{Ind} \forall x.\exists y.G(y,x)$ holds.

The presented results have been published as (Horbach and Weidenbach, 2009b,c).

6.2 Preliminaries

In this section, I will formally introduce the extended notion of *regular constraint clauses* mentioned in the introduction and define the semantics of these clauses. The basis of the extensions are *substitution expressions*, regular expressions built over substitutions by serial and parallel composition and iteration.

6.2.1 Substitution Expressions and Regular Constraint Clauses

Definition 6.2 (Substitution Expressions)
Let $\Sigma = (\mathcal{S}, \mathcal{F}, \mathcal{X}, \tau_\mathcal{S})$ be a signature. The set of Σ-*substitution expressions* (or simply *substitution expressions*) is the smallest set such that

(i) every Σ-substitution σ is a substitution expression,

(ii) if $\bar\sigma_1, \bar\sigma_2$ are substitution expressions, then so are $\bar\sigma_1 \circ \bar\sigma_2$, $\bar\sigma_1 | \bar\sigma_2$, and $\bar\sigma_1^*$.

6.2 Preliminaries

A substitution expression $\bar\sigma_1 \circ \bar\sigma_2$ is called a *composition*, $\bar\sigma_1|\bar\sigma_2$ a *disjunction*, and $\bar\sigma_1^*$ a *loop*. A composition $\bar\sigma_1 \circ \bar\sigma_2$ is often written more compactly as $\bar\sigma_1\bar\sigma_2$

Definition 6.3 (Domain and Variable Range)
The *domain* $\mathrm{dom}(\bar\sigma)$ and the *variable range* $\mathrm{VRan}(\bar\sigma)$ of a substitution expression are defined inductively as follows:

$$\mathrm{dom}(\sigma) = \{x_1, \ldots, x_n\}$$
$$\text{where } \sigma : \{x_1, \ldots, x_n\} \to \mathcal{T}(\Sigma, \mathcal{X})$$
$$\mathrm{dom}(\bar\sigma \circ \bar\tau) = \mathrm{dom}(\bar\sigma)$$
$$\mathrm{dom}(\bar\sigma_1|\bar\sigma_2) = \mathrm{dom}(\bar\sigma_1) \cup \mathrm{dom}(\bar\sigma_2)$$
$$\mathrm{dom}(\bar\sigma^*) = \mathrm{dom}(\bar\sigma)$$

$$\mathrm{VRan}(\sigma) = \mathrm{var}(x_1\sigma, \ldots, x_n\sigma)$$
$$\text{where } \sigma : \{x_1, \ldots, x_n\} \to \mathcal{T}(\Sigma, \mathcal{X})$$
$$\mathrm{VRan}(\bar\sigma \circ \bar\tau) = \mathrm{VRan}(\bar\tau)$$
$$\mathrm{VRan}(\bar\sigma_1|\bar\sigma_2) = \mathrm{VRan}(\bar\sigma_1) \cap \mathrm{VRan}(\bar\sigma_2)$$
$$\mathrm{VRan}(\bar\sigma^*) = \mathrm{dom}(\bar\sigma)$$

The definition of the variable range for a loop is admittedly dubious at this point. The idea behind the function VRan is that it maps a substitution expression $\bar\sigma$ to the set of variables that are introduced by *every* substitution represented by $\bar\sigma$, provided that $\bar\sigma$ is in some sense well-behaved (cf. Section 6.4.1).

A term t can be regarded as the image $x\sigma$ of a variable x under a substitution σ mapping x to t, which makes expressions of the form $x\bar\sigma$ a generalization of terms. Constraints and clauses are now extended in this spirit:

Definition 6.4 (Regular Constraints)
Let $\Sigma = (\mathcal{S}, \mathcal{F}, \mathcal{X}, \tau_\mathcal{S})$ be a signature and $\mathcal{V} = \{v_1, \ldots, v_n\} \subseteq \mathcal{X}$ be finite, where the v_i are pairwise distinct. A *regular equation* over Σ and $\mathcal{V}$ is a pair $(v, x\bar\sigma)$ where $v \in \mathcal{V}$, $x \in \mathcal{X}$ and $\bar\sigma$ is a substitution expression over Σ such that $x \in \mathrm{dom}(\bar\sigma)$. A *regular constraint* α over Σ and $\mathcal{V}$ is a multiset of regular equations such that

(i) every existential variable occurs exactly once in α and

(ii) all regular equations in α feature a common substitution expression $\bar\sigma$

(iii) existential variables do not occur in the image of any subexpression of $\bar\sigma$.

A regular constraint $v_1 {\simeq} x_1\bar\sigma, \ldots, v_n {\simeq} x_n\bar\sigma$ is also written as $\vec v {\simeq} \vec x\bar\sigma$.

Definition 6.5 (Regular Constraint Clauses)
A *regular constraint clause* $\alpha \parallel C$ over Σ and $\mathcal{V}$ consists of a regular constraint α over Σ and $\mathcal{V}$ and a clause C over Σ such that C does not contain any existential variables, i.e. $\mathrm{var}(C) \cap \mathcal{V} = \emptyset$.

To keep the presentation more concise, a regular constraint that is part of a regular constraint clause is often just called a *constraint*.

A regular constraint clause $\vec{v}{\simeq}\vec{x}\sigma \parallel C$ where σ maps x_i to t_i is written more compactly as $\vec{v}{\simeq}\vec{t} \parallel C$. In particular, it is written as $\vec{v}{\simeq}\vec{x} \parallel C$ if σ is the identity substitution on $\vec{x}$.

If $\bar{\sigma}$ is a variable renaming and C does not contain any variables of $\vec{v}{\simeq}\vec{x}\sigma$, then $\vec{v}{\simeq}\vec{x}\sigma \parallel C$ is abbreviated as $\parallel C$. A regular constraint clause $\parallel C$ is called *unconstrained* and identified with its clausal part C.

Now I will formalize which substitutions are represented by a given substitution expression.

6.2.2 Semantics of Regular Constraint Clauses

Definition 6.6 (Denotations)
Let Σ be a signature. The *denotation* $[\![.]\!]$ of a substitution expression is defined inductively as a set of substitutions as follows:

$$[\![\sigma]\!] = \{\sigma\}$$
$$[\![\bar{\sigma}_1 \circ \bar{\sigma}_2]\!] = \{\sigma_1\pi\sigma_2 \mid \sigma_1 \in [\![\bar{\sigma}_1]\!], \sigma_2 \in [\![\bar{\sigma}_2]\!] \text{ and } \pi \text{ is a variable renaming}$$
$$\pi : \mathrm{var}(\mathrm{im}(\sigma_1)) \setminus \mathrm{dom}(\sigma_2) \to \mathcal{X} \setminus \mathrm{var}(\mathrm{im}(\sigma_2))\}$$
$$[\![\bar{\sigma}_1 | \bar{\sigma}_2]\!] = [\![\bar{\sigma}_1]\!] \cup [\![\bar{\sigma}_2]\!]$$
$$[\![\bar{\sigma}^0]\!] = \{\{x \mapsto x \mid x \in \mathrm{dom}\,\bar{\sigma}\}\}$$
$$[\![\bar{\sigma}^{n+1}]\!] = [\![\bar{\sigma}^n \circ \bar{\sigma}]\!]$$
$$[\![\bar{\sigma}^*]\!] = \bigcup_{n \geq 0}[\![\bar{\sigma}^n]\!]$$

The expressions $\bar{\sigma}^n$ are only auxiliary constructs used in this definition, not full-fledged substitution expressions.

If $\vec{t}$ is a tuple of terms in $\mathcal{T}(\Sigma, \mathcal{X})$, define $\vec{t}[\![\bar{\sigma}]\!] = \{\vec{t}\sigma \mid \sigma \in [\![\bar{\sigma}]\!]\}$.

For a regular constraint clause $\vec{v}{\simeq}\vec{x}\sigma \parallel C$, let $[\![\vec{v}{\simeq}\vec{x}\bar{\sigma} \parallel C]\!]$ be the (potentially infinite) formula set $[\![\vec{v}{\simeq}\vec{x}\bar{\sigma} \parallel C]\!] = \{\forall \vec{y}. \vec{v}{\simeq}\vec{x}\sigma \to C \mid \sigma \in [\![\bar{\sigma}]\!]\}$, where the universal quantifier ranges over the variables of the term list $\vec{x}\sigma$ and of C.

For a set N of constrained clauses, let $[\![N]\!] = \bigcup_{(\vec{v}{\simeq}\vec{x}\bar{\sigma} \parallel C) \in N}[\![\vec{v}{\simeq}\vec{x}\bar{\sigma} \parallel C]\!]$.

The notion of VRan might now become clearer. For the above-mentioned *well-behaved* substitution expressions, $\mathrm{VRan}(\bar{\sigma})$ is the set of all variables that appear in the image of each element of $[\![\bar{\sigma}]\!]$. For the substitution $\sigma = \{x \mapsto f(x, y)\}$, for example, only x is contained in all terms $x\sigma^n$ (because $x[\![\sigma^0]\!] = \{x\}$), hence $\mathrm{VRan}(\sigma^*) = \{x\}$.

6.2 Preliminaries

The rationale behind the variable renaming introduced in the denotation of compositions is that compositions are supposed to accumulate the unifiers used in a series of inferences. Consider for example the inferences

$$\frac{v{\simeq}x \parallel P(x) \to \quad P(x') \to P(f(x',y'))}{v{\simeq}f(x,y) \parallel P(x) \to}$$

and

$$\frac{v{\simeq}f(x,y) \parallel P(x) \to \quad P(x') \to P(f(x',y'))}{v{\simeq}f(f(x,y),y') \parallel P(x) \to},$$

where the conclusion of the first inference is used as a premise in the second inference. Although in both inferences $P(x)$ and $P(f(x',y'))$ are unified using the same unifier $\sigma = \{x \mapsto f(x,y), x' \mapsto x, y' \mapsto y\}$, variables that do not occur in the unified atoms must be renamed in the second inference. So the constraint of the last clause is not $v{\simeq}x\sigma\sigma$, which would translate to $v{\simeq}f(f(x,y),y)$, but $v{\simeq}x\sigma\pi\sigma$, where π maps the variable y to a fresh variable.

Because of the associativity of set union, $[\![(\bar{\sigma}_1|\bar{\sigma}_2)|\bar{\sigma}_3]\!] = [\![\bar{\sigma}_1|(\bar{\sigma}_2|\bar{\sigma}_3)]\!]$, i.e. $|$ is associative. It is also easy to check that $[\![(\bar{\sigma}_1 \circ \bar{\sigma}_2) \circ \bar{\sigma}_3]\!] = [\![\bar{\sigma}_1 \circ (\bar{\sigma}_2 \circ \bar{\sigma}_3)]\!]$ holds. This justifies the following abbreviating notation:

Definition 6.7 (Abbreviations for Substitution Expressions)
Brackets are often omitted in the description of nested compositions and disjunctions. In particular, $\bar{\sigma}_1 \circ \bar{\sigma}_2 \circ \bar{\sigma}_3$ ambiguously denotes both $(\bar{\sigma}_1 \circ \bar{\sigma}_2) \circ \bar{\sigma}_3$ and $\bar{\sigma}_1 \circ (\bar{\sigma}_2 \circ \bar{\sigma}_3)$, and $\bar{\sigma}_1|\bar{\sigma}_2|\bar{\sigma}_3$ ambiguously denotes both $(\bar{\sigma}_1|\bar{\sigma}_2)|\bar{\sigma}_3$ and $\bar{\sigma}_1|(\bar{\sigma}_2|\bar{\sigma}_3)$.

I will now extend the notion of coverage to substitution expressions. To reach more natural and concise formulations later on, coverage is formally defined as a property of the substitution expressions themselves, not of regular constraints. The concrete connection between coverage of constraints and substitution expressions will be clarified in Lemma 6.9.

Definition 6.8 (Coverage)
A substitution expression $\bar{\sigma}$ over Σ and $\mathcal{X}$ with domain $\mathrm{dom}(\bar{\sigma}) = \{x_1, \ldots, x_n\}$ is *covering for a set* $T \subseteq \mathcal{T}(\Sigma, \mathcal{X})^n$ of n-tuples of terms if all ground instances of elements of T are instances of an element of $(x_1, \ldots, x_n)[\![\bar{\sigma}]\!]$. If $\bar{\sigma}$ is covering for $\mathcal{T}(\Sigma)^n$, then $\bar{\sigma}$ is simply called *covering*.

Lemma 6.9
A finite set $\{\alpha_1, \ldots, \alpha_n\}$ of positive constraints (*not* regular constraints) over Σ and $\mathcal{V}$ is covering in the sense of Definition 2.39 if, and only if, the substitution expression $\sigma_{\alpha_1}|\ldots|\sigma_{\alpha_n}$ is covering, where $\sigma_{\alpha_i} : \mathcal{V} \to \mathcal{T}(\Sigma)$ is the substitution mapping an existential variable v to t whenever $v{\simeq}t$ is an equation in α_i.

Example 6.10
Consider the signature Σ_{nat} and substitutions $\sigma = \{x \mapsto s(x)\}$, $\tau = \{x \mapsto 0\}$ and $\rho = \{x \mapsto s(x), y \mapsto z\}$. The substitution expressions $\sigma|\tau$, σ^* and ρ^* are covering. The substitution expressions σ, τ and ρ themselves are not covering because σ does not cover the term 0, τ does not cover the term $s(0)$, and ρ does not cover the pair $(0,0)$.

Definition 6.11 (Entailment)
An interpretation $\mathcal{I} = (U, I)$ *entails* a set N of regular constraint clauses over Σ and $\mathcal{X}$, written $\mathcal{I} \models N$, if, and only if, there is an assignment $\mu : \mathcal{V} \to U$ such that $\mathcal{I}, \mu \models \phi$ for every $\phi \in [\![N]\!]$. In this case, $\mathcal{I}$ is called a *model* of N. A set of regular constraint clauses is *satisfiable* if it has a model. If M and N are two sets of regular constraint clauses, the expression $N \models M$ means that each model of N is also a model of M. If N is Horn and satisfiable, then N has a unique minimal Herbrand model over Σ, and $N \models_{Ind} M$ denotes that this minimal model entails M.

In analogy to the case of constrained clauses, universal variables in regular constraint clauses can be renamed without changing the semantics. The main complication for regular constraint clauses is that this renaming cannot just be applied to the regular constraints, because applying a substitution to a substitution expression is not defined. Instead, the involved substitution expressions must be extended by concatenating the renaming and then denotations must be compared.

Definition 6.12 (Variants)
Two regular constraint clauses $\vec{v} \simeq \vec{x}\bar{\sigma} \parallel C$ and $\vec{v} \simeq \vec{y}\bar{\sigma}' \parallel C'$ are *variants* if there is a variable renaming $\pi : \text{VRan}(\bar{\sigma}) \cup \text{var}(C) \to \text{VRan}(\bar{\sigma}') \cup \text{var}(C')$ such that

(i) π maps the variables of $\text{VRan}(\bar{\sigma})$ to $\text{VRan}(\bar{\sigma}')$,

(ii) $C\pi = C'$, and

(iii) $\vec{x}[\![\bar{\sigma}\pi]\!] = \vec{y}[\![\bar{\sigma}']\!]$.

If both C and C' are unconstrained, this reduces to the usual notion of variants. Indeed, the denotations of variants agree up to a renaming of bound variables. This justifies the abbreviation $\parallel C$ of Definition 6.5 because all regular constraint clauses that are abbreviated as $\parallel C$ are variants.

Example 6.13
Let $\sigma = \{x \mapsto s(x)\}$, $\tau_1 = \{y \mapsto s(y)\}$ and $\tau_2 = \{y \mapsto s(s(y))\}$. The two regular constraint clauses $v \simeq x\sigma^* \parallel \to P(x)$ and $v \simeq y(\tau_2^*|(\tau_1\tau_2^*)) \parallel \to P(y)$ are variants because of the variable renaming $\pi = \{x \mapsto y\}$: The denotation of σ^* comprises exactly the substitutions of the form $x \mapsto s^n(x)$ and $\tau_2^*|(\tau_1\tau_2^*)$

those of the form $y \mapsto s^n(y)$. So both $\vec{x}[\![\sigma^*\pi]\!]$ and $\vec{y}[\![\tau_2^*|(\tau_1\tau_2^*)]\!]$ consist of the terms of the form $s^n(y)$.

6.2.3 Inferences and Redundancy

The notions of *inferences*, *inference rules*, *inference calculi* and *derivations* from Definition 2.44 carry over naturally to regular constraint clauses. However, the same does not hold for the notion of *redundancy* from Definition 2.45. The main reason is that the accumulative nature of regular constraints allows for a new redundancy notion based on subset relations between the denotations of regular constraints.

Definition 6.14 (Redundancy and Saturation)
A regular constraint clause $\vec{v} \simeq \vec{x}\vec{\sigma} \parallel C$ is *redundant with respect to a set* N of regular constraint clauses if

(i) C is a tautology or

(ii) there is a variant $\vec{v} \simeq \vec{x}\vec{\tau} \parallel C$ of a regular constraint clause in N such that $[\![\vec{\sigma}]\!] \subsetneq [\![\vec{\tau}]\!]$.

An inference is *redundant with respect to* N if its conclusion is redundant with respect to N or if a premise $\alpha \parallel C$ of the inference is redundant with respect to N. A set of regular constraint clauses N is *saturated* with respect to a given inference calculus if each inference in the calculus with premises in N is redundant with respect to N.

Redundancy usually defines a well-founded partial ordering on clauses. The notion of redundancy introduced here is not well-founded as, e.g., each regular constraint clause in the sequence

$$v \simeq x\sigma_1 \parallel C, \ v \simeq x(\sigma_1|\sigma_2) \parallel C, \ v \simeq x(\sigma_1|\sigma_2|\sigma_3) \parallel C, \ \ldots$$

with pairwise different substitutions $\sigma_i : \{x\} \to \mathcal{T}(\Sigma)$ is redundant with respect to its successor. Hence the termination of saturation for calculi in the context of regular constraint clauses cannot be proved by using such a property. This will affect the termination proof in Section 6.3.3.

6.3 A Resolution Calculus for Regular Constraint Clauses

I will now introduce an inference system for regular constraint clauses. This inference system is based on the calculus **SFD** presented in Chapter 4. In

Chapter 6: Generic Superposition-based Decidability of Minimal Model Validity

Section 6.3.1, I will show how SFD behaves in the predicative Horn setting described in the introduction. I will then identify an adaption of SFD using a constraint melting rule, called ORM, that allows to decide the class of so-called existential query problems. Soundness, refutational completeness and termination of ORM for existential query problems are proved in Sections 6.3.2 and 6.3.3.

The running example in this section will be representation of the "one greater than" relation that was introduced in the introduction. I will shortly recall how this example is translated into the language of regular constraint clauses:

Example 6.15
In the example of the "one greater than" relation, where the set of existential variables is $V = \{v\}$, the correspondence between the components of the initial problem and their respective representations as regular constraint clauses is as follows (σ_x denotes the substitution $\sigma_x = \{x \mapsto x\}$):

$$
\begin{array}{rl}
\to G(s(s(0)), s(0)) \,\hat{=}\, v{\simeq}x\sigma_x \| & \to G(s(s(0)), s(0)) \\
G(x,y) \to G(s(x), s(y)) \,\hat{=}\, v{\simeq}x\sigma_x \| & G(y_1, y_2) \to G(s(y_1), s(y_2)) \\
G(s(x), s(y)) \to G(x,y) \,\hat{=}\, v{\simeq}x\sigma_x \| G(s(y_1), s(y_2)) \to G(y_1, y_2) \\
\text{negation of } \forall x.\exists y.G(y,x) \,\hat{=}\, v{\simeq}x\sigma_x \| & G(y,x) \to
\end{array}
$$

Since I usually omit the explicit mentioning of σ_x and of constraint equations the variables of which do not occur in the clausal part (cf. Definition 6.5), this can also be written as follows:

$$
\begin{array}{rl}
\to G(s(s(0)), s(0)) \,\hat{=}\, \| & \to G(s(s(0)), s(0)) \\
G(x,y) \to G(s(x), s(y)) \,\hat{=}\, \| & G(y_1, y_2) \to G(s(y_1), s(y_2)) \\
G(s(x), s(y)) \to G(x,y) \,\hat{=}\, \| G(s(y_1), s(y_2)) \to G(y_1, y_2) \\
\text{negation of } \forall x.\exists y.G(y,x) \,\hat{=}\, v{\simeq}x \| & G(y,x) \to
\end{array}
$$

6.3.1 Melting and the Calculus ORM

The negation of a query of the form $\forall \vec{x}.\exists \vec{y}.\phi$ with positive and quantifier-free ϕ corresponds to a set of regular constraint clauses of the form $\vec{v}{\simeq}\vec{x} \| \Gamma \to$, i.e. with empty succedent. This motivates the following definition:

Definition 6.16 (Existential Query Problems)
An *existential query problem* is a set of regular constraint clauses all of which are of the form

(i) $\quad \| \Gamma \to A$ or
(ii) $\vec{v}{\simeq}\vec{x} \| \Gamma \to .$

6.3 A Resolution Calculus for Regular Constraint Clauses

Ordered Query Resolution:

$$\frac{\Gamma_1 \to A_1 \quad \vec{v} \simeq \vec{x}\sigma \parallel \Gamma_2, A_2 \to \Delta_2}{\vec{v} \simeq \vec{x}\bar\sigma\tau' \parallel \Gamma_1\tau, \Gamma_2\tau \to \Delta_2\tau}$$

where

(i) τ is the most general unifier of A_1 and A_2,
(ii) $\tau' : \mathrm{VRan}(\bar\sigma) \to \mathcal{T}(\Sigma, \mathcal{X})$ maps y to $y\tau$ if $y \in \mathrm{dom}(\tau)$ and to y otherwise, and
(iii) $A_1\tau$ is strictly maximal in $(\Gamma_1 \to A_1)\tau$ and $A_2\tau$ is maximal in $(\Gamma_2, A_2 \to \Delta_2)\tau$, where Δ_2 is either empty or contains a single atom.

Figure 6.1: The Ordered Query Resolution Rule

The only useful rule of SFD in a non-equational Horn setting is Left Superposition (followed by an elimination of the equation $c_{\mathrm{true}} \simeq c_{\mathrm{true}}$ in the antecedent): Equality Resolution, Constraint Superposition, and Equality Elimination are never applicable if all atoms are of the form $f_P(\vec{t}) \simeq c_{\mathrm{true}}$ (which is abbreviated as $P(\vec{t})$) and Equality Factoring is not applicable to Horn clauses. Right Superposition might be applicable, but it only creates clauses that contain a positive atom $c_{\mathrm{true}} \simeq c_{\mathrm{true}}$ and are tautologies.

When inferences are drawn between regular constraint clauses in an equational query problem, the resulting regular constraint clauses are still either unconstrained or have an empty succedent, i.e. are of the form

(i) $\parallel \Gamma \to A$ or
(ii) $\vec{v} \simeq \vec{x}\sigma \parallel \Gamma \to$.

Hence the first premise of a Left Superposition inference between regular constraint clauses derived from an existential query problem always has an empty constraint. Written down its predicative form and adapted to this setting and to regular constraints, Left Superposition becomes the Ordered Query Resolution rule presented in Figure 6.1.

Note that Ordered Query Resolution can as usual be restricted by means of a literal selection function. Moreover, the (unconstrained) Ordered Resolution rule is included as the restriction of Ordered Query Resolution to unconstrained clauses.

The main weakness of the calculus SFD, and also of Ordered Query Resolution alone, is that it does not terminate even in very simple cases.

Example 6.17
Consider again the example of the "one greater" relation defined by the unconstrained clauses

$$\to G(s(s(0)), s(0))$$
$$G(x, y) \to G(s(x), s(y))$$
$$G(s(x), s(y)) \to G(x, y)$$

and the query $\forall x.\exists y.G(y, x)$.

Starting from the translation of the problem into the language of regular constraint clauses in Example 6.15, a possible derivation with Ordered Query Resolution (or with **SFD**) runs as follows. Remember that I omit constraints whose variables do not occur in the clausal part.

clauses defining G: 1 :	||		$\to G(s(s(0)), s(0))$
2 :	||	$G(y_1, y_2) \to G(s(y_1), s(y_2))$
3 :	||	$G(s(y_1), s(y_2)) \to G(y_1, y_2)$
negated query: 4 :	$v \simeq x$	||	$G(y, x) \to$
resolve(1,3) = 5 :		||	$\to G(s(0), 0)$
resolve(5,4) = 6 :	$v \simeq 0$	||	$\square$
resolve(2,4) = 7 :	$v \simeq s(x)$	||	$G(y, x) \to$
resolve(5,7) = 8 :	$v \simeq s(0)$	||	$\square$
resolve(2,7) = 9 :	$v \simeq s(s(x))$	||	$G(y, x) \to$
resolve(5,9) = 10 :	$v \simeq s(s(0))$	||	$\square$
resolve(2,9) = 11 :	$v \simeq s(s(x))$	||	$G(y, x) \to$
resolve(5,11) = 12 :	$v \simeq s(s(s(0)))$	||	$\square$
...			

Clause 2 can now be resolved with clause 11 (and its descendants) an arbitrary number of times, and clause 5 can be resolved with each of the conclusions. So similar regular constraint clauses will now be computed with ever increasing regular constraints, making the derivation non-terminating.

A human observer of the previous example will quickly see that regular constraint clauses with empty clausal part, i.e. contradictions, will be derived successively for all regular constraints of the form $v \simeq s^n(0)$, where $s^n(0)$ denotes the n-fold application $s(\ldots s(0) \ldots)$ of s to 0. He might thus replace all these infinitely many constrained clauses by only one constrained "super" clause, writing it, e.g., as $v \simeq s^*(0) \parallel \square$. In fact, I will show that such repetitive behavior is the only reason for non-termination, and that the melting of the repeated clauses into one regular constraint clause subsuming them all can be automated.

To do so, I now extend the calculus **SFD** to an inference system consisting of Ordered Query Resolution and a rule that executes this melting.

6.3 A Resolution Calculus for Regular Constraint Clauses

Melting:
$$\frac{\vec{v}{\simeq}\vec{x}\bar{\sigma} \parallel C \quad \vec{v}{\simeq}\vec{x}\bar{\sigma}\bar{\tau}' \parallel C'}{\vec{v}{\simeq}\vec{x}\bar{\sigma}'' \parallel C}$$

where

(i) $\vec{v}{\simeq}\vec{x}\bar{\sigma} \parallel C$ is an ancestor of $\vec{v}{\simeq}\vec{x}\bar{\sigma}\bar{\tau}' \parallel C'$,
(ii) there is a substitution expression $\bar{\tau}$ such that $\vec{v}{\simeq}\vec{x}\bar{\sigma}\bar{\tau}' \parallel C'$ is a variant of $\vec{v}{\simeq}\vec{x}\bar{\sigma}\bar{\tau} \parallel C$, and
(iii) a) either $\bar{\sigma}$ is of the form $\bar{\sigma} = \bar{\sigma}_1\bar{\sigma}_2^*$ and $\bar{\sigma}'' = \bar{\sigma}_1(\bar{\sigma}_2|\bar{\tau})^*$, or
b) $\bar{\sigma}$ is not of this form and $\bar{\sigma}'' = \bar{\sigma}\bar{\tau}^*$.

Figure 6.2: The Melting Rule

Definition 6.18 (Ancestors and ORM)
Let $\succ$ be a well-founded strict reduction ordering on atoms over Σ that is total on ground atoms. To define the Melting inference rule, every regular constraint clause is annotated with a set of regular constraint clauses, called its *ancestors*. The *Ordered Resolution Calculus with Melting* ORM consists of the two rules in Figures 6.1 and 6.2, where all (strict) maximality constraints have to be considered with respect to $\succ$.

A regular constraint clause that serves as the rightmost premise of a Melting inference is called *meltable*. The leftmost premise of a Melting inference is called the *base clause* for the melting, and the conclusion the *melted clause*.

As before, I will implicitly assume that a well-founded strict reduction ordering $\succ$ on atoms over Σ that is total on ground atoms is fixed for all following considerations.

Example 6.19
With Melting, it is possible to combine the two regular constraint clauses $v{\simeq}x \parallel G(y,x) \to$ and $v{\simeq}x\sigma \parallel G(y,x) \to$, as they appeared in the introduction and in Example 6.17, into the regular constraint clause $v{\simeq}x\sigma^* \parallel G(y,x) \to$:

$$\frac{v{\simeq}x \parallel G(y,x) \to \quad v{\simeq}x\sigma \parallel G(y,x) \to}{v{\simeq}x\sigma^* \parallel G(y,x) \to}$$

The Melting rule is in general unsound. For example, the two regular constraint clauses $v{\simeq}x \parallel G(y,x) \to$ and $v{\simeq}x\sigma \parallel G(y,x) \to$ by themselves do not imply $v{\simeq}x\sigma^* \parallel G(y,x) \to$; it is only the context in which they appear that validates the melting. Hence the choice of the ancestor sets of the regular constraint clauses appearing in a ORM derivation has to ensure that Melting is sound:

Definition 6.20 (Existential Query Derivations)
A ORM derivation $N_0, N_1, \ldots$ is an *existential query derivation* if
(i) N_0 is an existential query problem and
(ii) The ancestors of the regular constraint clauses in the derivation are defined as follows:
   a) For every regular constraint clause in N_0, the ancestor set in N_0 is empty.
   b) For every regular constraint clause in N_{i+1} that is also contained in N_i, the set of ancestors in N_{i+1} is the set of ancestors in N_i.
   c) If $N_{i+1} = N_i \cup \{\alpha \,\|\, C\}$ and $\alpha \,\|\, C \notin N_i$ is the conclusion of an Ordered Query Resolution inference between regular constraint clauses in N_i, then the ancestors of $\alpha \,\|\, C$ in N_{i+1} are the rightmost premise of the inference and all of its ancestors in N_i.
   d) If $N_{i+1} = N_i \cup \{\alpha \,\|\, C\}$ and $\alpha \,\|\, C \notin N_i$ is the conclusion of a Melting inference between regular constraint clauses in N_i, then the ancestors of $\alpha \,\|\, C$ in N_{i+1} are ancestors of the base clause of the inference in N_i (but not the base clause itself).

Note that if a regular constraint clause is an element of two sets N_i and N_j in a derivation, its ancestors as an element of N_i and of N_j may be different, for example because the regular constraint clause was at some point in the derivation deleted and later re-derived. However, this will usually not occur, and I will simply speak of *ancestors* of a regular constraint clause if no ambiguities arise from this.

Example 6.21
A possible existential query derivation for the introductory example looks as follows, where the substitutions σ and τ are defined by $\sigma = \{x \mapsto s(x)\}$ and $\tau = \{x \mapsto 0\}$:

$$
\begin{array}{rlll}
\text{clauses defining } G: \;\; 1: & & \| & \to G(s(s(0)), s(0)) \\
2: & & \| & G(x,y) \to G(s(x), s(y)) \\
3: & & \| & G(s(x), s(y)) \to G(x,y) \\
\text{negated query: } 4: & v \simeq x & \| & G(y, x) \to \\
\text{resolve}(1,3) = 5: & & \| & \to G(s(0), 0) \\
\text{resolve}(5,4) = 6: & v \simeq x\tau & \| & \square \\
\text{resolve}(2,4) = 7: & v \simeq x\sigma & \| & G(y,x) \to \\
\text{melt}(4,7) = 8: & v \simeq x\sigma^* & \| & G(y,x) \to \\
\text{resolve}(5,8) = 9: & v \simeq x\sigma^*\tau & \| & \square \\
\end{array}
$$

The only regular constraint clauses with non-empty ancestor set are 5, 6, 7, and 9, with ancestors {3}, {4}, {4}, and {8}, respectively. The set of regular constraint clauses {1,...,9} is saturated with respect to ORM.

6.3.2 Soundness and Completeness of ORM

To establish the soundness of ORM in existential query derivations, I have to show the soundness of the two rules Ordered Query Resolution and Melting. While the former is easy, the main objective will be to prove that all elements of the conclusion's denotation in a Melting inference step are really consequences of the premises.

Lemma 6.22 (Soundness of Ordered Query Resolution)
The Ordered Query Resolution rule is sound.

Proof. For an inference

$$\frac{\Gamma_1 \to A_1 \quad \vec{v} \simeq \vec{x}\bar{\sigma} \parallel \Gamma_2, A_2 \to \Delta_2}{\vec{v} \simeq \vec{x}\bar{\sigma}\tau' \parallel \Gamma_1\tau, \Gamma_2\tau \to \Delta_2\tau}$$

to be sound, it suffices that each inference

$$\frac{\Gamma_1 \to A_1 \quad \vec{v} \simeq \vec{x}\sigma \parallel \Gamma_2, A_2 \to \Delta_2}{\vec{v} \simeq \vec{x}\sigma\tau' \parallel \Gamma_1\tau, \Gamma_2\tau \to \Delta_2\tau}$$

for $\sigma \in [\![\bar{\sigma}]\!]$ is sound. This is the case because of the soundness of the SFD rule Left Superposition (or its ORFD counterpart Ordered Resolution), c.f. Proposition 4.15. ◊

The soundness of Melting is not that obvious: The Melting rule introduces regular constraint clauses that do not follow from the premises. For example, the two regular constraint clauses $v \simeq x \parallel G(y,x) \to$ and $v \simeq x\sigma \parallel G(y,x) \to$ by themselves do not imply $v \simeq x\sigma^* \parallel G(y,x) \to$. In fact, the soundness of Melting strongly depends on the context, e.g. on the clauses it is applied to but also on other available inference. Above all, the requirement that the left-most premise of Ordered Query Resolution inferences is unconstrained is imperative:

Example 6.23
Assume that Ordered Resolution inferences in the style of ORFD were allowed (cf. Chapter 5), i.e. with a constrained first premise. Consider an inference between the two regular constraint clauses $v \simeq s(x) \parallel P(x) \to P(s(x))$ and $v \simeq x \parallel P(x) \to$:

$$\frac{v \simeq s(x) \parallel P(x) \to P(s(x)) \quad v \simeq x \parallel P(x) \to}{v \simeq s(x) \parallel P(x) \to}$$

The application of Melting to the regular constraint clause $v{\simeq}x \parallel P(x) \rightarrow$ as an ancestor of $v{\simeq}s(x) \parallel P(x) \rightarrow$ is unsound, because $v{\simeq}s(s(x)) \parallel P(x) \rightarrow$ is not implied by the given constrained clauses.

To establish the soundness of Melting for existential query derivations, observe the following:

(i) Since the leftmost premise of each Ordered Query Resolution inference is unconstrained (by definition), an Ordered Query Resolution inference with rightmost premise $\vec{v}{\simeq}\vec{x}\bar{\sigma} \parallel C$ and conclusion $\vec{v}{\simeq}\vec{x}\bar{\sigma}\tau \parallel D$ can also be made with any other regular constraint clause $\vec{v}{\simeq}\vec{x}\bar{\sigma}' \parallel C$ with the same clausal part but a different constraint, then resulting in the regular constraint clause $\vec{v}{\simeq}\vec{x}\bar{\sigma}'\tau \parallel D$:

$$\frac{\Gamma \rightarrow A \quad v{\simeq}x\bar{\sigma} \parallel C}{\vec{v}{\simeq}\vec{x}\bar{\sigma}\tau \parallel D} \quad \rightsquigarrow \quad \frac{\Gamma \rightarrow A \quad v{\simeq}x\bar{\sigma}' \parallel C}{\vec{v}{\simeq}\vec{x}\bar{\sigma}'\tau \parallel D}$$

If the former inference is sound, so is the latter.

(ii) The second observation is that, if a ORM derivation starts from an existential query problem, i.e. from regular constraint clauses that do not contain any loops $\bar{\sigma}^*$, then all loops appearing in constraints during the derivation have been introduced by Melting steps.

Lemma 6.24 (Soundness of Melting)
For existential query derivations, the Melting rule is sound.

Proof. Melting derivations can take one of two shapes, corresponding to the two side conditions (ii,a) and (ii,b).

Consider a derivation step from a set N of regular constraint clauses to N' where a Melting inference

$$\frac{\vec{v}{\simeq}\vec{x}\bar{\sigma}_1\bar{\sigma}_2^* \parallel C \quad \vec{v}{\simeq}\vec{x}\bar{\sigma}_1\bar{\sigma}_2^*\bar{\tau}' \parallel C'}{\vec{v}{\simeq}\vec{x}\bar{\sigma}_1(\bar{\sigma}_2|\bar{\tau})^* \parallel C}$$

of type (ii,b) is performed. I will show that, for each integer $n \geq 0$, the regular constraint clause $\vec{v}{\simeq}\vec{x}\bar{\sigma}_1(\bar{\sigma}_2|\bar{\tau})^n \parallel C$ is implied by the regular constraint clauses in N.

Since the derivation started from regular constraint clauses whose constraints do not contain any loops, the regular constraint clause $\vec{v}{\simeq}\vec{x}\bar{\sigma}_1\bar{\sigma}_2^* \parallel C$ must have been derived from some regular constraint clause $\vec{v}{\simeq}\vec{x}\bar{\sigma}_1 \parallel C$ or $\vec{v}{\simeq}\vec{x}\bar{\sigma}_1\bar{\sigma}'^* \parallel C$ to account for the loop around $\bar{\sigma}_2$.

So the case $n = 0$ is trivial.

6.3 A Resolution Calculus for Regular Constraint Clauses

If $n > 0$, assume that the regular constraint clause $\vec{v} \simeq \vec{x} \bar{\sigma}_1 (\bar{\sigma}_2|\bar{\tau})^{n-1} \parallel C$ is implied. Moreover, inductively assume that all previous steps in the derivation are sound.

Following the remarks preceding this lemma, the same set of inference steps needed to derive $\vec{v} \simeq \vec{x} \bar{\sigma}_1 \bar{\sigma}_2^* \parallel C$ from $\vec{v} \simeq \vec{x} \bar{\sigma}_1 \parallel C$ could be used to derive the regular constraint clause $\vec{v} \simeq \vec{x} \bar{\sigma}_1 (\bar{\sigma}_2|\bar{\tau})^{n-1} \bar{\sigma}_2^* \parallel C$ from $\vec{v} \simeq \vec{x} \bar{\sigma}_1 (\bar{\sigma}_2|\bar{\tau})^{n-1} \parallel C$. This regular constraint clause directly implies $\vec{v} \simeq \vec{x} \bar{\sigma}_1 (\bar{\sigma}_2|\bar{\tau})^{n-1} \bar{\sigma}_2 \parallel C$.

Along the same lines, the same set of inference steps needed to derive $\vec{v} \simeq \vec{x} \bar{\sigma}_1 \bar{\sigma}_2^* \bar{\tau} \parallel C$ from $\vec{v} \simeq \vec{x} \bar{\sigma}_1 \bar{\sigma}_2^* \parallel C$ could be used to derive $\vec{v} \simeq \vec{x} \bar{\sigma}_1 (\bar{\sigma}_2|\bar{\tau})^{n-1} \bar{\tau} \parallel C$.

Thus, both $\vec{v} \simeq \vec{x} \bar{\sigma}_1 (\bar{\sigma}_2|\bar{\tau})^{n-1} \bar{\sigma}_2 \parallel C$ and $\vec{v} \simeq \vec{x} \bar{\sigma}_1 (\bar{\sigma}_2|\bar{\tau})^{n-1} \bar{\tau} \parallel C$ are implied regular constraint clauses, and hence also $\vec{v} \simeq \vec{x} \bar{\sigma}_1 (\bar{\sigma}_2|\bar{\tau})^{n-1} (\bar{\sigma}_2|\bar{\tau}) \parallel C$ is implied.

If the Melting inference is of type (ii,a), i.e. of the shape

$$\frac{\vec{v} \simeq \vec{x} \bar{\sigma}_1 \parallel C \quad \vec{v} \simeq \vec{x} \bar{\sigma}_1 \bar{\tau}' \parallel C'}{\vec{v} \simeq \vec{x} \bar{\sigma}_1 \bar{\tau}^* \parallel C} \quad ,$$

the argumentation is analogous, except that the suffix $\bar{\sigma}_2$ need not be re-derived. ◇

Concerning completeness, I can make use of the following proposition:

Proposition 6.25 (Completeness)
Let N be a finite existential query problem, let N^* be a finite saturation of N with respect to Ordered Query Resolution, and let $\vec{v} \simeq \vec{x} \bar{\sigma}_1 \parallel \square, \ldots, \vec{v} \simeq \vec{x} \bar{\sigma}_m \parallel \square$ be the regular constraint clauses in N^* with empty clausal part. Then N has a Herbrand model if, and only if, $\bar{\sigma}_1 | \ldots | \bar{\sigma}_m$ is not covering.

Proof. By Lemma 6.9, that links coverage of constraints and of substitution expressions, this proposition is an instance of Theorem 4.12. ◇

As the Ordered Query Resolution rule alone is already complete, the same holds for the combination of Ordered Query Resolution and Melting.

Hence, provided saturation with ORM terminates, I can express the initial problem whether $N \models_{Ind} \forall \vec{x}. \exists \vec{y}. \phi$ for positive and quantifier-free ϕ in terms of a coverage problem:

Corollary 6.26
Let N be a satisfiable set of unconstrained Horn clauses, let N^* be a finite saturation of the set $N \cup \{\vec{v} \simeq \vec{x} \parallel A_{11}, \ldots, A_{1m_1} \to, \ldots, \vec{v} \simeq \vec{x} \parallel A_{n1}, \ldots, A_{nm_n} \to\}$ with respect to ORM, and let $\vec{v} \simeq \vec{x} \bar{\sigma}_1 \parallel \square, \ldots, \vec{v} \simeq \vec{x} \bar{\sigma}_m \parallel \square$ be the set of regular constraint clauses in N^* with empty clausal part. Then the following are equivalent:

(i) $N \models_{Ind} \forall \vec{x}. \exists \vec{y}. \bigvee_i \bigwedge_j A_{ij}$

(ii) $\bar{\sigma}_1 | \ldots | \bar{\sigma}_m$ is not covering.

6.3.3 Termination of ORM

I now show that, if a clause set $N \cup \{\Gamma_1 \to, \ldots, \Gamma_n \to\}$ can be finitely saturated by Ordered Resolution (modulo variants and tautologies), then the calculus ORM finitely saturates the set $N \cup \{\vec{v} \simeq \vec{x} \,\|\, \Gamma_1 \to, \ldots, \vec{v} \simeq \vec{x} \,\|\, \Gamma_n \to\}$. Termination also ensures that derivations are *fair*, i.e. that every possible inference between derived regular constraint clauses will finally be redundant.

The derivation strategy that ensures termination of existential query derivations proceeds in two stages. First a set of regular constraint clauses is derived using Ordered Query Resolution only, then (the constraints of) these clauses are updated by meltings in such a way that the resulting clause set is saturated:

Derivation Strategy 6.27
Proceed according to the following two stages:

(i) Perform inferences by Ordered Query Resolution on the initial set of regular constraint clauses $N \cup \{\vec{v} \simeq \vec{x} \,\|\, \Gamma_1 \to, \ldots, \vec{v} \simeq \vec{x} \,\|\, \Gamma_n \to\}$ according to the given strategy that would finitely saturate the unconstrained set $N \cup \{\Gamma_1 \to, \ldots, \Gamma_n \to\}$. Whenever a meltable regular constraint clause is derived, do not consider this clause for any further Ordered Query Resolution inferences.

(ii) When no more inferences as in (i) are possible, start melting: Perform a (non-redundant) Melting inference and *update* the derivation: Repeat, starting from the melted clause, all previous (non-redundant) Ordered Query Resolution inferences that have the base clause as an ancestor and all (non-redundant) Melting inferences that are possible with the newly derived regular constraint clauses, as well as all deletion steps. This is called an *elementary update*. Afterwards continue recursively with updates for the repeated Meltings.

When the update is finished, reiterate this stage with another Melting inference.

When updates have been performed for all Meltings, terminate.

An update can be viewed as a generalization of the constraints expressions of previously derived regular constraint clauses. When this happens, the "old" regular constraint clauses with their more specific regular constraints become redundant. This means that they can and will be ignored for the rest of the derivation and are effectively *replaced* by their more general counterparts.

Lemma 6.28
If regular constraint clauses in an existential query derivation are arranged in

6.3 A Resolution Calculus for Regular Constraint Clauses

a graph defined by the direct ancestor relation, then this graph is a forest (a set of trees).

Proof. Initially, each regular constraint clause forms its own tree. These initial regular constraint clauses are and remain roots of the forest.

Recall that the ancestors of a regular constraint clause do not form a binary tree but a line, because basically one premise is always ignored. Because of this, each inference by Ordered Query Resolution extends the tree of the rightmost premise by one fresh leaf.

In Melting inferences, the conclusion becomes a sibling of the base clause, i.e. it either becomes a fresh leaf in the tree of the base clause or, if the base clause is a root, it forms a new root of its own.

In any case, no inference can connect existing trees or introduce loops. ◊

Example 6.29
For Example 6.17, the graph looks as follows, where regular constraint clauses are represented by their numbers:

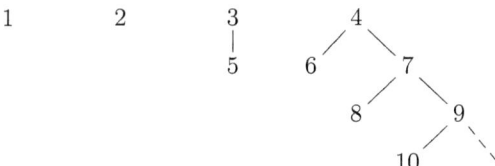

For Example 6.21, which in fact follows Strategy 6.27, the graph looks as follows. The dotted lines are not part of the graph but illustrate replacements caused by the melting of clauses 4 and 7 into clause 8 and the following update:

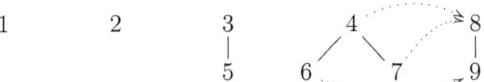

Lemma 6.30 (Termination of Updates)
The update following a Melting inference step in an existential query derivation following Strategy 6.27 terminates.

Proof. Each elementary update is terminating, since there are only finitely many inferences to repeat. I show that the number of elementary updates in an update is finite and proceed by induction over the depth of the base clause in the ancestor-based forest.

Consider the case of a Melting inference as follows:
$$\frac{\vec{v}\simeq\vec{x}\bar{\alpha}\bar{\sigma}^* \parallel C \quad \vec{v}\simeq\vec{x}\bar{\alpha}\bar{\sigma}^*\bar{\tau}' \parallel C'}{\vec{v}\simeq\vec{x}\bar{\alpha}(\bar{\sigma}|\bar{\tau})^* \parallel C}$$

Let
$$\frac{\vec{v}\simeq\vec{x}\bar{\beta} \parallel E \quad \vec{v}\simeq\vec{x}\bar{\beta}\bar{\rho}' \parallel E'}{\vec{v}\simeq\vec{x}\bar{\beta}_1(\bar{\beta}_2|\bar{\rho})^* \parallel E}$$

be a Melting inference that is redundant before the current elementary update. There are several possible cases, depending on whether and where one of the premises of the initial Melting inference appears as an ancestor of $\vec{v}\simeq\vec{x}\bar{\beta}\bar{\rho}' \parallel E'$:

- $\vec{v}\simeq\vec{x}\bar{\alpha}\bar{\sigma}^* \parallel C$ is not an ancestor of $\vec{v}\simeq\vec{x}\bar{\beta}\bar{\rho} \parallel E$. Then this Melting inference is not affected by the elementary update.

- $E = C$. Then also $\bar{\beta} = \bar{\alpha}\bar{\sigma}^*$, and the first elementary update leads to a Melting candidate
$$\frac{\vec{v}\simeq\vec{x}\bar{\alpha}(\bar{\sigma}|\bar{\tau})^* \parallel C \quad \vec{v}\simeq\vec{x}\bar{\alpha}(\bar{\sigma}|\bar{\tau})^*\bar{\rho} \parallel C}{\vec{v}\simeq\vec{x}\bar{\beta}(\bar{\sigma}|\bar{\tau}|\bar{\rho})^* \parallel C}$$
Since the original Melting inference was redundant before, $\llbracket\bar{\rho}\rrbracket \subseteq \llbracket\bar{\sigma}\rrbracket$. So the new Melting candidate is also redundant and this branch of the update stops before the Melting inference.

- $\vec{v}\simeq\vec{x}\bar{\alpha}\bar{\sigma}^* \parallel C$ is an ancestor of $\vec{v}\simeq\vec{x}\bar{\beta} \parallel E$, but not vice versa. Then $\bar{\beta} = \bar{\alpha}\bar{\sigma}^*\bar{\pi}$ and the elementary update leads to a Melting candidate
$$\frac{\vec{v}\simeq\vec{x}\bar{\alpha}(\bar{\sigma}|\bar{\tau})^*\bar{\pi} \parallel E \quad \vec{v}\simeq\vec{x}\bar{\alpha}(\bar{\sigma}|\bar{\tau})^*\bar{\pi}\bar{\rho} \parallel E}{\vec{v}\simeq\vec{x}\bar{\alpha}(\bar{\sigma}|\bar{\tau})^*\bar{\pi}_1(\bar{\pi}_2|\bar{\rho})^* \parallel E}$$
where $\bar{\pi} = \bar{\pi}_1\bar{\pi}_2^*$. Since the original Melting inference was redundant before, $\llbracket\bar{\rho}\rrbracket \subseteq \llbracket\bar{\pi}_2\rrbracket$. So the new Melting candidate is also redundant and this branch of the update stops before the Melting inference.

- $\vec{v}\simeq\vec{x}\bar{\beta} \parallel E$ is an ancestor of $\vec{v}\simeq\vec{x}\bar{\alpha}\bar{\sigma}^* \parallel C$. Then this Melting inference has a base that lies strictly above the base of the originally inspected Melting inference in the ancestor-based clause forest. Because of Lemma 6.28, it may inductively be assumed that the update initiated by the Melting of $\vec{v}\simeq\vec{x}\bar{\beta} \parallel E$ terminates.

This shows that the number of elementary updates is finite in this case. The case of a Melting inference
$$\frac{\vec{v}\simeq\vec{x}\bar{\alpha} \parallel C \quad \vec{v}\simeq\vec{x}\bar{\alpha}\bar{\tau}' \parallel C'}{\vec{v}\simeq\vec{x}\bar{\alpha}\bar{\tau}^* \parallel C}$$
works similarly. $\diamond$

6.3 A Resolution Calculus for Regular Constraint Clauses

Lemma 6.31 (Saturation)
Let $N \cup \{\Gamma_1 \to, \ldots, \Gamma_n \to\}$ be a finite set of Horn clauses. If an existential query derivation that uses Strategy 6.27 and starts from the set $N \cup \{\vec{v}{\simeq}\vec{x} \,\|\, \Gamma_1 \to, \ldots, \vec{v}{\simeq}\vec{x} \,\|\, \Gamma_n \to\}$ terminates with a set N^*, then N^* is saturated with respect to ORM.

Proof. I have to show that all Melting and Ordered Query Resolution inferences with premises in N^* are redundant.

All possible Melting inferences with premises in N^* are redundant because, by assumption, the second stage of the derivation terminates.

For any given Melting inference, redundancy can have one of three reasons, all of which imply that the leftmost premise of the Melting inference is redundant: If the conclusion is redundant, then so are both premises. If the rightmost premise is redundant, then so is the leftmost, because it was derived from a redundant regular constraint clause. Or finally, the leftmost premise itself might be redundant.

All in all, each meltable regular constraint clause in N^* is redundant, which means that also all Ordered Query Resolution inferences with a meltable clause are redundant.

The same holds for all Ordered Query Resolution inferences with premises that are not meltable: They are redundant by construction after the first stage and this can easily be seen to be maintained by each elementary update.

So all ORM inferences with premises in N^* are redundant, which means that N^* is saturated. ◊

Theorem 6.32 (Termination)
Let $N \cup \{\Gamma_1 \to, \ldots, \Gamma_n \to\}$ be a finite set of Horn clauses that can be finitely saturated by Ordered Resolution, where deletion steps are restricted to the deletion of variants and tautologies. Then ORM finitely saturates the set $N \cup \{\vec{v}{\simeq}\vec{x} \,\|\, \Gamma_1 \to, \ldots, \vec{v}{\simeq}\vec{x} \,\|\, \Gamma_n \to\}$ of regular constraint clauses using Strategy 6.27.

Proof. Because Lemma 6.31 shows that the strategy yields a saturated set, it remains to show termination of the existential query derivation starting from the constrained clause set $N \cup \{\vec{v}{\simeq}\vec{x} \,\|\, \Gamma_1 \to, \ldots, \vec{v}{\simeq}\vec{x} \,\|\, \Gamma_n \to\}$. I do so by proving the termination of each stage:

(i) Let M be the (possibly infinite) set of constrained clauses obtained after the first stage of the existential query derivation starting from the initial set $N \cup \{\vec{v}{\simeq}\vec{x} \,\|\, \Gamma_1 \to, \ldots, \vec{v}{\simeq}\vec{x} \,\|\, \Gamma_n \to\}$. I first show that M is finite. To do so, I show that the ancestor-based forest G for M is finite, i.e. it has only finitely many roots, is of finite depth, and is finitely branching.

Chapter 6: Generic Superposition-based Decidability of Minimal Model Validity

- Only the finitely many regular constraint clauses in the initial existential query problem $N \cup \{\vec{v} \simeq \vec{x} \,\|\, \Gamma_1 \to, \ldots, \vec{v} \simeq \vec{x} \,\|\, \Gamma_n \to\}$ can appear as roots.

- Let N_0^* be a finite saturation of $N \cup \{\Gamma_1 \to, \ldots, \Gamma_n \to\}$ with respect to Ordered Resolution.

  Consider two clauses $\vec{v} \simeq \vec{x}\bar{\sigma} \,\|\, C$ and $\vec{v} \simeq \vec{x}\bar{\sigma}\bar{\tau} \,\|\, C'$ lying on a common branch, such that none of them is a leaf. Because of the strategy of forbidding ordered query resolution inferences with clauses that can be melted with an ancestor, the two clauses cannot be melted. So there is no substitution expression $\bar{\tau}'$ such that $\vec{v} \simeq \vec{x}\bar{\sigma}\bar{\tau} \,\|\, C'$ is a variant of $\vec{v} \simeq \vec{x}\bar{\sigma}\bar{\tau}' \,\|\, C$.

  This means that every branch in G contains only a finite number of inner nodes for each element C of N_0^*: There is at most one for each subset of $\mathrm{var}(C)$, since these correspond to the possibilities for $\mathrm{VRan}(\bar{\sigma}\bar{\tau}) \cap \mathrm{var}(C)$ and hence to regular constraint clauses with clausal part C that are not variants and hence cannot be melted.

  So the graph is of finite depth.

- Finally, each node in G has a finite arity, as only finitely many inferences into the regular constraint clause at this node have been possible (namely from some of the finitely many unconstrained clauses only).

Since G is finite, and the same holds for M.

(ii) It remains to show that the second stage terminates.

The number of meltable regular constraint clauses is finite when stage (1) is left, because M is finite. There are only finitely many iterations of stage (2), because each such iteration decreases the number of unreplaced meltable regular constraint clauses by one: The initial Melting inference replaces both its premises (and in particular one meltable and unreplaced regular constraint clause), and each inference step in an update keeps the number of unreplaced meltable regular constraint clauses constant.

Moreover, I have proved in Lemma 6.30 that each update, i.e. each iteration, terminates.

So the whole second stage terminates.

Since both stages terminate, so does the whole derivation. ◇

6.4 Generalized Substitutions as Clause Sets

To make use of the completeness result Corollary 6.26, the task remains to decide whether a finite disjunction $\bar\sigma_1|\dots|\bar\sigma_n$ of substitution expressions is covering.

For a finite disjunction $\sigma_1|\dots|\sigma_n$ of substitutions (or equivalently a finite set of constraints), I have shown that this can be done using the predicate completion algorithm PC (Theorem 4.6). To do so, the problem is considered as a disunification problem and reduced to an emptiness problem that is trivially decidable.

For the general case of substitution expressions, there is no obvious translation of coverage into a disunification problem. Instead, I follow a related approach. I will introduce a predicate $P_{\bar\sigma}$ for every substitution expression $\bar\sigma$ that is defined by a Horn clause set $N_{\bar\sigma}$ in such a way that a ground atom $P_{\bar\sigma}(\vec{s})$ holds in the minimal model of $N_{\bar\sigma}$ if, and only if, $\vec{s}$ lies in $\vec{x}[\![\bar\sigma]\!]$, where $\vec{x}$ is the domain of $\bar\sigma$. A clause $P_{\bar\sigma}(\vec{s}) \to P_{\bar\tau}(\vec{t})$ will mean that if a ground instance $\vec{s}\rho$ of $\vec{s}$ is a ground instance of an element of $\vec{x}[\![\bar\sigma]\!]$, then every ground instance of $\vec{t}\rho$ is a ground instance of an element of $\vec{y}[\![\bar\tau]\!]$, where $\vec{x},\vec{y}$ are the respective domains.

In particular, this means that $\bar\sigma$ is covering if, and only if, $P_{\bar\sigma}$ is the total relation in the minimal model of $N_{\bar\sigma}$, i.e. if, and only if, $N_{\bar\sigma} \models_{Ind} \forall \vec{x}.P_{\bar\sigma}(\vec{x})$.

A variation of the predicate completion procedure, the *Negating Predicate Completion Algorithm* NPC (see Definition 6.46), will generate a Horn clause set $\check{N}_{\bar\sigma}$ for the complement of $P_{\bar\sigma}$, named $\check{P}_{\bar\sigma}$, such that $P_{\bar\sigma}$ is total in the minimal model of $N_{\bar\sigma}$ if, and only if, $\check{P}_{\bar\sigma}$ is empty in the minimal model of $\check{N}_{\bar\sigma}$. The completion procedure ensures that $\check{N}_{\bar\sigma}$ has only one Herbrand model over the given signature, which means that emptiness of $\check{P}_{\bar\sigma}$ in the minimal model of $\check{N}_{\bar\sigma}$ is equivalent to the emptiness of $\check{P}_{\bar\sigma}$ in every Herbrand model of $\check{N}_{\bar\sigma}$. Since $\check{N}_{\bar\sigma}$ is composed of unconstrained clauses, the problem can even be considered as a first-order problem that can be decided by ordered resolution. This is, for example, a direct consequence of Proposition 4.25.

I will start the discussion by establishing the link between substitution expressions and clauses. Afterwards, I will recall the predicate completion procedure and explain how to adapt it to substitution expressions, and finally show that it permits to decide the coverage of substitution expressions (Section 6.4.2).

Definition 6.33 (Substitutions and Predicates)
Given a substitution expression $\bar\sigma$, assign a predicate $P_{\bar\tau}$ to every occurrence of a substitution expression $\bar\tau$ that is a subexpression of $\bar\sigma$:

Chapter 6: Generic Superposition-based Decidability of Minimal Model Validity

- If $\bar{\tau}$ is a substitution or disjunction or loop, then $P_{\bar{\tau}}$ is a fresh predicate of arity $|\mathrm{dom}(\bar{\tau})|$.

- If $\bar{\tau} = \bar{\tau}_1 \bar{\tau}_2$ is a concatenation, then $P_{\bar{\tau}} = P_{\bar{\tau}_1}$.

Note that predicates are assigned not to substitution expressions themselves but to *occurrences* of substitution expressions. For example in a substitution expression like $\{x \mapsto x\} \circ \{x \mapsto x\}$, two *different* predicates are assigned to the two occurrences of $\{x \mapsto x\}$.

Example 6.34
Consider the two substitutions $\sigma = \{x \mapsto s(x)\}$ and $\tau = \{x \mapsto 0\}$ appearing in Example 6.21. For the substitution expression $\sigma^*\tau$, fresh predicates P_σ, P_τ and P_{σ^*} are assigned to σ, τ and σ^* and the predicate $P_{\sigma^*\tau}$ assigned to $\sigma^*\tau$ is identical to P_{σ^*}.

Definition 6.35 (Substitutions and Clauses)
Translate substitution expressions $\bar{\sigma}$ to clause sets $N_{\bar{\sigma}}^0$ (which is just an intermediate representation) and $N_{\bar{\sigma}}$ as follows: Let P_{glue} be a fresh predicate of arity 0. This predicate will be used as a means to glue together the sets corresponding to different (occurrences of) substitution expressions. Assume a strict ordering $\prec$ on the set $\mathcal{X}$ of variables and write $\vec{x} = \mathrm{dom}(\bar{\sigma})$ if $\mathrm{dom}(\bar{\sigma}) = \{x_1, \ldots, x_n\}$ and $x_1 \prec \ldots \prec x_n$.

Let $N[B/A]$ denote textual replacement of every occurrence of the atom A in the clause set N by the atom B.

$$N_\sigma^0 = \{P_{\mathrm{glue}} \to P_\sigma(\vec{x}\sigma)\} \text{ where } \vec{x} = \mathrm{dom}(\sigma)$$
$$N_{\bar{\sigma}\bar{\tau}}^0 = N_{\bar{\tau}}^0 \cup N_{\bar{\sigma}}^0[P_{\bar{\tau}}(\mathrm{dom}(\bar{\tau}))/P_{\mathrm{glue}}]$$
$$N_{\bar{\sigma}^*}^0 = \{P_{\mathrm{glue}} \to P_{\bar{\sigma}^*}(\mathrm{dom}(\bar{\sigma}))\}$$
$$\cup\ N_{\bar{\sigma}}^0[P_{\bar{\sigma}^*}(\mathrm{dom}(\bar{\sigma}))/P_{\mathrm{glue}}]$$
$$\cup\ \{P_{\bar{\sigma}}(\mathrm{dom}(\bar{\sigma})) \to P_{\bar{\sigma}^*}(\mathrm{dom}(\bar{\sigma}))\}$$
$$N_{\bar{\sigma}_1|\bar{\sigma}_2}^0 = N_{\bar{\sigma}_1}^0 \cup \{P_{\bar{\sigma}_1}(\vec{x}_1) \to P_{\bar{\sigma}_1|\bar{\sigma}_2}(\vec{y})\}$$
$$\cup\ N_{\bar{\sigma}_2}^0 \cup \{P_{\bar{\sigma}_2}(\vec{x}_2) \to P_{\bar{\sigma}_1|\bar{\sigma}_2}(\vec{y})\}$$
$$\text{where } \vec{x}_i = \mathrm{dom}(\bar{\sigma}_i) \text{ and } \vec{y} = \mathrm{dom}(\bar{\sigma}_1|\bar{\sigma}_2)$$

6.4 Generalized Substitutions as Clause Sets

The set $N_{\bar{\sigma}}$ arises from $N_{\bar{\sigma}}^0$ by deletion of all occurrences of P_{glue}:

$$N_\sigma = \{ \to P_\sigma(\vec{x}\sigma)\} \text{ where } \vec{x} = \text{dom}(\sigma)$$
$$N_{\bar{\sigma}\bar{\tau}} = N_{\bar{\tau}} \cup N_{\bar{\sigma}}^0[P_{\bar{\tau}}(\text{dom}(\bar{\tau}))/P_{\text{glue}}]$$
$$N_{\bar{\sigma}^*} = \{ \to P_{\bar{\sigma}^*}(\text{dom}(\bar{\sigma}))\}$$
$$\cup\, N_{\bar{\sigma}}^0[P_{\bar{\sigma}^*}(\text{dom}(\bar{\sigma}))/P_{\text{glue}}]$$
$$\cup\, \{P_{\bar{\sigma}}(\text{dom}(\bar{\sigma})) \to P_{\bar{\sigma}^*}(\text{dom}(\bar{\sigma}))\}$$
$$N_{\bar{\sigma}_1|\bar{\sigma}_2} = N_{\bar{\sigma}_1} \cup \{P_{\bar{\sigma}_1}(\vec{x}_1) \to P_{\bar{\sigma}_1|\bar{\sigma}_2}(\vec{y})\}$$
$$\cup\, N_{\bar{\sigma}_2} \cup \{P_{\bar{\sigma}_2}(\vec{x}_2) \to P_{\bar{\sigma}_1|\bar{\sigma}_2}(\vec{y})\}$$
$$\text{where } \vec{x}_i = \text{dom}(\bar{\sigma}_i) \text{ and } \vec{y} = \text{dom}(\bar{\sigma}_1|\bar{\sigma}_2)$$

Example 6.36
Consider the two substitutions $\sigma = \{x \mapsto s(x)\}$ and $\tau = \{x \mapsto 0\}$ appearing in Examples 6.21 and 6.34 as parts of the substitution expression $\sigma^*\tau$. Then $N_\tau^0 = \{P_{\text{glue}} \to P_\tau(0)\}$, and $N_\sigma^0 = \{P_{\text{glue}} \to P_\sigma(s(x))\}$. Hence

$$N_{\sigma^*}^0 = \{\quad P_{\text{glue}} \to P_{\sigma^*}(x)\quad ,$$
$$P_{\sigma^*}(x) \to P_\sigma(s(x))\quad ,$$
$$P_\sigma(x) \to P_{\sigma^*}(x)\quad \}$$

and finally (note that $P_{\sigma^*\tau} = P_{\sigma^*}$ as seen in Example 6.34)

$$N_{\sigma^*\tau}^0 = \{\quad P_{\text{glue}} \to P_\tau(0),$$
$$P_\tau(x) \to P_{\sigma^*\tau}(x)\quad ,$$
$$P_{\sigma^*\tau}(x) \to P_\sigma(s(x))\quad ,$$
$$P_\sigma(x) \to P_{\sigma^*\tau}(x)\quad \}\,.$$

As the predicate P_{glue} is only used to glue clause sets together, its occurrences can be thrown away. This leads to the final representation of $\sigma^*\tau$ as a clause set:

$$N_{\sigma^*\tau} = \{\quad \to P_\tau(0),$$
$$P_\tau(x) \to P_{\sigma^*\tau}(x)\quad ,$$
$$P_{\sigma^*\tau}(x) \to P_\sigma(s(x))\quad ,$$
$$P_\sigma(x) \to P_{\sigma^*\tau}(x)\quad \}$$

The set $N_{\sigma^*\tau}$ can be regarded as building terms in $x[\![\sigma^*\tau]\!]$ a bottom-up approach: The first clause creates the constant 0 (which is the only term in $x[\![\tau]\!]$), the second clause enters the σ loop, and the last two clauses allow to repeatedly wrap applications of $s(\ )$ around a term (corresponding to the terms $s^n(0)$ in $x[\![\sigma^*\tau]\!]$).

Chapter 6: Generic Superposition-based Decidability of Minimal Model Validity

6.4.1 Equivalence of Substitution Expressions and Clause Sets

I will now show that each clause set $N_{\bar{\sigma}}$ describes exactly the (instances of the) term tuples generated by the respective substitution expression $\bar{\sigma}$, provided that this substitution stems from a suitable derivation.

Definition 6.37 (Derivation Substitution)
Let $\vec{v}{\simeq}\vec{x}\bar{\sigma}_1,\ldots,\vec{v}{\simeq}\vec{x}\bar{\sigma}_n$ be finitely many constraints appearing in an existential query derivation. Then $\bar{\sigma}_1|\ldots|\bar{\sigma}_n$ is called a *derivation substitution*.

Such substitution expressions are especially well-behaved. For example, if disjunctions $\bar{\sigma}_1|\bar{\sigma}_2$ appear, then $\bar{\sigma}_1$ and $\bar{\sigma}_2$ share the same domain.

Lemma 6.38
Let $\bar{\sigma}$ be a derivation substitution. Then $\mathrm{VRan}(\bar{\tau}_1) = \mathrm{dom}(\bar{\tau}_2)$ for all subexpressions $\bar{\tau}_1 \circ \bar{\tau}_2$.

Proof. This is true initially and can be easily seen to be maintained during each inference step. ◇

Lemma 6.39
Let $\bar{\sigma}$ be a derivation substitution. Then $\mathrm{dom}(\bar{\tau}_1) = \mathrm{dom}(\bar{\tau}_2)$ for all subexpressions $\bar{\tau}_1|\bar{\tau}_2$.

Proof. If the derivation substitution $\bar{\sigma} = \bar{\sigma}_1|\ldots|\bar{\sigma}_n$ was created from the regular constraints $\vec{v}{\simeq}\vec{x}\bar{\sigma}_1,\ldots,\vec{v}{\simeq}\vec{x}\bar{\sigma}_n$, then the domains of all $\bar{\sigma}_i$ are equal by definition. A disjunction $\bar{\tau}_1|\bar{\tau}_2$ inside $\bar{\sigma}_i$ can only have been introduced during a Melting inference of type (ii,b) involving two constraints $\vec{v}{\simeq}\vec{x}\bar{\sigma}'\bar{\tau}_1^*$ and $\vec{v}{\simeq}\vec{x}\bar{\sigma}'\bar{\tau}_1^*\bar{\tau}_2$. Hence $\mathrm{dom}(\bar{\tau}_2) = \mathrm{VRan}(\bar{\tau}_1^*) = \mathrm{dom}(\bar{\tau}_1)$ by Lemma 6.38 and the definition of VRan. ◇

Lemma 6.40
Let $\bar{\sigma}$ be a substitution expression. Then in each clause in $N_{\bar{\sigma}}^0$ of the form $P_{\mathrm{glue}} \to P(t_1,\ldots,t_n)$, the atom $P(t_1,\ldots,t_n)$ contains all variables in the set $\mathrm{VRan}(\bar{\sigma})$.

Proof. This follows directly from the definitions. ◇

The clauses in $N_{\bar{\sigma}}^0$ and $N_{\bar{\sigma}}$ are particularly simple. On the one hand, all terms appearing in the antecedent of a (Horn) clause in N_{σ}^0 and N_σ are variables, on the other hand, I will now show that the clauses are universally reductive, i.e. all antecedent variables also occur in the succedent, a property that is necessary for the applicability of predicate completion.

176

6.4 Generalized Substitutions as Clause Sets

Proposition 6.41 (Universal Reductiveness of $N_{\bar{\sigma}}$)
Let $\bar{\sigma}$ be a derivation substitution. Then all clauses in $N_{\bar{\sigma}}$ are universally reductive.

Proof. If the clauses in $N_{\bar{\sigma}}^0$ are universally reductive, then obviously so is $N_{\bar{\sigma}}$. Hence it suffices to show that the clauses in $N_{\bar{\sigma}}^0$ are universally reductive. I proceed by structural induction on the derivation substitution.

The clause $P_{\text{glue}} \to P_\sigma(x_1\sigma, \ldots, x_n\sigma)$ for a single substitution σ is universally reductive because no variables occur in the antecedent.

In a conjunction $\bar{\sigma}\bar{\tau}$, inductively, the clauses in $N_{\bar{\sigma}}^0$ and $N_{\bar{\tau}}^0$ are universally reductive. Moreover, $\text{VRan}(\bar{\sigma}) = \text{dom}(\bar{\tau})$ by Lemma 6.38, so the clauses in $N_{\bar{\sigma}}^0[P_{\bar{\tau}}(\text{dom}(\bar{\tau}))/P_{\text{glue}}]$ are also universally reductive by Lemma 6.40.

The same argument applies to $N_{\bar{\sigma}*}^0$, except that in this case $\text{VRan}(\bar{\sigma}) = \text{dom}(\bar{\sigma})$ by definition of VRan.

For $\bar{\sigma}_1|\bar{\sigma}_2$, inductively, the clauses in both $N_{\bar{\sigma}_1}^0$ and $N_{\bar{\sigma}_2}^0$ are universally reductive. Moreover, since $\text{dom}(\bar{\sigma}_1), \text{dom}(\bar{\sigma}_2) \subseteq \text{dom}(\bar{\sigma}_1|\bar{\sigma}_2)$, the newly introduced clauses are also universally reductive. ◊

In the following propositions, I write $N \vdash^* A$ if N is a Horn clause set and A is an atom and either a variant of A is contained in N or A can be derived from the clause set N by a finite number of Resolution inference steps.

Lemma 6.42 (Derivation Decomposition)
Let $\bar{\sigma}$ be a derivation substitution. Let M be a clause set that does not contain any predicates of $N_{\bar{\sigma}}$, and let P be a predicate appearing in M. For terms $\vec{s}$, the following are equivalent:

(i) $N_{\bar{\sigma}}^0[P(\vec{y})/P_{\text{glue}}] \cup M \vdash^* P_{\bar{\sigma}}(\vec{s})$.

(ii) There are terms $\vec{s}_1, \vec{r}$, such that
- $\text{var}(\vec{s}_1) \cap \text{var}(\vec{r}) \subseteq \vec{y}$,
- $\vec{s} = \vec{s}_1\{y_1 \mapsto r_1, \ldots, y_n \mapsto r_n\}$,
- $M \vdash^* P(\vec{r})$ and
- $N_{\bar{\sigma}} \vdash^* P_{\bar{\sigma}}(\vec{s}_1)$.

This lemma formalizes a generalization of the idea that, if derivation substitutions are properly described by the corresponding clause sets, e.g. every atom $P_{\sigma_1}(\vec{s})$ that can be derived by $N_{\bar{\sigma}_1\bar{\sigma}_2}$ should correspond to an element of $\vec{x}[\![\bar{\sigma}_1\bar{\sigma}_2]\!]$ and hence be composed as $P_{\sigma_1}(\vec{s}) = P_{\sigma_1}(\vec{x}\sigma_1\sigma_2)$ with $\sigma_i \in [\![\bar{\sigma}_i]\!]$, such that $P_{\sigma_1}(\vec{x}\sigma_1)$ can be derived by $N_{\bar{\sigma}_1}$ and $P_{\sigma_2}(\vec{y}\bar{\sigma}_2)$ can be derived by $N_{\bar{\sigma}_2}$.

Proposition 6.43 (Equivalence of Derivation Substitutions and Clauses)
Let $\bar{\sigma}$ be a derivation substitution. Then $N_{\bar{\sigma}} \vdash^* P_{\bar{\sigma}}(\vec{t})$ if, and only if, there is a variable renaming π such that $\vec{t}\pi \in \vec{x}[\![\bar{\sigma}]\!]$.

Chapter 6: Generic Superposition-based Decidability of Minimal Model Validity

I prove Lemma 6.42 and Proposition 6.43 in parallel. The proofs rely on each other, however they do so in a well-founded way: The proof of Proposition 6.43 for a given substitution $\bar{\sigma}$ uses Lemma 6.42 only for strict subexpressions of $\bar{\sigma}$, and the proof of Lemma 6.42 for $\bar{\sigma}$ uses Proposition 6.43 for (possibly non-strict) subexpressions of $\bar{\sigma}$. In both proofs, I use existential quantifiers on the meta-level to denote the existence of terms with a given property.

Proof of Lemma 6.42. Proceed by induction over the structure of the substitution expression. Throughout this proof, I will abbreviate the application of a substitution $\{y_1 \mapsto r_1, \ldots, y_n \mapsto r_n\}$ to a term tuple $\vec{s}$ as $\vec{s}\{\vec{y} \mapsto \vec{r}\}$.

- Consider a substitution σ with $N_\sigma^0 = \{P_{\text{glue}} \to P_\sigma(\vec{x}\sigma)\}$. If $\{P(\vec{y}) \to P_\sigma(\vec{x}\sigma)\} \cup M \vdash^* P_\sigma(\vec{s})$, then the last step in the derivation must have used the clause $P(\vec{y}) \to P_\sigma(\vec{x}\sigma)$, i.e. $M \vdash^* P(\vec{r})$ for some $\vec{r}$ (for which without loss of generality $\text{var}(\vec{r}) \cap \text{var}(\vec{x}\sigma) \subseteq \vec{y}$) and $\vec{s}$ is of the form $\vec{s} = \vec{s}_1\{\vec{y} \mapsto \vec{r}\}$ for $\vec{s}_1 = \vec{x}\sigma$. Quite obviously, $\{\to P_\sigma(\vec{x}\sigma)\} \vdash^* P_\sigma(\vec{s}_1)$.

  For the other direction assume that $\{\to P_\sigma(\vec{x}\sigma)\} \vdash^* P_\sigma(\vec{s}_1)$ and $M \vdash^* P(\vec{r})$. Then clearly $\{P(\vec{y}) \to P_\sigma(\vec{x}\sigma)\} \cup M \vdash^* P_\sigma(\vec{s}_1)\{\vec{y} \mapsto \vec{r}\}$.

- In the case of a concatenation $\bar{\sigma}\bar{\tau}$ with $\text{VRan}(\bar{\sigma}) = \text{dom}(\bar{\tau}) = \vec{z}$ (cf. Lemma 6.38), I make excessive use of the induction hypotheses (i.h.):

$$\exists \vec{s}_1, \vec{r}. \ \text{var}(\vec{r}) \cap \text{var}(\vec{s}_1) \subseteq \vec{y} \text{ and } \vec{s} = \vec{s}_1\{\vec{y} \mapsto \vec{r}\}$$
$$\text{and } N_{\bar{\sigma}\bar{\tau}} \vdash^* P_{\bar{\sigma}}(\vec{s}_1) \text{ and } M \vdash^* P(\vec{r})$$
$$\iff \exists \vec{s}_1, \vec{r}. \ \text{var}(\vec{r}) \cap \text{var}(\vec{s}_1) \subseteq \vec{y} \text{ and } \vec{s} = \vec{s}_1\{\vec{y} \mapsto \vec{r}\}$$
$$\text{and } N_{\bar{\sigma}}^0[P_{\bar{\tau}}(\vec{z})/P_{\text{glue}}] \cup N_{\bar{\tau}} \vdash^* P_{\bar{\sigma}}(\vec{s}_1) \text{ and } M \vdash^* P(\vec{r})$$
$$\stackrel{\text{i.h.}}{\iff} \exists \vec{s}_1, \vec{r}, \vec{s}_2, \vec{t}. \ \text{var}(\vec{r}) \cap \text{var}(\vec{s}_1) \subseteq \vec{y} \text{ and } \text{var}(\vec{t}) \cap \text{var}(\vec{s}_2) \subseteq \vec{z}$$
$$\text{and } \vec{s} = \vec{s}_1\{\vec{y} \mapsto \vec{r}\} \text{ and } \vec{s}_1 = \vec{s}_2\{\vec{z} \mapsto \vec{t}\}$$
$$\text{and } N_{\bar{\sigma}} \vdash^* P_{\bar{\sigma}}(\vec{s}_2) \text{ and } N_{\bar{\tau}} \vdash^* P_{\bar{\tau}}(\vec{t}) \text{ and } M \vdash^* P(\vec{r})$$
$$\stackrel{\text{i.h.}}{\iff} \exists \vec{s}_1, \vec{r}, \vec{s}_2, \vec{t}. \ \text{var}(\vec{r}) \cap \text{var}(\vec{s}_1) \subseteq \vec{y} \text{ and } \text{var}(\vec{t}) \cap \text{var}(\vec{s}_2) \subseteq \vec{z}$$
$$\text{and } \vec{s} = \vec{s}_1\{\vec{y} \mapsto \vec{r}\} \text{ and } \vec{s}_1 = \vec{s}_2\{\vec{z} \mapsto \vec{t}\}$$
$$\text{and } N_{\bar{\sigma}} \vdash^* P_{\bar{\sigma}}(\vec{s}_2) \text{ and } N_{\bar{\tau}}[P(\vec{y})/P_{\text{glue}}] \cup M \vdash^* P_{\bar{\tau}}(\vec{t}\{\vec{y} \mapsto \vec{r}\})$$
$$\stackrel{\text{i.h.}}{\iff} N_{\bar{\sigma}}^0[P_{\bar{\tau}}(\vec{z})/P_{\text{glue}}] \cup N_{\bar{\tau}}[P(\vec{y})/P_{\text{glue}}] \cup M \vdash^* P_{\bar{\sigma}}(\vec{s})$$
$$\iff N_{\bar{\sigma}\bar{\tau}}^0[P(\vec{y})/P_{\text{glue}}] \cup M \vdash^* P_{\bar{\sigma}}(\vec{s})$$

- In the case of a loop $\bar{\sigma}^*$, let $I(\vec{t}_1)$ be the minimal number of times the clause $P_{\bar{\sigma}}(\vec{x}) \to P_{\bar{\sigma}^*}(\vec{x}) \in N_{\bar{\sigma}^*}$ is needed in a derivation $N_{\bar{\sigma}^*} \vdash^* P_{\bar{\sigma}^*}(\vec{t}_1)$,

178

6.4 Generalized Substitutions as Clause Sets

and let $J(\vec{t}_1)$ be the minimal number of times this clause is needed in a derivation $N^0_{\bar{\sigma}^*}[P(\vec{y})/P_{\text{glue}}] \cup M \vdash^* P_{\bar{\sigma}^*}(\vec{t}_1)$, provided that such a derivation exists. If there is no such derivation, then $I(\vec{t}_1)$ or $J(\vec{t}_1)$ is undefined.

Proceed by induction over $I(\vec{t}_1)$, showing that for all n, the following are equivalent:

(i) $N^0_{\bar{\sigma}^*}[P(\vec{y})/P_{\text{glue}}] \cup M \vdash^* P_{\bar{\sigma}^*}(\vec{t})$ and $J(\vec{t}) = n$
(ii) there are terms $\vec{t}_1$ and $\vec{r}$ such that $\vec{t} = \vec{t}_1\{\vec{x} \mapsto \vec{r}\}$ and $N_{\bar{\sigma}^*} \vdash^* P_{\bar{\sigma}^*}(\vec{t}_1)$ and $M \vdash^* P(\vec{r})$ and $I(\vec{t}_1) = n$.

For $I(\vec{t}_1) = 0$, the following equivalences hold:

$\exists \vec{t}_1, \vec{r}.\ \text{var}(\vec{r}) \cap \text{var}(\vec{t}_1) \subseteq \vec{y}$ and $\vec{t} = \vec{t}_1\{\vec{y} \mapsto \vec{r}\}$
  and $N_{\bar{\sigma}^*} \vdash^* P_{\bar{\sigma}^*}(\vec{t}_1)$ and $M \vdash^* P(\vec{r})$ and $I(\vec{t}_1) = 0$
$\iff \exists \vec{t}_1, \vec{r}.\ \text{var}(\vec{r}) \cap \text{var}(\vec{t}_1) \subseteq \vec{y}$ and $\vec{t} = \vec{t}_1\{\vec{y} \mapsto \vec{r}\}$
  and $N^0_{\bar{\sigma}}[P_{\bar{\sigma}^*}(\vec{y})/P_{\text{glue}}] \cup \{P_{\bar{\sigma}^*}(\vec{y})\} \vdash^* P_{\bar{\sigma}^*}(\vec{t}_1)$ and $M \vdash^* P(\vec{r})$
$\iff \exists \vec{t}_1, \vec{r}.\ \text{var}(\vec{r}) \cap \text{var}(\vec{t}_1) \subseteq \vec{y}$ and $\vec{t} = \vec{t}_1\{\vec{y} \mapsto \vec{r}\}$
  and $\{P_{\bar{\sigma}^*}(\vec{y})\} \vdash^* P_{\bar{\sigma}^*}(\vec{t}_1)$ and $M \vdash^* P(\vec{r})$
$\overset{\text{i.h.}}{\iff} \{P(\vec{y}) \to P_{\bar{\sigma}^*}(\vec{y})\} \cup M \vdash^* P_{\bar{\sigma}^*}(\vec{t})$
$\iff N^0_{\bar{\sigma}^*}[P(\vec{y})/P_{\text{glue}}] \cup M \vdash^* P_{\bar{\sigma}^*}(\vec{t})$ and $J(\vec{t}) = 0$

For $I(\vec{t}_1) = n+1$, let $\bar{\sigma}'$ be a copy of $\bar{\sigma}$, such that $N_{\bar{\sigma}}$ and $N_{\bar{\sigma}'}$ do not share any predicate symbols. From Proposition 6.43, it follows that $[\![\bar{\sigma}^*]\!] \setminus [\![\bar{\sigma}]\!] = [\![\bar{\sigma}^*\sigma']\!]$. In particular it follows that $N_{\bar{\sigma}^*} \vdash^* P_{\bar{\sigma}^*}(\vec{t}_1)$ with $I(\vec{t}_1) > 0$ if, and only if, $N_{\bar{\sigma}^*\bar{\sigma}'} \vdash^* P_{\bar{\sigma}^*}(\vec{t}_1)$, and that $N_{\bar{\sigma}^*\bar{\sigma}'}[P(\vec{y})/P_{\text{glue}}] \cup M \vdash^* P_{\bar{\sigma}^*}(\vec{t})$ if, and only if, $N_{\bar{\sigma}^*\bar{\sigma}'}[P(\vec{y})/P_{\text{glue}}] \cup M \vdash^* P_{\bar{\sigma}^*}(\vec{t})$. The use of Proposition 6.43 for $\bar{\sigma}^*$ is sound, since the proof of that proposition uses the current lemma only for strict subexpressions (in this case: $\bar{\sigma}$).

$\exists \vec{t}_1, \vec{r}.\ \text{var}(\vec{r}) \cap \text{var}(\vec{t}_1) \subseteq \vec{y}$ and $\vec{t} = \vec{t}_1\{\vec{y} \mapsto \vec{r}\}$ and $I(\vec{t}_1) = n+1$
  and $N_{\bar{\sigma}^*} \vdash^* P_{\bar{\sigma}^*}(\vec{t}_1)$ and $M \vdash^* P(\vec{r})$
$\iff \exists \vec{t}_1, \vec{r}.\ \text{var}(\vec{r}) \cap \text{var}(\vec{t}_1) \subseteq \vec{y}$ and $\vec{t} = \vec{t}_1\{\vec{y} \mapsto \vec{r}\}$ and $I(\vec{t}_1) = n+1$
  and $N_{\bar{\sigma}^*\bar{\sigma}'} \vdash^* P_{\bar{\sigma}^*}(\vec{t}_1)$ and $M \vdash^* P(\vec{r})$
$\iff \exists \vec{t}_1, \vec{r}.\ \text{var}(\vec{r}) \cap \text{var}(\vec{t}_1) \subseteq \vec{y}$ and $\vec{t} = \vec{t}_1\{\vec{y} \mapsto \vec{r}\}$ and $I(\vec{t}_1) = n+1$
  $N^0_{\bar{\sigma}^*}[P_{\bar{\sigma}'}(\vec{y})/P_{\text{glue}}] \cup N_{\bar{\sigma}'} \vdash^* P_{\bar{\sigma}^*}(\vec{t}_1)$ and $M \vdash^* P(\vec{r})$

Chapter 6: Generic Superposition-based Decidability of Minimal Model Validity

$\overset{\text{i.h.}}{\iff} \exists \vec{t_1}, \vec{r}, \vec{s_1}, \vec{t_2}.\ \text{var}(\vec{r}) \cap \text{var}(\vec{t_1}) \subseteq \vec{y} \text{ and } \text{var}(\vec{s_1}) \cap \text{var}(\vec{t_2}) \subseteq \vec{y}$
and $\vec{t} = \vec{t_1}\{\vec{y} \mapsto \vec{r}\}$ and $\vec{t_1} = \vec{t_2}\{\vec{y} \mapsto \vec{s_1}\}$ and $I(\vec{t_2}) = n$
and $N_{\bar{\sigma}^*} \vdash^* P_{\bar{\sigma}^*}(\vec{t_2})$ and $N_{\bar{\sigma}'} \vdash^* P_{\bar{\sigma}'}(\vec{s_1})$ and $M \vdash^* P(\vec{r})$

$\overset{\text{i.h.}}{\iff} \exists \vec{t_1}, \vec{r}, \vec{s_1}, \vec{t_2}.\ \text{var}(\vec{r}) \cap \text{var}(\vec{t_1}) \subseteq \vec{y} \text{ and } \text{var}(\vec{s_1}) \cap \text{var}(\vec{t_2}) \subseteq \vec{y}$
and $\vec{t} = \vec{t_1}\{\vec{y} \mapsto \vec{r}\}$ and $\vec{t_1} = \vec{t_2}\{\vec{y} \mapsto \vec{s_1}\}$ and $I(\vec{t_2}) = n$
and $N_{\bar{\sigma}^*} \vdash^* P_{\bar{\sigma}^*}(\vec{t_2})$ and $N^0_{\bar{\sigma}'}[P(\vec{y})/P_{\text{glue}}] \cup M \vdash^* P_{\bar{\sigma}'}(\vec{s_1}\{\vec{y} \mapsto \vec{r}\})$

$\overset{\text{i.h.}}{\iff} \exists \vec{t_1}, \vec{r}, \vec{s_1}, \vec{t_2}.\ \text{var}(\vec{r}) \cap \text{var}(\vec{t_1}) \subseteq \vec{y} \text{ and } \text{var}(\vec{s_1}) \cap \text{var}(\vec{t_2}) \subseteq \vec{y}$
and $\vec{t} = \vec{t_1}\{\vec{y} \mapsto \vec{r}\}$ and $\vec{t_1} = \vec{t_2}\{\vec{y} \mapsto \vec{s_1}\}$ and $J(\vec{t_2}) = n$
and $N^0_{\bar{\sigma}^*}[P_{\bar{\sigma}'}(\vec{y})/P_{\text{glue}}] \cup N^0_{\bar{\sigma}^*}[P(\vec{y})/P_{\text{glue}}] \cup M$
$\vdash^* P_{\bar{\sigma}^*}(\vec{t_2}\{\vec{y} \mapsto \vec{s_1}\{\vec{y} \mapsto \vec{r}\}\})$

$\overset{\text{i.h.}}{\iff} \exists \vec{t_1}, \vec{r}, \vec{s_1}, \vec{t_2}.\ \text{var}(\vec{r}) \cap \text{var}(\vec{t_1}) \subseteq \vec{y} \text{ and } \text{var}(\vec{s_1}) \cap \text{var}(\vec{t_2}) \subseteq \vec{y}$
and $\vec{t} = \vec{t_1}\{\vec{y} \mapsto \vec{r}\}$ and $\vec{t_1} = \vec{t_2}\{\vec{y} \mapsto \vec{s_1}\}$ and $J(\vec{t_2}) = n$
and $N^0_{\bar{\sigma}^* \bar{\sigma}'}[P(\vec{y})/P_{\text{glue}}] \cup M \vdash^* P_{\bar{\sigma}^*}(\vec{t_2}\{\vec{y} \mapsto \vec{s_1}\{\vec{y} \mapsto \vec{r}\}\})$

$\iff J(\vec{t}) = n+1$ and $N^0_{\bar{\sigma}^*}[P(\vec{y})/P_{\text{glue}}] \cup M \vdash^* P_{\bar{\sigma}^*}(\vec{t})$

- In the case of a disjunction $\bar{\sigma}_1 | \bar{\sigma}_2$ with $\text{dom}(\bar{\sigma}_1) = \text{dom}(\bar{\sigma}_2) = \vec{x}$, the two clause sets $N_{\bar{\sigma}_1}$ and $N_{\bar{\sigma}_2}$ do not share any predicate symbols. The proof if the lemma in this case proceeds as follows:

$\exists \vec{s_1}, \vec{r}.\ \text{var}(\vec{r}) \cap \text{var}(\vec{s_1}) \subseteq \vec{y} \text{ and } \vec{s} = \vec{s_1}\{\vec{y} \mapsto \vec{r}\}$
and $M \vdash^* P(\vec{r})$ and $N_{\bar{\sigma}_1 | \bar{\sigma}_2} \vdash^* P_{\bar{\sigma}_1 | \bar{\sigma}_2}(\vec{s_1})$

$\iff \exists \vec{s_1}, \vec{r}.\ \text{var}(\vec{r}) \cap \text{var}(\vec{s_1}) \subseteq \vec{y} \text{ and } \vec{s} = \vec{s_1}\{\vec{y} \mapsto \vec{r}\}$
and $M \vdash^* P(\vec{r})$ and $\exists i.\ N_{\bar{\sigma}_i} \cup \{P_{\bar{\sigma}_i}(\vec{x}) \to P_{\bar{\sigma}_1 | \bar{\sigma}_2}(\vec{x})\} \vdash^* P_{\bar{\sigma}_1 | \bar{\sigma}_2}(\vec{s_1})$

$\overset{\text{i.h.}}{\iff} \exists \vec{s_1}, \vec{r}.\ \text{var}(\vec{r}) \cap \text{var}(\vec{s_1}) \subseteq \vec{y} \text{ and } \vec{s} = \vec{s_1}\{\vec{y} \mapsto \vec{r}\}$
and $M \vdash^* P(\vec{r})$ and $\exists i.\ N_{\bar{\sigma}_i} \vdash^* P_{\bar{\sigma}_i}(\vec{s_1})$

$\iff \exists i.\ \exists \vec{s_1}, \vec{r}.\ \text{var}(\vec{r}) \cap \text{var}(\vec{s_1}) \subseteq \vec{y} \text{ and } \vec{s} = \vec{s_1}\{\vec{y} \mapsto \vec{r}\}$
and $M \vdash^* P(\vec{r})$ and $N_{\bar{\sigma}_i} \vdash^* P_{\bar{\sigma}_i}(\vec{s_1})$

$\overset{\text{i.h.}}{\iff} \exists i.\ N^0_{\bar{\sigma}_i}[P(\vec{y})/P_{\text{glue}}] \cup M \vdash^* P_{\bar{\sigma}_i}(\vec{s})$

$\overset{\text{i.h.}}{\iff} \exists i.\ N^0_{\bar{\sigma}_i}[P(\vec{y})/P_{\text{glue}}] \cup M \cup \{P_{\bar{\sigma}_i}(\vec{x}) \to P_{\bar{\sigma}_1 | \bar{\sigma}_2}(\vec{x})\} \vdash^* P_{\bar{\sigma}_1 | \bar{\sigma}_2}(\vec{s})$

$\iff N^0_{\bar{\sigma}_1}[P(\vec{y})/P_{\text{glue}}] \cup \{P_{\bar{\sigma}_1}(\vec{x}) \to P_{\bar{\sigma}_1 | \bar{\sigma}_2}(\vec{x})\}$
$\cup N^0_{\bar{\sigma}_2}[P(\vec{y})/P_{\text{glue}}] \cup \{P_{\bar{\sigma}_2}(\vec{x}) \to P_{\bar{\sigma}_1 | \bar{\sigma}_2}(\vec{x})\}) \cup M \vdash^* P_{\bar{\sigma}_1 | \bar{\sigma}_2}(\vec{s})$

$\iff N_{\bar{\sigma}_1 | \bar{\sigma}_2}[P(\vec{y})/P_{\text{glue}}] \cup M \vdash^* P_{\bar{\sigma}_1 | \bar{\sigma}_2}(\vec{s})$

This completes the proof. ◇

6.4 Generalized Substitutions as Clause Sets

Proof of Proposition 6.43. I again proceed by structural induction on the substitution expression. Whenever the symbols π and ρ occur in the proof, they denote variable renamings.

- The validity of the proposition is obvious for substitutions.

- In the case of a concatenation $\bar{\sigma}\bar{\tau}$ with $\text{dom}(\bar{\sigma}) = \vec{x}$ and $\text{dom}(\bar{\tau}) = \vec{y}$, the following equality holds:

$$\{\vec{s}\mid N_{\bar{\sigma}\bar{\tau}} \vdash^* P_{\bar{\sigma}}(\vec{s})\}$$
$$= \{\vec{s}\mid N_{\bar{\sigma}}^0[P_{\bar{\tau}}(\vec{y})/P_{\text{glue}}] \cup N_{\bar{\tau}} \vdash^* P_{\bar{\sigma}}(\vec{s})\}$$
$$\stackrel{6.42}{=} \{\vec{s}\mid \exists \vec{t}, \vec{s}_1.\ \text{var}(\vec{t}) \cap \text{var}(\vec{s}_1) \subseteq \vec{y} \text{ and } \vec{s} = \vec{s}_1\{\vec{y} \mapsto \vec{t}\}$$
$$\quad \text{and } N_{\bar{\tau}} \vdash^* P_{\bar{\tau}}(\vec{t}) \text{ and } N_{\bar{\sigma}} \vdash^* P_{\bar{\sigma}}(\vec{s}_1)\}$$
$$\stackrel{\text{i.h.}}{=} \{\vec{s}\mid \exists \vec{t}, \vec{s}_1, \pi, \rho.\ \text{var}(\vec{t}) \cap \text{var}(\vec{s}_1) \subseteq \vec{y} \text{ and } \vec{s} = \vec{s}_1\{\vec{y} \mapsto \vec{t}\}$$
$$\quad \text{and } \vec{t}\pi \in \vec{y}[\![\bar{\tau}]\!] \text{ and } \vec{s}_1\rho \in \vec{x}[\![\bar{\sigma}]\!]\}$$
$$= \{\vec{s}\mid \exists \pi.\ \vec{s}\pi \in \vec{x}[\![\bar{\sigma}\bar{\tau}]\!]\}$$

- In the case of a loop $\bar{\sigma}^*$ with $\text{dom}(\bar{\sigma}) = \vec{x}$, I show inductively that $\vec{x}[\![\bar{\sigma}^n]\!]$ is the subset of $\{\vec{s}\mid N_{\bar{\sigma}^*} \vdash^* P_{\bar{\sigma}^*}(\vec{s})\}$ of those term tuples $\vec{s}$ for which n is the minimal number of times the iteration clause $P_{\bar{\sigma}}(\vec{x}) \to P_{\bar{\sigma}^*}(\vec{x})$ is needed in a derivation $N_{\bar{\sigma}^*} \vdash^* P_{\bar{\sigma}^*}(\vec{s})$, denoted $I(\vec{s}) = n$. For $I(\vec{s}) = 0$, the following equality holds:

$$\{\vec{s}\mid N_{\bar{\sigma}^*} \vdash^* P_{\bar{\sigma}^*}(\vec{s}) \text{ and } I(\vec{s}) = 0\}$$
$$= \{\vec{s}\mid N_{\bar{\sigma}}^0[P_{\bar{\sigma}^*}(\vec{x})/P_{\text{glue}}] \cup \{\to P_{\bar{\sigma}^*}(\vec{x})\} \vdash^* P_{\bar{\sigma}^*}(\vec{s})\}$$
$$= \{\vec{s}\mid \{\to P_{\bar{\sigma}^*}(\vec{x})\} \vdash^* P_{\bar{\sigma}^*}(\vec{s})\}$$
$$= \{\vec{s}\mid \exists \pi.\ \vec{s}\pi \in \vec{x}[\![\bar{\sigma}^0]\!]\}$$

For $I(\vec{s}) = n+1$, split a derivation $N_{\bar{\sigma}^*} \vdash^* P_{\bar{\sigma}^*}(\vec{s})$ at the point where the clause $P_{\bar{\sigma}}(\vec{x}) \to P_{\bar{\sigma}^*}(\vec{x})$ is used for the last time:

$$\{\vec{s}\mid N_{\bar{\sigma}^*} \vdash^* P_{\bar{\sigma}^*}(\vec{s}) \text{ and } I(\vec{s}) = n+1\}$$
$$= \{\vec{s}\mid \exists \vec{t}.\ N_{\bar{\sigma}^*} \vdash^* P_{\bar{\sigma}^*}(\vec{t}) \text{ and } I(\vec{t}) = n$$
$$\quad \text{and } N_{\bar{\sigma}}^0[P_{\bar{\sigma}^*}(\vec{x})/P_{\text{glue}}] \cup \{\to P_{\bar{\sigma}^*}(\vec{t})\} \vdash^* P_{\bar{\sigma}}(\vec{s})\}$$
$$\stackrel{\text{i.h.}}{=} \{\vec{s}\mid \exists \vec{t}, \pi.\ \vec{t}\pi \in \vec{x}[\![\bar{\sigma}^n]\!]$$
$$\quad \text{and } N_{\bar{\sigma}}^0[P_{\bar{\sigma}^*}(\vec{x})/P_{\text{glue}}] \cup \{\to P_{\bar{\sigma}^*}(\vec{t})\} \vdash^* P_{\bar{\sigma}}(\vec{s})\}$$

$$\stackrel{6.42}{=} \{\vec{s} \mid \exists \vec{t}, \vec{s}_1, \pi. \ \text{var}(\vec{t}) \cap \text{var}(\vec{s}_1) \subseteq \vec{x} \text{ and } \vec{s} = \vec{s}_1\{\vec{x} \mapsto \vec{t}\}$$
$$\text{and } \vec{t}\pi \in \vec{x}[\![\bar{\sigma}^n]\!] \text{ and } N_{\bar{\sigma}} \vdash^* P_{\bar{\sigma}}(\vec{s}_1)\}$$
$$\stackrel{\text{i.h.}}{=} \{\vec{s} \mid \exists \vec{t}, \vec{s}_1, \pi, \rho. \ \text{var}(\vec{t}) \cap \text{var}(\vec{s}_1) \subseteq \vec{x} \text{ and } \vec{s} = \vec{s}_1\{\vec{x} \mapsto \vec{t}\}$$
$$\text{and } \vec{t}\pi \in \vec{x}[\![\bar{\sigma}^n]\!] \text{ and } \vec{s}_1\rho \in \vec{x}[\![\bar{\sigma}]\!]\}$$
$$= \{\vec{s} \mid \exists \pi. \ \vec{s}\pi \in \vec{x}[\![\bar{\sigma}^{n+1}]\!]\}$$

- Finally, in the case of a disjunction $\bar{\sigma}_1 | \bar{\sigma}_2$ with domains $\text{dom}(\bar{\sigma}_1) = \text{dom}(\bar{\sigma}_2) = \vec{x}$ (cf. Lemma 6.39), the following equality holds, where I use that $N_{\bar{\sigma}_1}$ and $N_{\bar{\sigma}_2}$ do not share any predicate symbols:

$$\{\vec{s} \mid N_{\bar{\sigma}_1 | \bar{\sigma}_2} \vdash^* P_{\bar{\sigma}}(\vec{s})\}$$
$$= \{\vec{s} \mid N_{\bar{\sigma}_1} \cup \{P_{\bar{\sigma}_1}(\vec{x}) \to P_{\bar{\sigma}}(\vec{x})\} \vdash^* P_{\bar{\sigma}}(\vec{s})$$
$$\text{or } N_{\bar{\sigma}_2} \cup \{P_{\bar{\sigma}_2}(\vec{x}) \to P_{\bar{\sigma}}(\vec{x})\} \vdash^* P_{\bar{\sigma}}(\vec{s})\}$$
$$\stackrel{6.42}{=} \{\vec{s} \mid N_{\bar{\sigma}_1} \vdash^* P_{\bar{\sigma}_1}(\vec{s}) \text{ or } N_{\bar{\sigma}_2} \vdash^* P_{\bar{\sigma}_2}(\vec{s})\}$$
$$\stackrel{\text{i.h.}}{=} \{\vec{s} \mid \exists \pi. \ \vec{s}\pi \in \vec{x}[\![\bar{\sigma}_1]\!] \text{ or } \vec{s}\pi \in \vec{x}[\![\bar{\sigma}_2]\!]\}$$
$$= \{\vec{s} \mid \exists \pi. \ \vec{s}\pi \in \vec{x}[\![\bar{\sigma}_1]\!] \cup \vec{x}[\![\bar{\sigma}_2]\!]\}$$
$$= \{\vec{s} \mid \exists \pi. \ \vec{s}\pi \in \vec{x}[\![\bar{\sigma}_1 | \bar{\sigma}_2]\!]\}$$

This completes the proof. ◇

Since Resolution is complete for first-order reasoning over Horn clauses, the term tuples $\vec{t}$ for which $P_{\bar{\sigma}}(\vec{t})$ is entailed by $N_{\bar{\sigma}}$ are exactly those covered by $\bar{\sigma}$:

Corollary 6.44 (Equivalence of $\bar{\sigma}$ and $N_{\bar{\sigma}}$)
Let $\bar{\sigma}$ be a derivation substitution. Then $N_{\bar{\sigma}} \models P_{\bar{\sigma}}(\vec{t})$ if, and only if, $\bar{\sigma}$ is covering for $\{\vec{t}\}$, i.e. the set $\{\vec{t} \mid N_{\bar{\sigma}} \models P_{\bar{\sigma}}(\vec{t})\}$ is the maximal set for which $\bar{\sigma}$ is covering.

6.4.2 Predicate Completion for Substitution Expressions

Now that it is clear how to transform $\bar{\sigma}$ into an equivalent set $N_{\bar{\sigma}}$ of Horn clauses, I will concentrate on how to decide whether $P_{\bar{\sigma}}$ is the total relation in the minimal model of $N_{\bar{\sigma}}$. To do so, I will transform I will this problem into an emptiness problem. This transformation will again employ predicate completion.

Since I have shown that $N_{\bar{\sigma}}$ is universally reductive if $\bar{\sigma}$ is a derivation substitution (Proposition 6.41), predicate completion is applicable to $N_{\bar{\sigma}}$. However, as already mentioned, the resulting clause set usually does not inherit desirable properties like being Horn.

6.4 Generalized Substitutions as Clause Sets

Example 6.45
The clause set $\{P(x) \to Q(x),\ R(x) \to Q(x)\}$ is completed by the non-Horn clause $Q(x) \to P(x), R(x)$. The clause set $\{\to S(x,x)\}$ is completed by $S(x,y) \to x{\simeq}y$, a clause that is not even predicative; if the sort of the variable x contains infinitely many ground terms, then the clause can also not be represented by finitely many predicative clauses.

For derivation substitutions, there is a simple trick to alleviate this complication, namely to express, intuitively, the completion as a set of clauses over negated atoms:

Definition 6.46 (Negating Prediacte Completion and $\check{N}$)
Let $\Sigma = (\mathcal{P}, \mathcal{F})$ be a signature and let N be a finite set of Horn clauses over Σ. Let $\check{\mathcal{P}} = \{\check{P} : S_1, \ldots, S_n \mid (P : S_1, \ldots, S_n) \in \mathcal{P}\}$ be a set of fresh predicate symbols.

The *Negating Predicate Completion Algorithm* **NPC** works as follows, where the decisive difference to **PC** lies in the additional step (iii):

(i) For $P \in \mathcal{P}$, let $N_P \subseteq N$ be the set of clauses in N of the form $\Gamma \to P(\vec{t})$. Combine all these clauses into the single formula $\forall \vec{x}.(\phi_P \to P(\vec{x}))$ where

$$\phi_P = \exists \vec{y}. \bigvee_{\Gamma \to P(\vec{t}) \in N_P} (x_1 {\simeq} t_1 \wedge \ldots \wedge x_n {\simeq} t_n \wedge \bigwedge_{A \in \Gamma} A),$$

the y_i are the variables appearing in N_P, and the x_j are fresh variables.

(ii) In the interpretation $\mathcal{I}_N$, the formula $\forall \vec{x}.(\phi_P \to P(\vec{x}))$ is equivalent to the formula $\forall \vec{x}.(\neg \phi_P \to \neg P(\vec{x}))$. Transform $\neg \phi_P$ using the algorithm **PDU** into an equivalent formula ϕ'_P that does not contain any universal quantifiers.

(iii) Replace every literal $\neg Q(\vec{s})$ in ϕ'_P by $\check{Q}(\vec{s})$, resulting in a formula $\check{\phi}_P$.

(iv) Write the formula $\forall \vec{x}.(\check{\phi}_P \to \check{P}(\vec{x}))$ as a set finite $\check{N}_P$ of clauses over $(\check{\mathcal{P}}, \mathcal{F})$.

(v) Let $\check{N}$ be the union of all sets $\check{N}_P$, $P \in \mathcal{P}$.

In general, the result of the adapted completion procedure is a set of clauses of the form $\Gamma \to \Delta, \check{P}(\vec{t})$, where Δ is a multiset of (non-predicative) equations. When all appearing substitutions have a one-element domain and are linear, however, the clauses in $\check{N}$ do not contain any equations, and they fall into a class for which the emptiness of $\check{N}$ is decidable by (unconstrained) Ordered Resolution (Theorem 6.49).

Chapter 6: Generic Superposition-based Decidability of Minimal Model Validity

Proposition 6.47 (Clauses in the Completion)
Let $\bar{\sigma}$ be a derivation substitution such that all substitutions appearing in $\bar{\sigma}$ are linear. For the predicates in $N_{\bar{\sigma}}$, the predicate completion algorithm NPC computes clauses of the following types:

(i) $\to \check{P}(\vec{t})$

(ii) $\check{P}_1(\vec{x}) \to \check{P}(\vec{t})$

(iii) $\check{P}_1(\vec{x}), \check{P}_2(\vec{x}) \to \check{P}(\vec{x})$

The positive literal of each computed clause is linear.

Proof. A substitution predicate P_σ is defined by a single clause that is either of the shape $\to P_\sigma(\vec{t})$ or $P_\tau(\vec{x}) \to P_\sigma(\vec{t})$. Its completion consists of a finite set of linear clauses of the form $\to \check{P}_\sigma(\vec{s})$ describing the term tuples not covered by $\vec{t}$ and, in the second case, additionally the clause $\check{P}_\tau(\vec{x}) \to \check{P}_\sigma(\vec{t})$.

A loop predicate $P_{\bar{\sigma}^*}$ is defined by the clause $P_{\bar{\sigma}}(\vec{x}) \to P_{\bar{\sigma}^*}(\vec{x})$ and either $\to P_{\bar{\sigma}^*}(\vec{x})$ or $P_{\bar{\tau}}(\vec{x}) \to P_{\bar{\sigma}^*}(\vec{x})$. The completion is the empty set in the first case (as $P_{\bar{\sigma}^*}$ is total) and $\{\check{P}_{\bar{\sigma}}(\vec{x}), \check{P}_{\bar{\tau}}(\vec{x}) \to \check{P}_{\bar{\sigma}^*}(\vec{x})\}$ in the second case.

The two clauses defining a disjunction predicate $P_{\bar{\sigma}_1 | \bar{\sigma}_2}$ are completed by the single clause $\check{P}_{\bar{\sigma}_1}(\vec{x}), \check{P}_{\bar{\sigma}_2}(\vec{x}) \to \check{P}_{\bar{\sigma}_1 | \bar{\sigma}_2}(\vec{x})$. ◊

The fact that all negative literals contain only variables is inherited from $N_{\bar{\sigma}}$. That no equations appear is due to the linearity of the positive literals in $N_{\bar{\sigma}}$.

Example 6.48
In Example 6.36, the following clause set $N_{\sigma*\tau}$ was derived:

$$\to P_\tau(0)$$
$$P_{\sigma*\tau}(x) \to P_\sigma(s(x))$$
$$P_\tau(x) \to P_{\sigma*\tau}(x)$$
$$P_\sigma(x) \to P_{\sigma*\tau}(x)$$

Hence $\check{N}_{\sigma*\tau}$ consists of the following clauses:

$$\to \check{P}_\tau(s(x))$$
$$\to \check{P}_\sigma(0)$$
$$\check{P}_{\sigma*\tau}(x) \to \check{P}_\sigma(s(x))$$
$$\check{P}_\tau(x), \check{P}_\sigma(x) \to \check{P}_{\sigma*\tau}(x)$$

6.4 Generalized Substitutions as Clause Sets

In this example, all appearing predicates are monadic. When there is more than one existential variable in the initial existential query problem or when the signature contains function symbols of arity at least two, predicates of higher arity appear also in N_σ and $\check{N}_\sigma$.

Theorem 6.49 (Decidability of Coverage)
Let $\bar{\sigma}$ be a derivation substitution over a signature Σ such that all substitutions in $\bar{\sigma}$ have a unary domain and are linear. It is decidable whether $\bar{\sigma}$ is covering.

Proof. Translate $\bar{\sigma}$ into a clause set $N_{\bar{\sigma}}$. All predicates in $N_{\bar{\sigma}}$ are unary. By Proposition 6.47, the resulting clause set $\check{N}_{\bar{\sigma}}$ defining the completion of all appearing predicates again contains only clauses of the form $\check{P}_1(x), \ldots, \check{P}_n(x) \to \check{P}(t)$. Weidenbach (1999) showed that such a clause set is equivalent to a so-called *sort theory*, a clause set in which additionally all clauses are shallow. For sort theories, emptiness is decidable by ordered resolution (Weidenbach, 1999; Seidl and Verma, 2004). Emptiness of $\check{P}_{\bar{\sigma}}$ in $\mathcal{I}_{\check{N}_{\bar{\sigma}}}$ in turn is equivalent to totality of $P_{\bar{\sigma}}$ in $\mathcal{I}_{N_{\bar{\sigma}}}$ (Theorem 3.34), which is equivalent to the coverage of the substitution expression $\bar{\sigma}$ (Corollary 6.44). ◊

Example 6.50
I shortly illustrate the final step of the proof using the running example (Examples 6.21, 6.34 and 6.48). Here, all clauses in $\check{N}_{\sigma*\tau}$ are already shallow. The predicate $P_{\sigma*\tau}$ is interpreted as the empty relation in $\mathcal{I}_{\check{N}_{\sigma*\tau}}$ if, and only if, $\check{N}_{\sigma*\tau} \not\models_{Ind} \exists x. \check{P}_{\sigma*}(x)$.

Choose an ordering $\succ$ on atoms such that $P_{\sigma*\tau}(x) \succ P_\tau(x), P_\sigma(x)$ and $P_\sigma(s(x)) \succ P_{\sigma*\tau}(x)$ and saturate $\check{N}_{\sigma*\tau} \cup \{\check{P}_{\sigma*\tau}(x) \to\}$ using Ordered Resolution. The derivation runs as follows:

$$
\begin{aligned}
\text{clauses in } \check{N}_{\sigma*\tau}: \quad 1 &: \quad \to \check{P}_\tau(s(x)) \\
2 &: \quad \to \check{P}_\sigma(0) \\
3 &: \quad \check{P}_{\sigma*\tau}(x) \to \check{P}_\sigma(s(x)) \\
4 &: \quad \check{P}_\tau(x), \check{P}_\sigma(x) \to \check{P}_{\sigma*\tau}(x) \\
\text{negated query}: \quad 5 &: \quad \check{P}_{\sigma*\tau}(x) \to \\
\text{resolve}(4,5) = 6 &: \quad \check{P}_\tau(x), \check{P}_\sigma(x) \to \\
\text{resolve}(1,6) = 7 &: \quad \check{P}_\sigma(s(x)) \to \\
\text{resolve}(2,6) = 8 &: \quad \check{P}_\tau(0) \to
\end{aligned}
$$

At this point, the clause set is saturated. It is consistent, so $\check{N}_{\sigma*\tau} \not\models \exists x. \check{P}_{\sigma*}(x)$. Since first-order and minimal model validity coincide for Horn clause sets and positive existential queries, this implies that $\check{P}$ is empty in the minimal model of $\check{N}_{\sigma*\tau}$. So $\sigma*\tau$ is covering and $N \models_{Ind} C$.

6.5 Decidability of Minimal Model Validity

As a combination of the complete and terminating calculus ORM for constrained clauses and the completion-based treatment of the substitution expressions that can appear during saturation, the following decidability result emerges:

Theorem 6.51 (Decidability of Minimal Model Validity)
Let N be a set of predicative Horn clauses and let A_{ij} be predicative atoms over a signature Σ, where

(i) all function symbols in Σ are at most unary,

(ii) all positive literals in N are linear, and

(iii) $N \cup \{A_{11}, \ldots, A_{1m_1} \to, \ldots, A_{n1}, \ldots, A_{nm_n} \to\}$ belongs to a class that can be finitely saturated by ordered resolution, where deletion steps are restricted to the deletion of variants and tautologies.

Let $\{x, y_1, \ldots, y_m\}$ be the set of variables that appear in the A_{ij}. It is decidable whether $N \models_{Ind} \forall x. \exists y_1, \ldots, y_m. \bigvee_i \bigwedge_j A_{ij}$.

Proof. Corollary 6.26 and Theorem 6.32 imply that the constrained clause set

$$N \cup \{\vec{v} \simeq \vec{x} \,\|\, A_{11}, \ldots, A_{1m_1} \to, \ldots, \vec{v} \simeq \vec{x} \,\|\, A_{n1}, \ldots, A_{nm_n} \to\}$$

can be finitely saturated by ORM, such that the finitely many deduced regular constraint clauses $v \simeq x\bar{\sigma}_1 \,\|\, \square, \ldots, v \simeq x\bar{\sigma}_k \,\|\, \square$ with empty clausal part in the saturated set correspond to a substitution expression $\bar{\sigma} = \bar{\sigma}_1 | \ldots | \bar{\sigma}_k$ that is covering if, and only if, $N \models_{Ind} \forall x. \exists y_1, \ldots, y_m. \bigvee_i \bigwedge_j A_{ij}$.

Since the domain $\text{dom}(\bar{\sigma}) = \{x\}$ of the derivation substitution $\bar{\sigma}$ contains only one element and Σ contains only unary function symbols, the domain of all substitutions appearing in $\bar{\sigma}$ has cardinality 1. These substitutions are also linear because all positive literals in N are linear and hence the most general unifiers appearing in each resolution step are linear.

Hence coverage of $\bar{\sigma}$ is decidable by Theorem 6.49. ◇

Example 6.52
Reconsider the partial definition of the usual ordering on the naturals given by the clause set $N_{GT} = \{\to GT(s(0), 0),\ GT(x, y) \to GT(s(x), s(y))\}$ over the signature $\Sigma_{GT} = (\{GT\}, \{s, 0\})$, as shown in the introduction. In Example 4.27, I presented a first attempt at proving with SFD that $N_{GT} \models_{\Sigma_{GT}} \forall x. GT(s(x), x)$. This attempt failed due to the non-termination of saturation.

I will now use the method described in this chapter to prove fully automatically that the proposition $\forall x. GT(s(x), x)$ holds in the minimal model of N_{GT}. Proposition 4.26 then implies that it also holds in every Herbrand model of N_{GT} over Σ_{GT}.

A possible saturation of $N_{GT} \cup \{v \simeq x \parallel GT(s(x),x)\}$ with ORM runs as follows, where $\tau = \{x \mapsto 0\}$ and $\sigma = \{x \mapsto s(x)\}$:

clauses in N:	$1:$	$\parallel$	$\to GT(s(0),0)$
	$2:$	$\parallel GT(x,y)$	$\to GT(s(x),s(y))$
negated conjecture:	$3: \ v \simeq x$	$\parallel GT(s(x),x)$	$\to$
Resolution(1,3) =	$4: \ v \simeq x\tau$	$\parallel$	$\square$
Resolution(2,3) =	$5: \ v \simeq x\sigma$	$\parallel GT(s(x),x)$	$\to$
Melting(3,5) =	$6: \ v \simeq x\sigma^*$	$\parallel GT(s(x),x)$	$\to$
Resolution(1,6) =	$7: \ v \simeq x\sigma^*\tau$	$\parallel$	$\square$

This set of regular constraint clauses is saturated, so it remains to show that the regular constraint $\sigma^*\tau$ is covering. (The regular constraint τ need not be considered because clause 4 has been replaced by 7, and so $[\![\tau]\!]$ is contained in $[\![\sigma^*\tau]\!]$.) This proof has been the subject of Examples 6.34, 6.48 and 6.50.

6.6 Conclusion

I have shown that the validity of a closed positive formula $\forall \exists^*. \bigvee_i \bigwedge_j A_{ij}$ in the minimal model of a predicative Horn clause set N is decidable whenever

(i) all function symbols in Σ are at most unary,

(ii) N is a finite set of predicative Horn clauses and all positive literals in N are linear, and

(iii) $N \cup \{A_{11}, \ldots, A_{1m_1} \to, \ldots, A_{n1}, \ldots, A_{nm_n} \to\}$ belongs to a class that can be finitely saturated by Ordered Resolution, where deletion steps are restricted to the deletion of variants and tautologies.

Note that such problems can in general not be represented by a class of (unconstrained or constrained) tree automata for which emptiness is decidable (Doner, 1970; Thatcher and Wright, 1968; Bogaert and Tison, 1992; Jacquemard et al., 2006), so this result cannot be mimicked using tree automata.

My proof is constructive and based on the Ordered Resolution Calculus with Melting ORM and a variant of predicate completion. Its first key ingredient are an extended notion of constraints, which can represent an infinite set of basic constraints, and the Melting rule that prevents the non-termination of Ordered Resolution (or in general of the algorithms SFD or ORFD) on the relevant fragment of constrained clauses, and allows me to reduce the problem to a simpler problem of minimal model validity (in particular: an emptiness problem of the form $N \models_{Ind} \forall x. \neg P(x)$), where the clause set N is further restricted to clauses with only monadic predicates and antecedents in which every atom is of the form $P(x)$ for a variable x.

Extensions of the approach might include a relaxation of its side conditions. Although both the superposition calculus SFD and the completion procedure PC are also applicable to clauses containing equality literals, it is not obvious how to extend this treatment of equality also to clauses containing generalized substitutions. The main problem here is that term rewriting, which is used in PC, cannot easily be extended to the rewriting of substitution expressions.

However, since both ORM and the PC work equally well on $\forall^*\exists^*$ queries, on clauses over an arbitrary signature, and on clauses containing non-linear positive atoms, the reduction to an emptiness problem is also possible in these extended settings. The resulting set $\check{N}$ may contain both non-monadic predicates and equational atoms. It is a natural next step to explore under which conditions these extensions lead to predicates $\check{P}$ that are nevertheless defined in such a way that emptiness remains decidable.

7 Conclusion

7.1 Resumé

I extended the state of the art concerning the applicability of disunification and predicate completion procedures, and developed saturation-based decision procedures for fixed domain and minimal model validity. In detail, my contributions are as follows:

- I extended disunification, i.e. the quantifier elimination-based computation of solutions of equational formulas, to so-called ultimately periodic interpretations, in which equations of the form $s^l(0){\simeq}s^k(0)$ hold. I showed that the validity of arbitrary equational formulas can be decided in such interpretations.

- I gave the first formal proof that disunification provides a means to complete predicates with respect to Herbrand interpretations with free constructors. I also extended predicate completion to ultimately periodic interpretations given by sets of universally reductive predicative clauses and equations of the form $s^l(x){\simeq}s^k(x)$, and I proved a unique Herbrand model property for completions of saturated sets of universally reductive predicative clauses.

- I introduced the concept of constrained clauses that allow for a treatment of existential variables without Skolemization and employed them for use in the refutationally complete superposition-based calculi SFD and SFD$^+$ for reasoning with respect to fixed domains. Those calculi are applicable to clause sets that do not fulfill any syntactic restrictions, and they are the first superposition calculi to handle an $\exists^*\forall^*$ quantifier alternation. Extended by a generic induction rule, which results in the calculus IS, the calculi can also be used for reasoning with respect to minimal models.

- I presented a translation of DIG (and ARM) representations of interpretations into the language of constrained clauses. Based on the calculi SFD and SFD$^+$, I developed the resolution calculus ORFD that spawns a variety of decision procedures for these representations. In particular, I showed that the following problems are decidable for DIG-represented interpretations $\mathcal{I}$:

- Equivalence of different DIG representations.
- Validity of ground atoms in $\mathcal{I}$.
- Validity in $\mathcal{I}$ of a range of classes of formulas of the form $\forall \vec{x}.\exists \vec{y}.\phi$ or $\exists \vec{x}.\forall \vec{y}.\phi$ with quantifier-free ϕ.
- For ARMs, validity in $\mathcal{I}$ of arbitrary formulas of the form $\forall \vec{x}.\exists \vec{y}.\phi$ or $\exists \vec{x}.\forall \vec{y}.\phi$ with quantifier-free ϕ.

- I proved a generic result reducing minimal model validity to (superposition-based) first-order validity: I have shown that the validity of a closed formula $\forall \exists^*. \bigvee_i \bigwedge_j A_{ij}$ in the minimal model of a predicative Horn clause set N is decidable whenever

  (i) all function symbols in Σ are at most unary,
  (ii) N is a finite set of predicative Horn clauses and all positive literals in N are linear, and
  (iii) $N \cup \{A_{11}, \ldots, A_{1m_1} \rightarrow, \ldots, A_{n1}, \ldots, A_{nm_n} \rightarrow\}$ belongs to a class that can be finitely saturated by Ordered Resolution, where clause deletion is restricted to the deletion of variants and tautologies.

  The basis of this result is an extended notion of constraints that do not only contain equations between terms but also feature regular expressions of substitutions, e.g. in the form $v \simeq x\{x \mapsto s(x)\}^*$, which enables the termination of saturation. The termination comes at a cost: In the setting of an extended constraint language, it is not obvious when a saturated set is satisfiable. To resolve this issue, I provide a reduction of this problem to a problem of minimal model validity that I prove to be decidable.

- One of the features of the presented decision procedures is that they can be implemented using general purpose first-order theorem provers and, apart from disunification, do not require specialized tools.

  The algorithms DU/PDU, PC and ORFD have been implemented on top of the automated first-order theorem prover SPASS. The implementation is available from the prototype section of the SPASS homepage (www.spass-prover.org/prototypes/). To my knowledge, this implementation constitutes the first publicly available implementation of disunification and predicate completion.

7.2 Outlook

There are several starting points for further research. In the area of disunification and predicate completion, the most obvious question is if there are more general classes of interpretations for which a correct and terminating disunification procedure can be defined. There are other attempts at finding such classes (Comon, 1988; Fernández, 1992), but decision procedures are only known for very restricted classes of equations like associativity and commutativity. There is also a more recent ansatz by Pichler (2003) who presented a disunification algorithm that is optimal in terms of worst case complexity. It would be interesting to see if the results developed here carry over to this algorithm.

The most severe restriction to predicate completion, the universal reductiveness condition on the input clauses, can probably not be lifted. The reason is that a clause like $P(x) \rightarrow Q(y)$ would have to be completed by a formula like $Q(y) \rightarrow \exists x.P(x)$, but for infinite sorts it does not seem possible to transform such a completion into a set of clauses. Even the constrained clauses developed in this work do not help because of the order of the quantifier alternation.

There are multiple prospects of further increasing the impact of the calculi SFD, IS, ORFD and ORM to derive more decidability results. For example, the ultimately periodic interpretations that arise as minimal models of predicative linear time temporal logic are very close to interpretations that are represented by DIGs. An extension of ORFD to such interpretations is easy (and in fact included in my implementation) and can semi-decide the satisfiability of queries similar to the ones that I have shown to be decidable for DIGs. Along the same lines, a combination of predicate completion and ORFD might provide a decision procedure for larger classes of interpretations.

The results in Chapter 6 are not yet completely satisfactory because of the restriction to signatures with at most unary function symbols. In particular, the calculus ORM operates on and is terminating for clauses over a signature that does not bear this restriction, and the reduction of the coverage of substitution expressions to an emptiness problem is also independent of the signature. Despite considerable work invested in solving this emptiness problem, it is yet unknown whether this problem is actually decidable.

Finally, it would be interesting to see in how far the calculus SFD and its derivatives are applicable to verification problems. In the analysis of security protocols, for example, the intended semantics is usually not the first-order semantics but a fixed domain semantics: Attacks that use non-signature symbols can be eliminated on a syntactical basis and are unable to undermine security. While there are attempts at protocol verification using interactive

Chapter 7: Conclusion

provers (e.g. Paulson, 1998) or terminating but incomplete automatic methods (Monniaux, 2003; Goubault-Larrecq, 2000), a fully automated verification procedure that is both terminating and complete would have obvious advantages and the presented calculi could play a role in this context.

Bibliography

Franz Baader and Wayne Snyder. Unification theory. In Alan Robinson and Andrei Voronkov, editors, *Handbook of Automated Reasoning*, volume 1, chapter 8, pages 445–532. Elsevier and MIT Press, 2001.

Leo Bachmair and Harald Ganzinger. On restrictions of ordered paramodulation with simplification. In Mark E. Stickel, editor, *Proceedings of the 10th International Conference on Automated Deduction, CADE-10*, volume 449 of *Lecture Notes in Computer Science*, pages 427–441. Springer, 1990.

Leo Bachmair and Harald Ganzinger. Completion of first-order clauses with equality by strict superposition. In Stéphane Kaplan and Mitsuhiro Okada, editors, *Proceedings of the 2nd International Workshop on Conditional and Typed Rewriting*, volume 516 of *Lecture Notes in Computer Science*, pages 162–180, Montreal, Canada, 1991. Springer.

Leo Bachmair and Harald Ganzinger. Rewrite-based equational theorem proving with selection and simplification. *Journal of Logic and Computation*, 4 (3):217–247, 1994. Revised version of Technical Report MPI-I-91-208, 1991.

Leo Bachmair and Harald Ganzinger. Resolution theorem proving. In John Alan Robinson and Andrei Voronkov, editors, *Handbook of Automated Reasoning*, volume 1, chapter 2, pages 19–99. Elsevier and MIT Press, 2001.

Leo Bachmair and David A. Plaisted. Associative path orderings. In Jean-Pierre Jouannaud, editor, *Proceedings of the First International Conference on Rewriting Techniques and Applications, RTA-85*, volume 202 of *Lecture Notes in Computer Science*, pages 241–254. Springer, 1985.

Leo Bachmair, Nachum Dershowitz, and David A. Plaisted. Completion without failure. In Hassan Aït-Kaci and Maurice Nivat, editors, *Rewriting Techniques*, volume 2 of *Resolution of Equations in Algebraic Structures*, chapter 1, pages 1–30. Academic Press, New York, 1989.

Leo Bachmair, Harald Ganzinger, and Uwe Waldmann. Superposition with simplification as a decision procedure for the monadic class with equality.

Bibliography

In Georg Gottlob, Alexander Leitsch, and Daniele Mundici, editors, *Proceedings of the Third Kurt Gödel Colloquium on Computational Logic and Proof Theory, KGC '93*, volume 713 of *Lecture Notes in Computer Science*, pages 83–96, London, UK, 1993. Springer.

Peter Baumgartner and Cesare Tinelli. The model evolution calculus. In Franz Baader, editor, *Proceedings of the 19th International Conference on Automated Deduction, CADE-19*, volume 2741 of *Lecture Notes in Computer Science*, pages 350–364. Springer, 2003.

Bruno Bogaert and Sophie Tison. Equality and disequality constraints on direct subterms in tree automata. In Alain Finkel and Matthias Jantzen, editors, *9th Annual Symposium on Theoretical Aspects of Computer Science, STACS'92*, volume 577 of *Lecture Notes in Computer Science*, pages 161–171. Springer, 1992.

Adel Bouhoula and Florent Jacquemard. Automated induction with constrained tree automata. In Alessandro Armando, Peter Baumgartner, and Gilles Dowek, editors, *Proceedings of the 4th International Joint Conference on Automated Reasoning, IJCAR 2008*, volume 5195 of *Lecture Notes in Computer Science*, pages 539–554. Springer, 2008.

Adel Bouhoula and Jean-Pierre Jouannaud. Automata-driven automated induction. In *Twelfth Annual IEEE Symposium on Logic in Computer Science, LICS'97*, pages 14–25. IEEE Computer Society Press, 1997.

Adel Bouhoula and Michaël Rusinowitch. Implicit induction in conditional theories. *Journal of Automated Reasoning*, 14(2):189–235, 1995.

Adel Bouhoula, Emmanuel Kounalis, and Michaël Rusinowitch. SPIKE, an automatic theorem prover. In Andrei Voronkov, editor, *Proceedings of the 3rd International Conference on Logic Programming and Automated Reasoning, LPAR'92*, volume 624 of *Lecture Notes in Computer Science*, pages 460–462. Springer, 1992.

Adel Bouhoula, Emmanuel Kounalis, and Michaël Rusinowitch. Automated mathematical induction. *Journal of Logic and Computation*, 5(5):631–668, 1995.

Daniel Brand. Proving theorems with the modification method. *SIAM Journal on Computing*, 4(4):412–430, 1975.

Bibliography

Ricardo Caferra and Nicolas Zabel. A method for simultaneous search for refutations and models by equational constraint solving. *Journal of Symbolic Computation*, 13(6):613–642, 1992.

Ricardo Caferra, Alexander Leitsch, and Nicholas Peltier. *Automated Model Building*, volume 31 of *Applied Logic Series*. Kluwer, 2004.

Keith L. Clark. Negation as failure. In Hervé Gallaire and Jack Minker, editors, *Logic and Data Bases*, pages 293–322, New York, 1977. Plenum Press.

Alain Colmerauer. Equations and inequations on finite and infinite trees. In *Proceedings of the International Conference on Fifth Generation Computer Systems, FGCS*, pages 85–99, 1984.

Hubert Comon. *Unification et Disunification: Théorie et applications*. PhD thesis, Institut National Polytechnique de Grenoble, July 1988.

Hubert Comon. Disunification: A survey. In Jean-Louis Lassez and Gordon D. Plotkin, editors, *Computational Logic: Essays in Honor of Alan Robinson*, pages 322–359. MIT Press, Cambridge, MA, 1991.

Hubert Comon. Inductionless induction. In John Alan Robinson and Andrei Voronkov, editors, *Handbook of Automated Reasoning*, volume 1, chapter 14, pages 913–962. Elsevier and MIT Press, 2001.

Hubert Comon and Catherine Delor. Equational formulae with membership constraints. *Information and Computation*, 112(2):167–216, 1994.

Hubert Comon and Florent Jacquemard. Ground reducability is exptime-complete. In *Twelfth Annual IEEE Symposium on Logic in Computer Science, LICS'97*, pages 26–34. IEEE Computer Society Press, 1997.

Hubert Comon and Pierre Lescanne. Equational problems and disunification. *Journal of Symbolic Computation*, 7(3-4):371–425, 1989.

Hubert Comon and Robert Nieuwenhuis. Induction = I-axiomatization + first-order consistency. *Information and Computation*, 159(1/2):151–186, 2000.

Nachum Dershowitz. Orderings for term-rewriting systems. *Theoretical Computer Science*, 17:279–301, 1982.

John Doner. Tree acceptors and some of their applications. *Journal of Computer and System Sciences*, 4(5):406–451, 1970.

Stephan Falke and Deepak Kapur. Inductive decidability using implicit induction. In Miki Hermann and Andrei Voronkov, editors, *Proceedings of the 13th International Conference on Logic for Programming, Artificial Intelligence and Reasoning (LPAR '06)*, Phnom Penh, Cambodia, volume 4246 of *Lecture Notes in Artificial Intelligence*, pages 45–59. Springer, 2006.

Christian G. Fermüller and Alexander Leitsch. Hyperresolution and automated model building. *Journal of Logic and Computation*, 6(2):173–203, 1996.

Christian G. Fermüller and Reinhard Pichler. Model representation via contexts and implicit generalizations. In Robert Nieuwenhuis, editor, *Proceedings of the 20th International Conference on Automated Deduction, CADE-20*, volume 3632 of *Lecture Notes in Computer Science*, pages 409–423. Springer, 2005.

Christian G. Fermüller and Reinhard Pichler. Model representation over finite and infinite signatures. *Journal of Logic and Computation*, 17(3):453–477, 2007.

Maribel Fernández. Narrowing based procedures for equational disunification. *Applicable Algebra in Engineering, Communication and Computing*, 3:1–26, 1992.

Harald Ganzinger and Hans De Nivelle. A superposition decision procedure for the guarded fragment with equality. In *Proceedings of the 14th Annual IEEE Symposium on Logic in Computer Science*, pages 295–305. IEEE Computer Society Press, 1999.

Harald Ganzinger and Jürgen Stuber. Inductive theorem proving by consistency for first-order clauses. In Michaël Rusinowitch and Jean-Luc Remy, editors, *Proceedings of the 3rd International Workshop on Conditional Term Rewriting Systems, CTRS-92*, volume 656 of *Lecture Notes in Computer Science*, pages 226–241. Springer, 1992. ISBN 3-540-56393-8.

Jürgen Giesl and Deepak Kapur. Deciding inductive validity of equations. In Franz Baader, editor, *Proceedings of the 19th International Conference on Automated Deduction, CADE-19*, volume 2741 of *Lecture Notes in Computer Science*, pages 17–31. Springer, 2003.

Kurt Gödel. Über formal unentscheidbare Sätze der Principia Mathematica und verwandter Systeme. *Monatshefte für Mathematik und Physik*, 38(1):173–198, 1931.

Joseph A. Goguen. How to prove algebraic inductive hypotheses without induction. In Wolfgang Bibel and Robert A. Kowalski, editors, *Proceedings of the 5th International Conference on Automated Deduction, CADE-5*, volume 87 of *Lecture Notes in Computer Science*, pages 356–373. Springer, 1980.

Warren D. Goldfarb. *Jacques Herbrand: Logical Writings*. Harward University Press, Cambridge, 1971.

Georg Gottlob and Reinhard Pichler. Working with ARMs: Complexity results on atomic representations of herbrand models. *Information and Computation*, 165(2):183–207, 2001.

Jean Goubault-Larrecq. A method for automatic cryptographic protocol verification. In José D. P. Rolim, editor, *IPDPS Workshops*, volume 1800 of *Lecture Notes in Computer Science*, pages 977–984. Springer, 2000.

Jacques Herbrand. Recherches sur la théorie de la démonstration. *Travaux de la Société des Sciences et des Lettres de Varsovie, Classe III Sciences Mathematiques et Physiques*, 33, 1930. Translated in Goldfarb (1971).

Thomas Hillenbrand and Christoph Weidenbach. Superposition for finite domains. Research Report MPI–I–2007–RG1–002, Max-Planck Institute for Informatics, Saarbrücken, Germany, April 2007.

Matthias Horbach. Disunification for ultimately periodic interpretations. In Edmund M. Clarke and Andrei Voronkov, editors, *Proceedings of the 16th International Conference on Logic for Programming, Artificial Intelligence, and Reasoning, LPAR-16*, volume 6355 of *Lecture Notes in Artificial Intelligence*, pages 290–311. Springer, 2010a. ISBN 978-3-642-17510-7.

Matthias Horbach. *Superposition-based Decision Procedures for Fixed Domain and Minimal Model Semantics*. PhD thesis, Max Planck Institute for Informatics and Saarland University, 2010b.

Matthias Horbach. Predicate completion for non-Horn clause sets. In Viorica Sofronie-Stockermans and Nikolaj Bjørner, editors, *Proceedings of the 23rd International Conference on Automated Deduction, CADE-23*, volume 6803 of *Lecture Notes in Artificial Intelligence*, pages 300–315. Springer, 2011a.

Matthias Horbach. System description: Spass-FD. In Viorica Sofronie-Stockermans and Nikolaj Bjørner, editors, *Proceedings of the 23rd International Conference on Automated Deduction, CADE-23*, volume 6803 of *Lecture Notes in Artificial Intelligence*, pages 316–322. Springer, 2011b.

Matthias Horbach and Christoph Weidenbach. Superposition for fixed domains. In Michael Kaminski and Simone Martini, editors, *Proceedings of the 17th Annual Conference of the European Association for Computer Science Logic, CSL 08*, volume 5213 of *Lecture Notes in Computer Science*, pages 293–307. Springer, 2008.

Matthias Horbach and Christoph Weidenbach. Decidability results for saturation-based model building. In Renate Schmidt, editor, *Proceedings of the 22nd International Conference on Automated Deduction, CADE-22*, volume 5663 of *Lecture Notes in Artificial Intelligence*, pages 404–420. Springer, 2009a.

Matthias Horbach and Christoph Weidenbach. Deciding the inductive validity of $\forall\exists^*$ queries. In Erich Grädel and Reinhard Kahle, editors, *Proceedings of the 18th Annual Conference of the European Association for Computer Science Logic, CSL 2009*, volume 5771 of *Lecture Notes in Computer Science*, pages 332–347. Springer, 2009b.

Matthias Horbach and Christoph Weidenbach. Deciding the inductive validity of $\forall\exists^*$ queries. Research Report MPI–I–2009–RG1–001, Max-Planck Institute for Informatics, Saarbrücken, Germany, May 2009c.

Matthias Horbach and Christoph Weidenbach. Decidability results for saturation-based model building. Research Report MPI–I–2009–RG1–004, Max-Planck Institute for Informatics, Saarbrücken, Germany, December 2009d.

Matthias Horbach and Christoph Weidenbach. Superposition for fixed domains. Research Report MPI–I–2009–RG1–005, Max-Planck Institute for Informatics, Saarbrücken, Germany, October 2009e.

Matthias Horbach and Christoph Weidenbach. Superposition for fixed domains. *ACM Transactions on Computational Logic*, 11(4):27:1–27:35, November 2010.

Jieh Hsiang and Michaël Rusinowitch. On word problems in equational theories. In Thomas Ottmann, editor, *Proceedings of the 14th International Colloquium on Automata, Languages and Programming, ICALP'87*, volume 267 of *Lecture Notes in Computer Science*, pages 54–71, Karlsruhe, Germany, 1987.

Gérard P. Huet and Jean-Marie Hullot. Proofs by induction in equational theories with constructors. In *Proceedings of the 21st Annual Symposium on*

Foundations of Computer Science, FOCS, pages 96–107. IEEE Computer Society Press, 1980.

Florent Jacquemard, Christoph Meyer, and Christoph Weidenbach. Unification in extensions of shallow equational theories. In Tobias Nipkow, editor, *Rewriting Techniques and Applications, 9th International Conference, RTA-98*, volume 1379 of *Lecture Notes in Computer Science*, pages 76–90. Springer, 1998.

Florent Jacquemard, Michaël Rusinowitch, and Laurent Vigneron. Tree automata with equality constraints modulo equational theories. In *Proceedings of the 3rd International Joint Conference on Automated Reasoning, IJCAR 2006*, volume 4130 of *Lecture Notes in Computer Science*, pages 557–571. Springer, 2006.

Jean-Pierre Jouannaud and Claude Kirchner. Solving equations in abstract algebras: A rule-based survey of unification. In Jean-Louis Lassez and Gordon Plotkin, editors, *Computational Logic - Essays in Honor of Alan Robinson*, pages 257–321. MIT Press, 1991.

Jean-Pierre Jouannaud and Hélène Kirchner. Completion of a set of rules modulo a set of equations. *SIAM Journal on Computing*, 15(4):1155–1194, 1986.

Deepak Kapur and Mahadevan Subramaniam. Extending decision procedures with induction schemes. In *Proceedings of the 17th International Conference on Automated Deduction, CADE-17*, volume 1831 of *Lecture Notes in Computer Science*, pages 324–345. Springer, 2000.

Deepak Kapur and Hantao Zhang. RRL: A rewrite rule laboratory. In Ewing L. Lusk and Ross A. Overbeek, editors, *Proceedings of the 9th International Conference on Automated Deduction, CADE-9*, volume 310 of *Lecture Notes in Computer Science*, pages 768–769. Springer, 1988.

Deepak Kapur, Paliath Narendran, and Hantao Zhang. Automating inductionless induction using test sets. *Journal of Symbolic Computation*, 11(1/2):81–111, 1991.

Donald E. Knuth and Peter B. Bendix. Simple word problems in universal algebras. In John Leech, editor, *Computational Problems in Abstract Algebra*, pages 263–297. Pergamon Press, 1970.

Bibliography

Emmanuel Kounalis. Testing for the ground (co-)reducibility property in term-rewriting systems. *Theoretical Computer Science*, 106(1):87–117, 1992.

D. S. Lankford. A simple explanation of inductionless induction. Memo mtp-14, Louisiana Technical University, Dep. of Math., Ruston, 1981.

Jean-Louis Lassez and Kim Marriott. Explicit representation of terms defined by counter examples. *Journal of Automated Reasoning*, 3(3):301–317, 1987.

Jean-Louis Lassez, Michael J. Maher, and Kim Marriott. Unification revisited. In *Foundations of Logic and Functional Programming*, volume 306 of *Lecture Notes in Computer Science*, pages 67–113. Springer, 1986.

Michel Ludwig and Ullrich Hustadt. Resolution-based model construction for PLTL. In Carsten Lutz and Jean-François Raskin, editors, *Proceedings of the 16th International Symposium on Temporal Representation and Reasoning, TIME 2009*, pages 73–80. IEEE Computer Society, 2009.

Michael J. Maher. Complete axiomatizations of the algebras of finite, rational and infinite trees. In *LICS*, pages 348–357. IEEE Computer Society, 1988.

Anatoly Ivanovich Mal'cev. Axiomatizable classes of locally free algebra of various type. In Benjamin Franklin Wells, editor, *The Metamathematics of Algebraic Systems: Collected Papers 1936–1967*, chapter 23, pages 262–281. North Holland, 1971.

David Monniaux. Abstracting cryptographic protocols with tree automata. *Science of Computer Programming*, 47(2–3):177–202, 2003.

David R. Musser. On proving inductive properties of abstract data types. In *Proceedings of the 7th ACM SIGPLAN-SIGACT symposium on Principles of Programming Languages, POPL 1980*, pages 154–162, New York, NY, USA, 1980. ACM Press.

Robert Nieuwenhuis. Basic paramodulation and decidable theories (extended abstract). In *Proceedings of the 11th IEEE Symposium on Logic in Computer Science, LICS'96*, pages 473–482. IEEE Computer Society Press, 1996.

Robert Nieuwenhuis and Albert Rubio. Paramodulation-based theorem proving. In John Alan Robinson and Andrei Voronkov, editors, *Handbook of Automated Reasoning*, volume 1, chapter 7, pages 371–443. Elsevier and MIT Press, 2001.

Lauwrence C. Paulson. The inductive approach to verifying cryptographic protocols. In *Journal of Computer Security*, volume 6, pages 85–128. IOS Press, 1998.

Nicolas Peltier. Model building with ordered resolution: extracting models from saturated clause sets. *Journal of Symbolic Computation*, 36(1-2):5–48, 2003.

Reinhard Pichler. On the complexity of equational problems in CNF. *Journal of Symbolic Computation*, 36(1-2):235–269, 2003.

David A. Plaisted. Semantic confluence tests and completion methods. *Information and Control*, 65(2/3):182–215, 1985.

Gordon Plotkin. Building in equational theories. In Bernard Meltzer and Donald Michie, editors, *Machine Intelligence 7*, pages 73–90. Edinburgh University Press, 1972.

Uday S. Reddy. Term rewriting induction. In Mark E. Stickel, editor, *Proceedings of the 10th International Conference on Automated Deduction, CADE-10*, volume 449 of *Lecture Notes in Computer Science*, pages 162–177. Springer, 1990.

George A. Robinson and Larry Wos. Paramodulation and theorem-proving in first-order theories with equality. In Bernard Meltzer and Donald Michie, editors, *Machine Intelligence 4*, pages 135–150. Edinburgh University Press, 1969.

John Alan Robinson. A machine-oriented logic based on the resolution principle. *Journal of the ACM*, 12(1):23–41, 1965.

Helmut Seidl and Kumar Neeraj Verma. Flat and one-variable clauses: Complexity of verifying cryptographic protocols with single blind copying. In *Proceedings of the 11th International Conference on Logic for Programming, Artificial Intelligence, and Reasoning, LPAR-11*, volume 3452 of *Lecture Notes in Computer Science*, pages 79–94. Springer, 2004.

Jürgen Stuber. Inductive theorem proving for Horn clauses. Master's thesis, Universität Dortmund, April 1991.

Geoff Sutcliffe. The TPTP problem library and associated infrastructure. *Journal of Automomated Reasoning*, 43(4):337–362, 2009.

Bibliography

James W. Thatcher and Jesse B. Wright. Generalized finite automata theory with an application to a decision problem of second-order logic. *Mathematical Systems Theory*, 2(1):57–81, 1968.

Christoph Weidenbach. Towards an automatic analysis of security protocols in first-order logic. In Harald Ganzinger, editor, *Proceedings of the 16th International Conference on Automated Deduction, CADE-16*, volume 1632 of *Lecture Notes in Artificial Intelligence*, pages 378–382. Springer, 1999.

Christoph Weidenbach. Combining superposition, sorts and splitting. In Alan Robinson and Andrei Voronkov, editors, *Handbook of Automated Reasoning*, volume 2, chapter 27, pages 1965–2012. Elsevier, 2001.

Christoph Weidenbach, Dilyana Dimova, Arnaud Fietzke, Rohit Kumar, Martin Suda, and Patrick Wischnewski. SPASS version 3.5. In Renate Schmidt, editor, *Proceedings of the 22nd International Conference on Automated Deduction, CADE-22*, volume 5663 of *Lecture Notes in Computer Science*, pages 140–145. Springer, 2009.

Hantao Zhang, Deepak Kapur, and Mukkai S. Krishnamoorthy. A mechanizable induction principle for equational specifications. In *Proceedings of the 9th International Conference on Automated Deduction*, pages 162–181, London, UK, 1988. Springer.

Index

A_N, 95
α_N, 95, 108, 130
ancestor, 163, 164
antecedent, 38
antisymmetric, 34
arity, 36
ARM, 25, 133
assignment, 46
    satisfying, 46
associative path ordering, 44
asymmetric, 34
atom, 37
    predicative, 45
atomic representation of a term model, 25, 133

base clause, 163
binary function symbol, 36

calculus, 52
    terminating, 54
clause, 38
    meltable, 163
    predicative, 45
clause normal form, 11
closed, 38
compatible with AC, 43
completely defined equality, 18
composition of substitution expressions, 155
conclusion, 12, 52
confluent, 44

congruence relation, 43
conjunction, 37
conjunctive normal form, 47
constant, 36
constrained clause, 39
    ground, 39
    unconstrained, 40
constraint, 39
    ground, 39
    positive, 39
contain, 38
covering, 28
    substitution expression, 157
covering constraint, 49

denotation, 156
derivation, 53, 159
derivation step, 52
derivation strategy, 53
derivation substitution, 176
DIG, 25, 133
    over P, 133
disequation, 37
disjunction, 37
disjunction of implicit generalizations, 25, 133
disjunction of substitution expressions, 155
disjunctive normal form, 48
disunification, 28
Disunification Calculus DU, 58
dom, 155

Index

domain
    of a substitution, 40
    of a substitution expression, 155
    of an interpretation, 45
DU, 58

element-of relation for multisets, 33
elementary update, 168
empty clause, 39
empty multiset, 33
entailment
    of a clause, 48
    of a clause set, 48
    of a constrained clause set, 50
    of a formula, 47
    of a set of regular constraint clauses, 158
equation, 37
equational, 45
equivalence class, 35
equivalence relation, 35
equivalent formulas, 47
    wrt. an interpretation, 47
existential closure, 38
existential query derivation, 164
existential query problem, 160
explosion level, 66
expression, 37
Extended Superposition Calculus for Fixed Domains SFD$^+$, 106

Factoring, 12
fair, 53
first-order interpretation, 45
fixed domain semantics, 16
formula, 37
    ground, 38
    positive, 37
    predicative, 45
    satisfiable, 47
    satisfiable in an interpretation, 47

free sort, 58
function symbols, 35

Herbrand interpretation, 46
Herbrand model, 16
Herbrand-satisfiable, 50
Herbrand-unsatisfiable, 50
Horn, 39

$\mathcal{I}_N$, 49, 96
$\mathcal{I}_N^\alpha$, 96
$\mathcal{I}_N^\succ$, 49
image of a substitution, 40
implementation, 81, 145
implicit generalization, 25, 133
    over P, 133
implicit induction, 19
inductive semantics, 16
Inductive Superposition Calculus IS(H), 119
inference, 51, 159
inference calculus, 52, 159
inference rule, 51, 159
interpretation, 45
inverse renaming, 40
irreducible, 44
IS(H), 119

linear substitution, 40
literal, 37
    negative, 37
    positive, 37
loop of substitution expressions, 155

many sorted signature, 35
maximal element, 34
meltable clause, 163
melted clause, 163
minimal element, 34
minimal model semantics, 16
minimal model wrt. α_N, 97

204

model, 158
    of a clause set, 48
    of a constrained clause set, 50
    of a formula, 47
monotonic, 43
most general unifier, 41
multiset, 33

$N_0(D)$, 134
$N(D)$, 135
Negating Predicate Completion Algorithm NPC, 183
negation, 37
negation normal form, 47
nested quantifiers, 70
normal form, 44
NPC, 183

occurs, 38
occurs freely, 38
Ordered Resolution Calculus for Fixed Domains ORFD, 130
Ordered Resolution Calculus with Melting ORM, 163
ordering, 34
ORFD, 130
ORM, 163

Paramodulation, 13
partial ordering, 33
    total, 34
path, 37
PC, 68
PDU, 58
Periodic Disunification Calculus PDU, 58
positive part, 39
positively constrained clause, 39
Post correspondence problem, 151
predicate completion, 29, 68
Predicate Completion Algorithm PC, 68

premise, 12, 52
produce
    clause produces rule, 21, 49
    constrained clause produces rule, 96
productive
    clause, 21, 49
    constrained clause, 96
proof by consistency, 18

quantifier-free, 38
quotient set, 35

recursive path ordering, 44
redex, 44
reducible, 44
reductio ad absurdum, 11
reduction ordering, 43
redundant, 13
    constrained clause, 52
    inference, 52, 159
    regular constraint clause, 159
reflexive, 34, 35
reflexive closure, 35
refutational theorem proving, 11
refutationally complete, 12, 53
regular constraint, 155
regular constraint clause, 156
regular equation, 155
Resolution, 11, 12
restriction of a substitution, 40
rewrite relation, 43
rewrite rule, 44
rewrite system, 44
    ground, 44
RLL, 20

satisfiable
    constraint, 49
saturated set, 11, 52, 159
selection function, 89

Index

set of ultimate periodicity equations, 58
SF, 73
SFD, 89
SFD$^+$, 106
signature, 35
simultaneous unifier, 41
size, 38
Skolemization, 27
solution of a formula, 47
solved form, 73
Solved Form Transformation Algorithm SF, 73
solved variable, 74
sort
    free, 58
    ultimately periodic, 58
sort assignment, 36
sort symbols, 35
sort theory, 147, 185
sound, 53
SPASS, 29, 30, 81, 145
SPIKE, 20
splitting, 147
stable under substitutions, 43
strict ordering, 34
strict partial ordering, 34
    total, 34
strict subexpression, 38
strictly maximal element, 35
strictly minimal element, 35
subexpression, 37
subformula, 38
substitution, 40
    grounding, 40
    linear, 40
substitution expression, 41, 153, 154
    covering, 157
subterm, 38, 39
subterm property, 43

succedent, 39
Superposition, 13
Superposition Calculus for Fixed Domains SFD, 89
symmetric, 35
symmetric closure, 35
syntactical tautology, 39
syntactically valid constraint, 49

tautology, 39
term, 36
    ground, 38
    in normal form, 44
    irreducible, 44
    of sort S, 36
    reducible, 44
terminating, 44
theorem proving derivation, 102
transitive, 34, 35

ultimate periodicity equation, 58
ultimately periodic interpretation, 29, 58
ultimately periodic sort, 58
unary function symbol, 36
unfailing completion, 13
unifiable, 41
unifier, 41
union of multisets, 33
universal closure, 38
universally reductive, 22, 43
universe, 45
unsolved variable, 74
update, 168
    elementary, 168

valid, 47
variable
    existential, 39
    solved, 74
    universal, 39
    unsolved, 74

variable range, 155
variable renaming, 40
variables, 35
    occurring, 39
    of a constraint, 39
    of a term, 38
variant, 158
VRan, 155

well-founded, 43

Die VDM Verlagsservicegesellschaft sucht für wissenschaftliche Verlage abgeschlossene und herausragende

Dissertationen, Habilitationen, Diplomarbeiten, Master Theses, Magisterarbeiten usw.

für die kostenlose Publikation als Fachbuch.

Sie verfügen über eine Arbeit, die hohen inhaltlichen und formalen Ansprüchen genügt, und haben Interesse an einer honorarvergüteten Publikation?

Dann senden Sie bitte erste Informationen über sich und Ihre Arbeit per Email an *info@vdm-vsg.de*.

Sie erhalten kurzfristig unser Feedback!

VDM Verlagsservicegesellschaft mbH
Dudweiler Landstr. 99　　　　　　Telefon　+49 681 3720 174
D - 66123 Saarbrücken　　　　　　Fax　　　+49 681 3720 1749
www.vdm-vsg.de

Die VDM Verlagsservicegesellschaft mbH vertritt

Printed by Books on Demand GmbH, Norderstedt / Germany